ANALYSES OF CONTEMPORARY SOCIETY

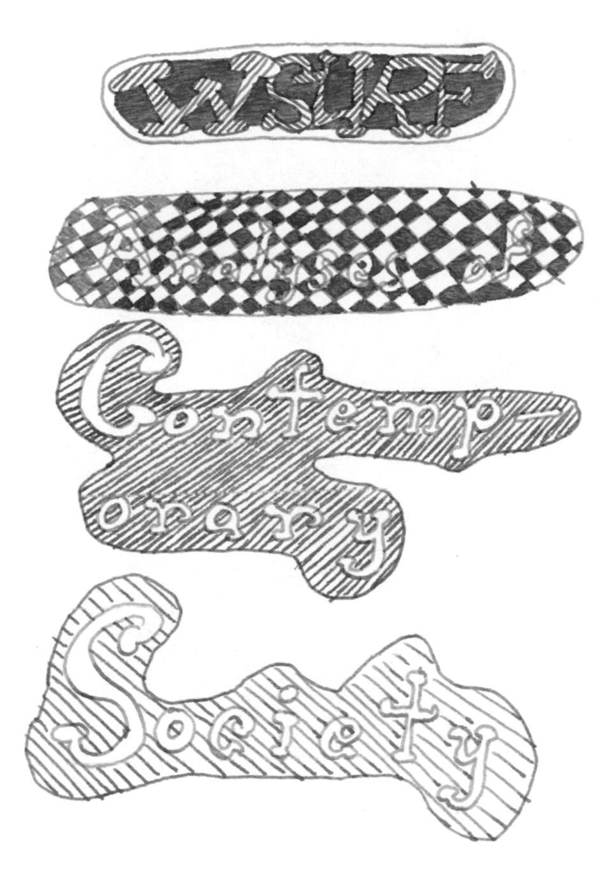

ANALYSES OF CONTEMPORARY SOCIETY

edited by
Bernard Rosenberg

THE CITY COLLEGE OF THE CITY UNIVERSITY
OF NEW YORK

THOMAS Y. CROWELL COMPANY
New York
Established 1834

FIRST PRINTING, APRIL, 1966
SECOND PRINTING, AUGUST, 1966
THIRD PRINTING, FEBRUARY, 1967
FOURTH PRINTING, JUNE, 1967

LIBRARY OF CONGRESS CATALOG CARD NUMBER: 66-20852

Designed by Judith Woracek Barry

MANUFACTURED IN THE UNITED STATES OF AMERICA

PREFACE

This book is intended to whet the reader's appetite. From having here sampled some of the best of contemporary sociological thought, he will go on, we hope, to enjoy a fuller feast. We have assembled substantial excerpts, not mere snippets, from the work of eight important thinkers. The reader will note that we have made a textual elision in only one excerpt, the first; throughout, we have omitted only such occasional footnotes as refer to sections of the original not reprinted here. In no case do we offer an excerpt as substitute for the whole text, which should be read in its entirety—as much for pleasure as instruction.

"What?" one can almost hear the self-styled humanist say. "Pleasure and instruction in *sociology*—that pretentious pseudo-science so little given to either learning or literacy?" As always, the skeptic has a case. In every field the genius quotient is modest, the output of trivia high. To those who have come to question the whole enterprise, sociology in its short life has seemed to contribute more than its fair share of nonsense.

But to reject all is to miss much that is valuable. A grand sociological tradition began in the nineteenth and early twentieth centuries. Having lain more or less dormant for a long time thereafter, it has in recent years come excitingly to life. In these readings are visible the bare bones of that tradition, a tradition largely extra-academic and beautifully amateurish. The conventional sociologist, striving for recognition within his closed fraternity, all too easily suffers an impairment of vision amid what Pitirim A. Sorokin has called the "fashions, fads, and foibles" of the profession. How often it has been the relatively untrained, untamed outsider who has seen past the unnecessary obscurities to the social reality he helps us grasp. Here, then, are eight men (there are others!) who have done much to rescue sociology—and the intelligent layman—from a regrettable fate.

B. R.

New York City
March, 1966

CONTENTS

THE QUEST FOR IDENTITY
Allen Wheelis

When they are unhappy, men tend either to idealize their past or to invest heavily in an indefinite but glorious future. This transitory life on earth is viewed as a vale of tears and laughter thrust upon us since our expulsion from Paradise. There once was a golden age, and some day there will be another. So said our Western forebears, whose theodicies vindicated their belief in an omniscient, omnipotent, and benevolent God by reconciling it with the presence of evil and misery. The waning of supernaturalism and, in Schiller's phrase, "the disenchantment of the world" produced secular theodicies. Messianism and redemption remained even as an anthropomorphic deity was dethroned. The religion of Man and the religion of Progress, the sanctification of Reason, and then of Science and Technology, helped to sustain civilization. Animated by the new faith, human beings could look hopefully to Utopia, to the good life that was in store for Everyman. Only lately has this elaborate ideological edifice crumbled. We are left to observe the ruins and ponder their meaning. From its inception in the nineteenth century, classical sociology has had scarcely any task but that of studying the rapid decomposition of traditional values. Most of the classicists clung to a secular religion; not many of their linear descendants are able to do so. For, to paraphrase Allen Wheelis, how can one take

Progress seriously—let alone worship its image—when simple survival is uppermost in our minds?

Although the odds seem unfavorable, we may manage the physical survival. But then what? It will still be necessary to face the appalling social wreckage that has accumulated all these years. In helping us pick our way through that wreckage, Wheelis is a knowing guide. He speaks simply and forthrightly to a condition most people feel and few articulate, a condition in which the individual lacks goals, loses all sense of purpose, and experiences deep feelings of emptiness and longing. The individual, by etymological definition indivisible, is nevertheless pulverized and atomized, set adrift in society. He is restless, potentially explosive, and ready for incorporation into mass movements.

When human character, individual personality, or the "social self" reaches this state, it approaches dissolution. Only then can a man ask the characteristic questions of our day: Who am I? What am I? Hitherto those on the fringe of society may well have wondered who and what they were; now a majority seem to have been cast onto the fringe. That modern men are, for the most part, hollow men wandering in the desert of their own despair, T. S. Eliot told us decades ago. If ever there had been reason to doubt the poet, today there is none. Who will fail to find a title like The Quest for Identity personally meaningful? Multitudes are engaged in that search.

Somewhat literary in his bent (he has shown a flair for fiction in several short stories and one novel), Allen Wheelis is obviously no T. S. Eliot. The reader will not thrill to soaring symbols in a book constructed, although with considerable art, of plain, grim prose. And the author's sociological conclusions can have been derived only in small part from his extensive reading. More often they derive from the clinic, where Wheelis has labored and prospered as a psychoanalyst. Trained in orthodox Freudian psychology, practicing it privately and as a staff member of the Austin

Riggs Center, and teaching it as an instructor in the San Francisco Psychoanalytic Institute, Wheelis discovered things that some of his colleagues may also have noted, but that he alone has had the courage to report in public. One discovery must have come as a shock: whereas psychoanalytic therapy is ideally suited to cases of hysteria, among today's patients one rarely encounters hysterics having the clear somatic symptoms that analysis can dispel. More typically the patient comes to his analyst complaining vaguely of unhappiness, of a generalized malaise, of lost identity. Freud described the therapeutic process as one in which layers of consciousness were gradually removed until the unconscious was reached. Wheelis found that after the layers were peeled, there was often—nothing—a great void that the analyst, though called upon to do so, could not possibly fill. This suggestive observation is the thread on which Wheelis strings his other insights. Not all are so novel, but no one has stated them with greater skill or precision. The sociologist cannot but stand in admiration of a psychoanalyst who, starting in his own special domain, has ranged so far and so brilliantly beyond it.

CHARACTER CHANGE AND CULTURAL CHANGE

Culture and Social Character

It is generally believed that our changing social character is symptomatic of crisis, that there was a period in the past—the Victorian period, for example—in which character was stable, and that there will be a corresponding period in the future in which society will have emerged from its present chaos, when stable traditions will again foster a stable character. The troubles which seem most crucial to an observer of any period are the troubles of his present; those receding into the past he views with detachment. The biggest wave is the one now striking the ship; toward the horizon, ahead or astern, the sea is level. And so our present, with its troubles and uncertainties, is seen as a temporary and perilous transition.

This belief will not bear scrutiny. Clearly character cannot remain fixed while the conditions of life change. And clearly the conditions of life have always been changing. Any culture tends to produce in individuals that social character which is fitted for survival in that culture;[1] and as a culture evolves, an evolution in the prevailing character of the individuals who adapt to it is to be expected. That there should have been a characterological change of some kind in western society during the past two generations occasions no surprise, nor should it. For the conditions of life have, during that time, undergone such radical alteration that it would be a greater mystery if no corresponding change in character had occurred. We know this in the same way we know that the Norman conquerors, the imperial Romans, the fabled Babylonians, and the stone age men must have been characterologically different, each from the others and each from ourselves. Since evolution has been intrinsic to culture for as long as we have any knowledge of culture, character, also, must always have been in a process of change.

Radical changes in the circumstances of life may befall man, as the several ice ages doubtless brought about different ways of life for peoples of the northern hemisphere. Such changes have, in the period of recorded history, become progressively less important: the changes brought about by man himself have provided the major problems of adaptation. It is the nature and continuity of these changes that are in question here.

The Institutional Process and the Instrumental Process

It is not possible to view the life of man apart from culture; for there is no man whose life has not been shaped from birth to death by its cultural matrix. An approximation of the life of

[1] Erich Fromm, "Individual and Social Origins of Neurosis," *American Sociological Review*, vol. 9 (1944), p. 380; reprinted in *Personality in Nature, Society and Culture*, edited by Clyde Kluckhohn and Henry Murray (New York: Alfred A. Knopf, 1948).

man without culture is afforded by those animals most closely related to man. Their lives consist of being born, eating, sleeping, playing, fighting, mating, procuring food, caring for young, and dying. All of these activities continue in the life of man, and are the life process for him as they are for other species. But in man—even the most primitive man—these activities are shaped by two superimposed modes of action which are distinctively human. These are the use of tools and the creation of myths. Culture is the product of these modes, and the distinction between them establishes the concepts with which culture may be analyzed and understood. These concepts were first indicated by Veblen, and have been elaborated and clarified by Dewey and Ayres. They are the instrumental process and the institutional process. Each of them encompasses a vast range of phenomena, yet they bear a precise meaning.

The instrumental process designates those activities dominated by an attitude which, if put in words, would be somewhat as follows: "Let us first examine the facts, and draw only such conclusions as the facts warrant. If no conclusion is warranted but some conclusion is necessary—since life does not wait on certainty—then let us hold the conclusion tentative and revise it as new evidence is gathered." Scientific method, therefore, approximates the essence of the matter; but the instrumental process is a larger concept. The origin of scientific method falls within recorded history, but the instrumental process is as old as man. It was a momentous event in this process when one of our remote forebears discovered by accident that fire can be maintained indefinitely by adding dry wood; but few persons would care to label this as science. The continuum of tools extends unbroken from the first flint knife to the latest atom-smasher, and this continuum is at the very heart of the concept; but, again, the instrumental process designates something more. Technology is usually taken to mean material artifacts, but the discovery and use of conceptual tools is an essential part of the instrumental process. It includes the differential calculus as well as the flying machine, the diatonic scale as well as the microscope. It includes, also, art, both fine and applied. For art, as all artists know, is a problem-solving activity in which answers are achieved by taking pains, not by revelation from on high or seizure by a muse. This is not to deny the existence or importance of chance insight or inspiration, either scientific or artistic; but chance, as Claude Bernard has remarked, favors the prepared mind. The authority of the instrumental process is rational, deriving from its demonstrable usefulness to the life process. The final appeal is to the evidence.

The institutional process designates all those activities which are dominated by the quest for certainty. Everything mundane is subject to change, and hence certainty is not to be found in the affairs of men. The searcher arrives at his goal, therefore, in a realm of being superordinate to man. Solomon put it succinctly: "Trust in the Lord with all thine heart; and lean not unto thine own understanding." Religion conveys the essence, but the institutional process is of greater scope. Religion was a relatively late development in the institutional process, as scientific method was a relatively late development in the instrumental process. Far older are animism and the alleged omnipotence of thought, which is magic. With these go rites, taboos, mores, and ceremonial compulsions. All of these belong to the institutional process and are part of a continuum which includes kingship, status, and the coercive power systems of such modern institutions as private property and the sovereign state. The authority of the institutional process is arbitrary; the final appeal is to force.

This instrumental process is bound to reality. Facts are facts, it seems to say. Ignoring them is of no avail. One doesn't have to like them, but he who would gratify his needs and secure himself from peril had better take them into account. Reality can be altered, particularly if it is closely observed. Indeed, the better one understands it and the more tools one has to deal with it, the more radically it can be changed. But it's there, for better or for worse, and the only way to make it better is to attend to it. The instrumental process is generally disparaged as mere problem-solving; for the security it creates, though real, is limited.

The institutional process is bound to human desire and fear. Wishing will make it so, it seems to say. It is unbearable that no one should care; so there must exist a heavenly Father who loves us. Activities of the institutional process do not, objectively, gratify any need or guard against any danger; incantation does not cause rain to fall or game to be plentiful. But such activities may engender a subjective sense of security, and this has always been a fact to be reckoned with—and, indeed, to be exploited. Honor and prestige accrue to the institutional process; for the security it creates, though illusory, is unlimited.

The Individual and the Social

Freud has described a mode of mental functioning, motivated by needs, which tolerates no deferment of gratification. The needs constitute an imperative which reality must meet or before which reality must give way. If the need-gratifying object is not immediately at hand it will be created in fantasy or by hallucination. This mode of mental functioning is characteristic of the unconscious, is apparent in dreams, and may be observed in the behavior of infants. Freud called it the primary process. It is to a greater or lesser degree replaced in the course of growth and development by another mode of mental functioning of which rational thought is an example. This mode, too, is motivated by needs, but the needs no longer constitute an imperative. Allegiance is given to reality as well, and the needs no longer warrant the fantasied creation or destruction of fact. This mode of mental functioning is characterized by tolerance of delay, attention to reality, detour activities, and compromise solutions. Freud called this the secondary process.

Clearly there is a striking parallel between the primary and secondary processes at the individual level of analysis, and the institutional and instrumental processes at the cultural level of analysis.

Such a correspondence appears to make possible the analysis of culture in terms of mental functions. Freud, for example, viewed culture as "a product of three independent variables: (1) necessity . . . imposed by nature; (2) the instinctual polarity in man: love and death . . . and (3) the institutions and ideals developed by society."[2] These concepts are not, however, coordinate, but refer to different levels of generalization. Scarcity is not an independent variable, but a function of the state of the industrial arts. Wild game was once the principal natural resource, but is so no longer. Arable land was hardly a natural resource before the discovery of agriculture. Coal became a natural resource only with the advent of tools with which it could be dug from the ground and of furnaces in which it could be used as fuel. And uranium has become a natural resource only in our own generation. Scarcity, therefore, has no meaning except as defined by a prevailing technology.

The instinctual drives of man are not a variable at all, but a constant. There is no evidence that they have changed in the course of man's known history, that a Carthaginian general was instinctually any different from an American businessman. The structural and instinctual nature of man would have to be invoked to explain why man creates civilizations, whereas apes do not; and without doubt any further evolutionary change in man's biological endowment would have profound effects on culture. With equal obviousness no society could long endure which wholly thwarted human needs. Any society which enforced exceptionless sexual continence or exacted the sacrifice of all newborn infants would cease to exist within a generation. But instinctual drives do not determine the patterns of culture; it is culture that determines the patterns of instinctual drives. To the problem of cultural change instinctual drives are ir-

[2] Hans Meyerhoff, "Freud and the Ambiguity of Culture," *Partisan Review*, vol. 24, no. 1 (1957), p. 119.

relevant, bearing the same relationship as does the law of gravity to the discovery and progress of aviation. The constant of biologically given needs cannot, therefore, explain the pageant of successive and diverse cultures in which these needs have achieved varying gratifications and suffered varying frustrations.

The frustration of human needs imposed by a culture may, of course, provide a starting point for the criticism of that culture. But if such criticism is to initiate cultural change it must proceed from the level of instinctual protest to the level of cultural process. It must enter, specifically, the instrumental process. The entire body of Freud's work is a landmark in this process and has thus been a force for cultural change.

Cultural change is a product of cultural forces. The analysis of this process, therefore, requires concepts on this level of generalization.

The separation of human activities into instrumental and institutional categories creates a dichotomy. As Ayres has pointed out, however, it does not create a dualism. It does not establish two realms of being, such as mind and body, but designates distinct aspects of a single and continuous life process. Both are present at all time. Both call upon and give expression to the entire range of human faculties. Both minister to human needs, in fact or in fantasy. In most human endeavors the two aspects are intricately interwoven. The governing of a state, for example, includes countless activities dominated by status and precedent, existing side by side with equally numerous processes of matter-of-fact problem-solving.[3]

The Dynamic of Cultural Change

The dynamic of cultural change is not to be found in politics, conquest, or revolution. Events in these areas are the visible expressions of a process of change that takes place continu-

[3] C. E. Ayres, *The Theory of Economic Progress* (Chapel Hill: The University of North Carolina Press, 1944), p. 101.

ously, and for the most part without notice, in the instrumental process. Acceleration is intrinsic to this process. The devices which transform man's environment—whether they be material, as the automobile, or intellectual, as the differential calculus—proliferate by geometric progression. The more tools in existence, the more new tool-combinations are possible. The introduction of keels into a culture that contains sails and rudders is likely to yield sailing ships. The perfection of an internal combustion engine by a culture that contains buggies and kites will certainly result in automobiles and airplanes. A historical chart of such devices, therefore, has the appearance of a logarithmic graph: the entries become most crowded together as one approaches the present.[4] This principle does not, of course, assert that the technological achievements of 1960 will be more numerous or more significant than those of 1950; its applicability is to time spans of greater length. Nor does it assert that the technological process is an imperative. Coercive institutional power may retard it, may, indeed, bring it to a complete stop, as is evidenced by the continuing existence of stone age culture in some parts of the world. Its validity is as a principle rather than a law. It asserts only that the instrumental process possesses an inherent dynamic of accelerating progression.

With these reservations, the principle fits the facts both of historical information and of contemporary observation. Of those periods of culture which are defined by the existing technology, the older the period the greater its length. The old stone age, for example, endured for a million years. The new stone age, brief in comparison, was still of a duration greater than all subsequent time. And in the "Dark" Ages—when, according to the old history books, the culture of Christendom was static—there were beginning to appear in western Europe those devices which prepared the way for the industrial revolution to follow—printing, gunpowder, the compass, the astro-

[4] *Ibid.*, Chap. VII.

labe, the symbol for zero, the mill wheel, and the clock.[5] At any time in the history of man the rate of technological development was greater than it had ever previously been; at present it is the fastest known.

The instrumental process, therefore, is the source of cultural change. This is not to deny that it might be maintained with equal truth that the source of change lies in the spirit of man that soareth upward; but it is in precisely such instrumental activities that the soaring and Promethean spirit of man is evidenced. For the instrumental process denotes, not only the material concatenation of devices and machines, but all of the problem-solving activities of the investigative and creative mind of man.

As change is the essence of the instrumental process, so standing pat is the essence of the institutional process. Institutions change only under duress, only under the impact, direct or remote, of the instrumental process. Revolutionary changes are implicit in the discovery of fire, agriculture, the wheel, and printing from movable type; but no impetus to change is to be found in the institutions of private property, the church, the divine right of kings, or human sacrifice to gods.

Institutions do, however, expand. They are coercive power systems, and they extend their authority to the furthest possible reach. The history of nations and of religions is a record of such expansions, their ebb and flow. The force of institutions, however, is unalterably opposed to developments in the instrumental process which give a new direction to culture and thereby threaten institutional authority.

Nevertheless institutions usually claim credit for those cultural changes which, in retrospect, seem to have been desirable. Capitalism, for example, is said to have made possible the industrial revolution; and the church is said to have made possible the colonization of the new world. Such claims—and

[5] *Ibid.*, p. 137.

these are representative—do not bear examination. The industrial revolution was the outcome of an advancing technology, particularly of power machinery which made large-scale productive operations more feasible than ever before. To the institution of capitalism belongs the credit only of not having halted the process, of having been permissive of its development. The Catholic Church certainly was active in converting the natives of New Spain; likewise the Spanish soldiers were active in plundering. The colonization of the new world might be credited with equal plausibility to the greed of individuals or nations, to the love of adventure, or to any other activity or motive evidenced by the colonists. Such claims proliferate easily, but miss the point. European settlements in the new world were a function of ships which could undertake Atlantic crossings. Without such ships there could be no settlements; with such ships it was only a matter of time until settlements were undertaken.

Cultural Lag

The instrumental impetus to change and the institutional insistence on rooted permanence constitute the dialectic of civilization. These contrary tendencies generate a growing discrepancy between technology and institutions and, consequently, a mounting social tension. Institutions change under the impact of technological progress. They change slowly and reluctantly, but they do change and make peace, finally, with the conditions which altered them. By then technology has moved on, and the laggard is still trailing. The discrepancy remains, only its position has shifted. This is the phenomenon of cultural lag. As a social problem it becomes increasingly crucial, because the lag itself increases. For, while technological progress is an accelerative progression, institutional malleability undergoes no such increase. Institutional practices, therefore, become progressively more at variance with the industrial arts.

The sovereign national state, for example, had become anachronistic by 1914. Developments in transportation and communication, in production and commerce, had rendered it dangerously at odds with industrial civilization. But though obsolete in principle, it was—and still is—very much alive. In the intervening forty-odd years sovereignty has been but minimally curtailed, while technological progress has veritably transformed the world. The discrepancy has consequently increased.

At times the discrepancy between institutions and technology becomes an incompatibility, and then one or the other must give way. The relatively straightforward course of western civilization during the past two thousand years is an indication that institutions have usually given way; but we have no guarantee that such will continue. If, as seems likely, the discrepancy between national sovereignty and prevailing technology has already become an incompatibility, and if this issue should be decided by force, we are in no way assured that it would be the institution of national sovereignty that would be destroyed. It might be—as we are frequently warned—industrial civilization itself which would disappear. Such a possibility lends unique urgency to the issue of cultural lag in our time.

Social Character and the Instrumental Process

Change in social character is to be related to change in the conditions of life; and change in the conditions of life is to be traced to the instrumental process. If these propositions are true, the emergent social character and the problem of identity must in some way correspond to the emergent consequences of the instrumental process. The nature of this correspondence, however, is not immediately clear. For social character is not fashioned out of the primary impact of technological change. Character is not molded by gadgets. New industrial procedures and scientific concepts do not directly alter personality.

The immediate causes of the characterological change are to be found in the secondary effects of technological change: the loss of the eternal verities and the fixed order, the weakening of traditions and institutions, the shifting values, the altered patterns of personal relationships. These changes directly mold character, and these changes occur with a continuity that is traceable to the continuity of the instrumental process.

Yet the belief that social character was formerly fixed and stable contains at least two elements of truth. The first of these is that character is now changing faster than it did in the past, a difference in rate that is easily mistaken for a difference in state. The second is that, during most of human history, change in the character of a people has proceeded so slowly as to be imperceptible during its occurrence. What is new is not the fact that social character is changing; this has always been in process. What is new is its occurrence at a more rapid rate than ever before and, thereby, our awareness of the change as it is taking place.

THE EMERGENT SOCIAL CHARACTER

Poised to Change

The social character now coming to prevail seems sculptured to fit a culture of change. In order to survive, it would appear that the individual must become progressively more able to modify himself, to alter his values, to change his reactions. The currently developing social character is equipped with precisely this potential. In it the light touch supplants the firm grip; the launcher of trial balloons replaces the committed man. One avoids final decisions, keeps everything subject to revision, and stands ready to change course when the winds change. The key words of our time are flexibility, adjustment, and warmth—as, for our grandfathers, they were work, thrift, and will.

Nevertheless, this character may not be best fitted for survival. That it exists at all is proof that it can survive in the present; that it is coming generally to prevail is proof that strong and widely-felt forces are participating in its formation. But these facts do not establish either that it is the only configuration of social character that could survive in the present or that, of all possible configurations, it is the one best fitted for survival, either in the present or in the long run. The social character which came to be dominant in Rome in the fourth century A.D. was quite possibly not the one best fitted for the survival of either the groups that exemplified it or the culture that formed it.

This is not to foretell disaster, but only to indicate that the characterological creations of culture are not necessarily most apt even for the culture that creates them. The fact that culture produces social character by the operation of pervasive and subtle influences that are superordinate to the conscious intent of individuals—a process which acquires thereby the status of an automatic mechanism—warrants no assumption of either purpose or infallibility. Cultures as well as individuals are full of automatic mechanisms that at times go dreadfully awry.

It might be inferred that a character fashioned by social conditions which require plasticity of character would not pursue distant goals. For goals, being the manifest expression of character, can hardly remain fixed while the character which they define changes. And what might be inferred can indeed be observed. The social character that is coming to prevail is not given to dedicated pursuits.[6] As the preoccupation with adjustment has increased, the drive for achievement has diminished. Idealism is on the wane; for the ideal, however variously conceived, is always at considerable distance from the actual. It is becoming more rare to believe, individually, with such conviction as to be willing, if necessary, to die for one's belief.

To commit allegiance and will and energy to valued ends

[6] David Riesman, *Faces in the Crowd* (New Haven: Yale University Press, 1952), p. 23.

means to define the self in terms of these ends and to find in them the enduring meaning and purpose of life. The social character of our time, being largely without goals, lacks this sense of meaning and purpose. This lack is experienced as futility, emptiness, and longing. It forms a reservoir of restless energy which seeks attachment, presses for discharge. It is the explosive fuel for, among other things, mass movements.[7] For when, from time to time, the level rises above a critical point, there appears a leader who can define a goal and force its acceptance, can exact allegiance, command the free energy, and can thereby give meaning to life and dispel the feeling of futility. Then one does have something for which he is willing to die. It is coming to be characteristic of our time that only in mass movements do goals become vital and vitalizing. The identity which is defined by their pursuit is firm and sharply circumscribed, but is not individually achieved. It is stamped out in millions by the modern production techniques of fanatic ideology.

Without meaningful goals modern man has, understandably, no sense of direction; for he does not look where he is going. Like an anxious soldier on a drill field he covertly watches those around him to make sure he stays in step. He sticks to the group, and where the group will go next nobody knows. He despairs of its zigzag course, but hesitates to strike out on his own in any direction because of the likelihood that no one direction can be long maintained. He adjusts to the group and keeps in step and executes the increasingly frequent maneuvers with increasing alacrity. Poised to wheel and turn, he pursues no ends, but rather perfects the instrument of achievement, his personality, which is kept flexible, alert, and perceptive. His character acquires a fine readiness for some unknown undertaking to which it is never committed. He is burdened by a sense of futility and longs for something or someone to give meaning to his life, to tell him who he is, to give him something to live for.

[7] Eric Hoffer, *The True Believer* (New York: Harper and Brothers, 1951).

Emergent social tasks are everywhere at hand, and the great social tasks of the past are still unfinished. Rousseau's stinging challenge, "Man is born free, and everywhere he is in chains," retains some pertinence for us after two hundred years. The old verities are still available, but may be found in libraries more readily than in the hearts of living men. They provide no answer for the man of today, and so make no valid claim on his allegiance. The religion of his parents has lost all meaning for him; the Marxism of his youth has become fatuous as well as dangerous. His grandfather was determined to blaze a trail, to become rich, to build a railroad, or to create a farm out of the wilderness. The grandson is not very interested in these things, or in their modern equivalents. He has become weary and skeptical. He is not seeking some *new* value; it is not novelty he needs, but durability. He is a seeker after something that will provide what values and goals have always provided; but he wants it to be different in kind. For values, he feels, cannot be made to stay. Their change is forced by a changing world, and he wants something that will last. But what can substitute for values except other values? What can function as goals except other goals? And on what basis could any possible value or goal be exempt from the engulfing flux?

There is, indeed, no escape from values and goals, or from their vulnerability. There is nothing different in kind but same in function. The effort to diminish the stress occasioned by accelerating change cannot eliminate goals and values. It can, however, force them to become subjective. One abandons the tasks of the world and bends one's efforts upon one's self. One gives up hope of changing the world and resigns one's self to the alteration only of one's reactions. This is the current guise of defeat. One seeks adjustment, a flexible personality, warm interpersonal relationships; and most particularly one cultivates an increasingly sensitive awareness of one's inner life and conflicts. But the energies of man drive for discharge; the direction of flow is outward. The cultivation only of one's self can command but a small fraction of one's potential motivation. The larger part remains dammed up, a reservoir of restless discontent.

Homogeneity, Heterogeneity, and Conformity

Observations of this kind have led to the designation of our time as an age of conformity, and our culture as one of increasing homogeneity. There is much to support this view. Traveling across the continent one sees a striking sameness. From Florida to Oregon people live in the same ranch style or tract houses, wear the same variety of clothes, read the same books, magazines, and editorials, see the same movies and television programs, listen to the same newscasts, discuss the same issues. From Tucson to Stockbridge they drive the same cars along the same superhighways, through towns which look alike, past the same billboards extolling the same beer, stop at the same motels, eat the same foods, use the same toothpaste, and go to sleep on the same foam-rubber mattresses. The traveler of fifty years ago would have found more diversity. From New England to the Oklahoma territory he would have observed striking differences in food, clothes, houses, recreation, education, manners, morals, customs, law and order. Most of those things which tend now toward uniformity were then diverse. This homogeneity is frequently cited as evidence of a growing need to conform. It is said that we, as individuals, are trying harder than ever to be like everybody else, that we are losing the potential for rebellion, for finding our own unique way in life.

The observations of homogeneity are beyond question, but in terms of individual experience they miss the point. For any individual the cultural change has been in precisely the opposite direction—from a relative homogeneity fifty years ago to a bewildering heterogeneity today. The apparent paradox is produced by a shifting point of view. It is only from a vantage point which scans the life of the entire country that the culture of fifty years ago appears heterogeneous; the vantage point of individuals living at that time permitted no such sweeping view. Their cultural horizons included but little more than the regions in which they lived, and within these limits the culture was relatively homogeneous. Technological change has since pushed back these horizons, has brought the culture of New York, Detroit, and Hollywood to people living anywhere in the land.

As the culture as a whole has become more uniform, the culture that impacts on any individual has become more diverse. The very changes that have brought about an over-all sameness to American life have enormously increased the variety of influences that play on the individual. As the culture as a whole gains in unity, the individual has a harder time maintaining a sense of personal unity and wholeness.

The present homogeneity of American life does not reflect a heightened tendency to conform. The observed facts are clearly a function of technological change, particularly the revolution in communication, transport, and mass production. If there has been any actual change in the tendency to conform, it is more likely to have decreased; for experience now is pluralistic, and choice is presented in areas that formerly permitted of only one course of action. The striking feature of present-day American life is precisely that there is no one over-all mode of conduct. As Daniel Bell has remarked, "One would be hard put to it to find today the 'conformity' *Main Street* exacted of Carol Kennicott thirty years ago."[8] School teachers are still well advised to be discreet in their personal relations, but surely they have a little more leeway now than in 1900.

The issue is not a change in the tendency to conform, but a change in the experienced value of what is conformed to. In the last century a person growing up in a small American town experienced a relatively homogeneous society. The

[8] Daniel Bell, "The Theory of Mass Society," *Commentary*, vol. 22, no. 1 (July, 1956), p. 82.

cultural boundaries were close at hand and the life they circumscribed was of a piece. The prevailing manners, morals, and customs were of stable value and were usually accepted without question. They provided the basis for the sense of identity. They defined—not one way of life among many—but *the* way of life, the right way. Following this way of life insured basic security. The approval of others was desirable, but not necessary. Conformity was more nearly automatic.

Today the village society has been replaced by the mass society. However small the town in which one lives, one's world is nevertheless expanded. Being exposed to heterogeneous manners, customs, and morals, their relativity can no longer be ignored. Eternal verities become mores. *The* way of life comes to be but one way among many. A fixed order of final truth has become a relative order of expedient truth. One conforms to some segment of this relative order, but conformity yields diminished security. The approval of others becomes essential. The perceived relativity of mores has diminished their experienced value.

Conformity may not have changed in degree, but our awareness of it has increased, and this entails a change in quality. Formerly it was not experienced as conformity at all, but rather as adherence to principle. One did not "conform" to the right way of life; one rather "elected"—proudly and with "free" will—to be honorable and upright. These categories did not appear to be defined by mores, but by divine revelation or self-evident truth. Today conformity is experienced more largely as such—namely, as adherence to custom. The change detracts from self-esteem as well as from security. Conformity to Southern Methodism was apt to yield a sense of righteousness; conformity to the *avant garde* is apt to yield a lurking sense of opportunism.

The change from coherent to conflicting mores accounts in large measure for the extended awareness of one's self and of others that is characteristic of the emergent social character. In a homogeneous society those motivations which run counter to mores are more apt to be excluded from individual awareness—as deviant sexual impulses were more apt to be repressed in Victorian society. In a heterogeneous society such repression is less likely. Not one way of life is offered, but many—and many of them incompatible. One conforms to those patterns which seem most appropriate, but continues to be exposed to diverse other influences. The mores that seem alien appeal to repressed motivations and facilitate the emergence of these motivations into consciousness.

This same change accounts, also, for the fact that it is becoming rare to value any belief more than life. To be willing to die for a belief means to be unable to conceive of an acceptable life outside the framework of that belief. The pluralistic and heterogeneous quality of present-day experience undermines such exclusive beliefs; for such a variety of values, standards, and ways of life are presented that no one of them seems indispensable. One *can* conceive of a tolerable life outside the framework of any ideology, and so is unwilling to die for any of them. In a mass movement, however, homogeneity may again be achieved, at least temporarily. The ideology may define the only acceptable life, and martyrdom again becomes possible.

Mores and Morals

Mores are usually distinguished from morals. "What is customary?" makes reference to mores. "What would be right?" makes reference to morals. Indeed, the difference in the verb form in these two questions indicates something of the difference between the subjects. Mores refer to the present, morals to all time. In morals one is not concerned with practice, but with principle.

Upon scrutiny, however, the principle proves to have originated in practice and to have a personal origin. The moral decision is the one which would be reached by a wise person of the past, were he in the same situation. This wise person, when exposed, usually turns out to be a parent—or a composite of both parents, and perhaps other older persons who were important in one's childhood. In reaching a moral decision, however, one does not usually make conscious reference to the person from whose practice the principle was derived; one makes reference only to the residue of that person which exists within one's self. This is one's conscience, a distillate of the past, the bearer of tradition. It is what one feels to be the best of his past, that most worthy of being preserved and honored. To act morally is to act in conformity to this residue of the past, even though such action be at odds with prevailing practice.

Mores, therefore, refer to prevailing practice, and the issue is one of adjustment. Morals refer to principles derived from the past, and the issue is one of integrity. This is the way the matter seems when viewed from within the confines of any culture. The distinction seems clear: what is customary is secular and temporary and relative; what is right is transcendent and permanent and absolute.

When, however, one views the same issue from the vantage point of a different culture, the distinction fades. Morals are seen to be simply the more durable mores, the mores which that particular culture deems most important. Sexual fidelity in marriage is, for us, a matter of morals; putting on one's best clothes to go to church, a matter of mores. One is a matter of right and wrong, the other a matter of custom. But from the vantage point of a different culture both practices are seen to possess only the same sanction: they are customary for our culture.

Mores, therefore, define what is right as well as what is customary. They establish what is worth striving for, cherishing, and protecting. And the authority of mores is simply that they exist. They are what they happen to be, and that is all they are. They possess no transcultural validity. They are the guiding agencies of life for those who are guided by them—and for none others. Billions of words have been written, and millions of persons have died, for the purpose of establishing a higher authority for mores, an authority rational or divine in nature, absolute in certainty, universal in scope, and eternal in duration; but the lives were wasted and the words are convincing only to those who already believe. The ineluctable fact is that the validity of mores is relative to the culture that supports them. The values that derive from them are likewise relative.

Moral behavior, therefore, is culturally relative and is defined by the mores. In any situation one will be acting morally if he acts as the "best" people of that culture act in that situation.[9] The "best" people are, of course, those of highest status. One who acts contrary to the most valued mores is immoral. If such action should lead to the downfall of existing mores and to the establishment of new ones, he may become known to later generations as a great moral leader. But at the time of the violation he is judged immoral. Moral behavior, therefore, is essentially imitative.

Since morals derive from mores, moral values are institutional in nature. There is no reason why they must necessarily be institutional; it is simply a matter of fact that they usually are. Instrumental values are relegated to an inferior realm. Indeed, if one performs a "good" act because of its demonstrable instrumental value, the act is not considered truly moral; it has, for most persons, the flavor of opportunism. Honesty is the best policy, we say; and this is an assertion of instrumental value. But we don't really expect people to be honest *because* it's the best policy. We expect them to be honest because it's *right,* and to console themselves for losses which the exercise of this virtue may entail by recalling that, in addition to being right, it is said to be to their advantage in the long run. Whenever we encounter a person who is honest only because he believes honesty to work to his ultimate ad-

[9] "Right is what the right people do publicly, and vice versa." C. E. Ayres, *op. cit.,* p. 215. If private and public actions are at variance, morality is hypocritical. In matters of money and sex, as Freud has remarked, such hypocrisy is the rule in western civilization.

vantage, we are apt to consider him morally inferior to one who is honest because of a belief that honesty is "right" in an absolute and transcendental sense.

In morals we hesitate to trust the processes of intelligent inquiry, fearing that our matter-of-fact considerations will be inadequate, that our purview of relevant facts will be short-range and misleading. Actually we believe that most of our morality has instrumental value, that its demonstrable consequences will be individually and socially beneficial. But we are loath to let it rest on that basis. For if it had no other sanction, then it would be open to question and to critical scrutiny. Alternate hypotheses would be formed, experiments undertaken; and when such processes get underway, change is certain. The changes might be to our great advantage, but we are afraid to risk it. We try to secure the good by making it an absolute, by placing it in a realm beyond the reach of intelligent inquiry. In this way morality is divorced from the instrumental process.

Ego and Superego

Though moral behavior is essentially imitative, it is not operationally imitative. In reaching a moral decision the inner experience is one of determining the application of basic principles to a unique situation. It is not important that the action to ensue be in accord with the behavior of contemporaries, but that it be in accord with eternal verities. Morality acquires this judicial and reflective quality by virtue of conscience, which is formed by the incorporation within the child of parental attitudes. These parental attitudes, having themselves been formed in the same way, reflect the mores. They reflect, specifically, those mores which society deems most important, those upon whose continuing integrity the continuance of orderly social life is thought to depend. Conscience becomes, therefore, the repository and the guardian of these mores. It is the carrier of tradition and the foe of change.

The executive department of personality is known as the

ego. It is a cohesive and more or less integrated group of functions; it is the locus of perception, evaluation, anticipation, and decision; it is largely, but not altogether, conscious. Impelled by basic needs and heedful of the strictures of conscience, it is the function of the ego to remain in touch with reality, to take note of changing conditions, to seize opportunities for gratification and security, and to initiate change in order to facilitate gratification and security.

The judicial department of personality is called the superego. What has been said of conscience could be said also of the superego; for conscience is part of the superego. Superego, therefore, is the more inclusive concept, being related to conscience as a whole is related to a part. Conscience may enter awareness; the superego is largely unconscious. Of conscience one may say that it carries into the present that which one feels to be the best of the past, that most deserving of being preserved and honored. Of the superego, particularly its unconscious aspects, one would have to say that it also carries into the present that which was most coercive and threatening in the past. The superego acts as a governor to the ego, administering both praise and blame, reward and punishment. It requires the ego to hew to the line, to keep its eye on eternal verities. Upon occasion it compels the ego to ignore opportunities for the safe gratification of impulse, forbids it to take advantage of changed conditions. Its dictum to the ego is, "What was good for your forefathers is good enough for you." The ego is the agency of change and adaptation; the superego is the carrier of tradition and the defender of mores.

At the psychological level of analysis, therefore, the ego and the superego parallel with curious exactness the instrumental process and the institutional process at the cultural level of analysis. This observation leads directly to a hypothesis: A society in which the prevailing social character is marked by a superego with authority of wide scope will offer relatively vigorous institutional opposition to technological change; and, conversely, a society in which the prevailing social character is marked by a superego with authority of diminished scope will offer diminished institutional opposition to technological change. Since technological change has flourished in America during the past fifty years as never before, this hypothesis would suggest that the change in social character during this period has involved a change in the superego. It suggests, specifically, that the superego has become weaker—either by diminished authority within its realm or, more probably, by a shrinking of the realm over which it exercises authority—and that the control of impulse now devolves more largely upon the ego. It is to the investigation of these propositions that the inquiry now proceeds.

The Decline of the Superego

Prior to the formation of the superego a child may refrain from a forbidden act because of the likelihood of being apprehended and punished; after its formation he will refrain because the act is "wrong." The rein on impulse is thereafter held by an agency within his own personality. The superego becomes relatively autonomous, functions largely on its own steam. Occasionally its autonomy in reference to other aspects of personality may be absolute, as when one elects to lose his life rather than betray his principles. But martyrdom is rare; usually the superego is only relatively independent, leaning heavily upon external support. This support is likely to remain unnoticed so long as it is continued. Only when it is lost does its extent and significance become manifest.

One who lives out his life in the town of his birth derives much superego support from proximity to family and relatives, and from their continuing expectations of him. They know what kind of person he is, and they expect him to continue being that kind of person. If the culture of the community is relatively homogeneous, conscience is strengthened also by the continuing pattern of known traditions, customs, and values. Unopposed mores are not subject to critical scrutiny, but are taken for granted. They comprise *the* way of life. The continuance in parents and in the community at large of the way of life from which the superego was derived continues to nourish and strengthen that superego. Life under such conditions is orderly and predictable.

Such conditions are becoming increasingly rare. Few persons these days live out their lives in the place of their birth or in proximity to parents. We move about the continent and, indeed, the world, with increasing freedom and speed; and such superego support as was formerly had from the continued presence of those persons from whom the superego was derived has been largely withdrawn. Immigrants have often been astonished to discover that a fellow immigrant of good repute and of humble station in the old world has, in the new world, acquired a past of remarkable grandeur—ancestral estates, titles, wealth, and close connections with those in high places. By the time the ship reaches the Statue of Liberty serious fractures of probity may already have occurred.

Probably there is no one who is not more liable to steal, to lie, or to commit adultery in a foreign land than at home. Some persons, indeed, travel for just this purpose—to lose an unwanted reinforcement of conscience. For them wanderlust is not a lust for wandering, but a wandering for lust—an effort to achieve abroad a license for which one could not forgive himself at home. Many persons do not need to go so far: the annual business convention in America is notorious in this respect. Things happen in motels that do not happen in homes, and towels are swiped in distant hotels by persons who would not steal a pin in their home towns. In these ways our increased mobility diminishes the external support for conscience.

Such support is withdrawn, also, by other changes. The rare person of today who does live out his life in the same town lives in a more heterogeneous culture than did his grandparents. The town has changed. Highways link it to the world; the products of faraway factories are for sale in its stores; in a thousand ways it has become connected with the larger society. The cultural horizons have receded; the diverse mores of distant cities seep in through each television antenna. Exposure to alien mores causes one to examine his native mores. And as soon as mores are examined they are seen to be relative; their claim to absolute validity evaporates. The superego is thus deprived of that support that had been provided by the unquestioning acceptance of an unopposed pattern of life.

The increase of leisure operates to the same effect. Work strengthens conscience; leisure facilitates impulse. Idle hands are used by the devil. Work, therefore, has been considered a necessary aid to the superego in its task of curbing sexual and aggressive impulses. It is because of the strength of impulse that one must live by the sweat of his brow; painful labor is both punishment for past sin and insurance against further sinning. Work is best able to implement the control of impulse if it is difficult and continuous. On the one day of rest the church, with its reminder of guilt and original sin, is supposed to serve in lieu of work as adjuvant to conscience. To the extent that work has become easy and leisure has increased, the superego has been deprived of support in its function of repression.

Formerly God was regularly a part of the superego. Behind the authority of one's father was the greater authority of God; behind the towering figure of one's father loomed the vast image of the Father of us all. Both were incorporated by the child in the formation of the superego. The function of God within the superego was steadily aided by the continued existence of God in the outside world, in the same way that continued nearness to one's earthly father augmented the authority of the internalized father. The decline of religious belief has sharply diminished this support. Statistics of church membership are clearly no index to this decline. Belief in the supernatural propositions of religion has, beyond any doubt, radically diminished during the past fifty years. The extent of decline measures the loss of one of the most important external supports to the superego.

. . . . .

The Diminished Unconscious

In these days the superego has become depersonalized.[10] It is no longer so predominantly the father who organizes life and value for the son; for the authority of the father has diminished. Culture contemporary to the child now plays a larger part; and since culture now presents diverse and conflicting mores, the superego that results is less well integrated and wields diminished authority. It is thereby less effective as a carrier of tradition. We do not escape the past altogether; but in the superego of the man of today the image of parents is fainter, their lifespan shorter.

With the decline of the superego, morality has changed in content. Many things at which our grandparents would have drawn the line now pass muster; and we balk at some things which caused them no compunction. But, apart from changes in the content of moral behavior, there have been changes in the source of morality, the mode of conformity to moral directives, and the site of moral authority.

Formerly morality was obedience to the verities instilled by parents; it is coming now to be compliance with the practices of one's peers.[11] In both instances the source of the standard is outside the individual; for moral principles, not being innate, must be somewhere acquired. In the nineteenth century they were learned from the older generation; now they are learned largely from contemporaries. This shift in source of moral directives is clearly a function of the accelerating rate of social change; for if social change of such magnitude as to require adaptive characterological change is occurring rapidly, the cues will be given first by one's contemporaries.

The change in conformity is less obvious. It is not that now

[10] "The repressive organization of the instincts seems to be *collective*, and the ego seems to be prematurely socialized by a whole system of extra-familial agents and agencies." Herbert Marcuse, *Eros and Civilization* (Boston: The Beacon Press, 1955), p. 97.

[11] David Riesman, Nathan Glazer, and Reuel Denney, *The Lonely Crowd* (New Haven: Yale University Press, 1950), Chap. II.

one conforms to the group whereas formerly one went his own way. Conformity is common to both modes: formerly one conformed to the precepts of parents; now one conforms to the expectations of contemporaries. Yet there is a difference in the style of conformity. When the source of morality is in the past one is more likely to abstract principles; when the source is in the present one is more likely to ape models. The change detracts from the reflective and judicial quality of moral action, discourages the examination of a unique situation with reference to a guiding principle, and fosters the adoption of total behavioral modes. This gives to morality an automaton quality. It tends, indeed, to make morality synonymous with adjustment.

The site of the moral standard has also changed. The group has gained in authority at the expense of the conscience. Formerly the standard whereby conduct was judged was within the individual. It was taken from the older generation, but the point is that it was *taken*. It was incorporated by the individual in his childhood and thereafter endured within him, beholden to no one, paying no tribute. Now the standard whereby conduct is judged is coming to be located in the group to which the individual adjusts. Specifically this means that the superego has become weaker, more susceptible to influence. The grounds on which it praises and prohibits are open to argument and, particularly, to example.

Consequent to the diminished authority of the superego, unconscious motivation has become less significant in human affairs—for the reason, simply, that there now is less of it. As the authority and stability of the superego have diminished, it has become less able to exclude psychic elements from consciousness. Therefore, there has occurred in society as a whole during the past two generations a development analogous to that which occurs in an individual during psychoanalysis, an expansion of awareness at the expense of the unconscious.

The contraction of the unconscious is empirical: it may be

observed. Many elements of motivation which were commonly repressed in the nineteenth century are now rarely repressed. The evidence concerning aggression is equivocal, but there is no doubt about the liberation of sexuality. The diminished incidence of hysteria is in line with these observations, and is similarly a matter of fact. Hysteria depends upon repression, and is becoming rare; character disorders reflect warped ego-functioning, and are becoming common. As clear-cut symptom neuroses disappear, vague conditions of aimlessness and futility become prevalent.

The contraction of the unconscious may also be theoretically derived from known cultural changes. For the superego, which is the instrument of repression, is the internal representative of the culture. As the culture changes, the superego necessarily changes; and as the superego changes, a change in the unconscious is to be expected. The superego does not, however, represent all aspects of culture; it is the representative only of those aspects of culture which have here been designated as the institutional process. The instrumental process develops at an accelerating pace, and the institutional process gives ground. The superego, being a precipitate of institutional verities, likewise gives ground. The contraction of the unconscious may thus be inferred from this reciprocal development.

In addition to the quantitative change in the unconscious, there has occurred also a qualitative change. Formerly the superego was the primary source of repression; now the ego is more commonly the agency that excludes perceptions and motivations from awareness. In the nineteenth century, man lived in a society of relatively stable values. These were transmitted to him by his parents and established within his character as a relatively permanent and autonomous agency. A drive conflicting with this agency was repressed. If sufficiently strong, this drive achieved a distorted symptomatic discharge which constituted the illness. Neurotic suffering in the present is coming more and more to derive from a quite different process. Society does not embody such generally accepted patterns of value, and the individual is caught in a dilemma: if out of the multitudinous choices of modern life he commits himself to certain values and with them builds a durable identity, he is apt to lose contact with a rapidly changing world; if he does not commit himself, but maintains an alert readiness to move with the current, he suffers a loss of the sense of self. Not knowing what he stands for, he does not know who he is. This occasions the anxiety which is coming to be the name of our age. Any development that threatens further to liquefy this already fluid sense of identity may increase anxiety to an unendurable pitch and hence prompt the ego to exclude the threatening wish or perception from awareness.

In the nineteenth century the unconscious consisted largely of superego rejects. Being the polar opposite of a known quantity, it was more homogeneous, more subject to inference. Nowadays the unconscious is comprised largely of ego rejects and is heterogeneous. In it sexual wishes, certainly, have lost their former pre-eminence. Being the product of the anxiety suffered by a fluid identity, it is the polar opposite of nothing definite.

Retreat from Reason

In the eighteenth century, having discarded the world view which had for centuries been imposed by the Church, man achieved by reason a blueprint of the universe. The great plan was seen in outline; it remained only to fill in the details. The universe was a precision instrument, a great clock that, having been set in motion, would continue forever. It functioned, not at the whim of God, but according to its own law. However cleverly hidden its secrets, they would all yield in time to the probing reason of enlightened man. Goodness, order, and uniformity were built into the nature of things. Progress would consist in approximating human nature and institutions to natural law.

Now there is no great plan or pattern. The blueprint has

been lost. Nothing is static. Everything evolves. We speak less of progress than of survival; and survival may be had only by adapting human nature and institutions to existing conditions of human life. The existing conditions undergo change at an accelerated rate, and seldom can a present problem be solved by a formula from the past.

From the eighteenth century until our own time it had seemed that reason could establish values of demonstrable validity, not only for the culture in which they arose, but for all peoples. In our time this position is being replaced by a cultural nihilism which reduces value to taste. It had seemed that precise science yielded absolute truth and that there was no limit to the penetrability of matter by science. Now the causal law is being replaced by the probability law, and our vision of the microcosmic world is limited in theory as well as practice. The currency of the phrase "indeterminacy principle" measures the appeal of its words rather than an understanding of the hypothesis, and the frequent allusions to this principle by social scientists bespeak an incipient readiness to give up the whole notion of a determined universe. The idea of progress has fallen into bad repute. It had seemed that technological progress would achieve progressive betterment of the human condition; now it is more common to regard the machine as the unruly and malevolent master of man. The atomic bomb and the assembly line are the present fruits of technology, and to many it appears a toss-up whether we shall die by blast or boredom. It had seemed that psychoanalysis would extend the realm of reason to include the most obscure and devious elements of mental life. Now Freud is claimed by the opposite camp. His greatest achievement, so it is said, is that of having exposed reason as the shoddy tissue of rationalizations that it is, and he is credited with having fathered the cult of the irrational.

Having lost faith in absolute values, we have become skeptical, also, of instrumental values. In the storm of change, we have jettisoned not only the excess baggage, but also the crucially important ballast. The retreat from reason, having gotten underway in the twenties, has so gained in speed and momentum that it is coming now to be known as a revolt.[12] "Man, having found that he cannot live by reason alone, seems determined that he will not live by reason at all."

The retreat from reason is reactive to the troubles of our times. Two world wars, a world depression, dictatorships, purges, and the present possibility of winding the whole thing up on the next slip—all this is within the lifetime of living men. Surveying this state of affairs, many persons find an explanation which appears obvious: science has imposed a godless materialism on western civilization, destroying those values which had provided for the support and security of man. Science, it may be allowed, has its place, but is out of place when it impinges on traditional values and institutions. In times of trouble the past is transformed, becomes an age of innocence and clarity. The evil was ushered in by change. Technology is the instrument of change. Behind technology stands science, behind science the method of rational inquiry, and, finally, reason itself. So science and reason are blamed, together and alone, for the evils of our day. Reason has had two hundred years in which to prove its right to direct the course of human affairs, and has brought us to the verge of universal destruction.

Those who are committed to reason are quick to point out that the accusation is both unfair and inconsistent. The social disasters of the twentieth century have issued out of economic and political practices and the relations between nations, and it is from precisely these areas that scientific method has been most rigorously excluded. When the findings of disinterested inquiry have run counter to vested interests, rational inquiry has usually been thrown out. Moreover the period prior to the last two centuries was not lacking in brutal wars, in purges, plagues, and starvation.

[12] Abraham Edel, "Revolt Against Reason," *The Nation*, vol. 181, no. 22 (Nov. 26, 1955), p. 459.

But the rebuttal does not convince, and more and more of those who are troubled by the crisis of our times call for a rebirth, in one form or another, of transcendental values.

Although reactive to the troubles of our times, the retreat from reason is not explained by those troubles. Past times have encountered comparable problems without being forced to flight. The retreat from reason, like the changing social character, is an outcome of the quickened and still accelerating rate of cultural change which is rendering obsolete many of the great intellectual systems of the past. Reason does not lose value, but fixed embodiments of reason become outdated. The goals which have held the allegiance of men and which have been superannuated by change have not all been products of faith. Many of them have been products of reason, and most of them have retained the guise of reason even after they have come to function as dogma.

But whatever guise it may wear, dogma claims finality. In its own domain it holds that its word is the last word, and any challenge of that word is heresy. Sooner or later changing conditions force the abandonment of such positions; and where dogma wears the guise of reason the discrediting of dogma discredits reason. For reason is not judged on its own merits; the products of reason are constantly transformed by the quest for certainty into articles of faith. They function then as a call to emotion rather than to critical intelligence. Being petrified into dogma they become the exact opposite of the rational inquiry that engendered them. But having remained for true believers as symbols of reason, their final collapse is taken as a collapse of reason.

Marxism is an example of such a development. Many Americans of this century passed from religion to Marxism during their college years, experiencing this as a transition from faith to reason, from transcendental values to rational values, from a mythological cosmogony to a scientific interpretation of history. There was much to support such a view.

Marx's analysis of capitalism was certainly an exercise of intelligence rather than faith; and the communist movement, so it seemed, was the direct outcome of that critical analysis. But although Marxism remained a symbol of rational inquiry, it ceased to be so in fact. It came indeed to be hostile to any disinterested review of the facts. It died as reason but lived as dogma, with its adherents remaining unaware of the change. When the developments of the last two decades forced the abandonment of the Marxian dream, many of the former dreamers felt that reason was bankrupt. It should occasion no surprise that ex-communists feel particularly drawn toward mysticism, Catholicism, and reactionary politics.

Institutional absolutes and the coercive power systems that protect them have never provided real security; but they create a subjective feeling of security. The chains that enslave also guard one from the unknown. The uses of reason have cut away most of our immemorial myths and superstitions, and without them we cringe in the sharp winds of uncertainty. We feel lost without the old ceremonial guarantees, afraid to trust our own processes of intelligent inquiry, for these seem too fallible. We have fallen victim to our own power to destroy our myths. Now we so miss the security of our former shackles that we are inclined to discard the sharp-edged tool that cut them. If we do, we shall not have long to wait before someone fits us out with a new set.

Clearly it is not reason that has failed. What has failed—as it has always failed, in all of its thousand forms—is the attempt to achieve certainty, to reach an absolute, to bind the course of human events to a final end. Reason cannot serve such a purpose and yet remain reason. By its nature it must be free to perceive emergent problems and meet them with new solutions. It is not reason that has promised to eliminate risk in human undertakings; it is the emotional needs of men, fastening onto the products of reason, that have made such promises. The vision of a state of universal peace and happiness, to be achieved by reason, is quite transparently the same old heavenly city which was to have been reached by faith and repentance.[13] The reason of the Enlightenment was, as Carl Becker has shown, a new religion. Natural law became a synonym for divine providence; the regularity of the universe was equivalent to the goodness of God; and the pursuit of truth was the new guise for the search for salvation. When a religion is built with the products of science it functions as does any other religion: it erects absolute truth as a dyke against the encompassing tides of change, risk, and uncertainty. Eventually such dykes crumble. In our time of quickened and rising tides they crumble faster than ever.

Adaptation to Change

Truth is hard to get in a net of words: some part of it slips through, or else one gets so much else besides that one cannot see truth whole and uncluttered. The view of life as change and flow appears at variance with the tragic view which finds the essentials of man's condition to be unchanging. "The thing that hath been, it is that which shall be; and that which is done is that which shall be done: and there is no new thing under the sun." The awareness of mortality, and of yearnings that would reach beyond death—this has always been man's fate. Grief and greed, desire and hate—these remain the same. To be born, to work, to suffer, to have fleeting joys, to die—these do not change.

The light of eternity does not illumine the temporal; by definition it reflects only the eternal. In this essay life is viewed in the light of every day, a level of abstraction at which the data assume a temporal and changing aspect. These two views do not conflict, do not contend for the same truth. One need not, and cannot, choose between them. They formulate distinct levels of experience.

The continuity of acceleration in the rate of cultural change

[13] Carl L. Becker, *The Heavenly City of the Eighteenth-Century Philosophers* (New Haven: Yale University Press, 1932), p. 51.

is the clue to the emergent social character. The character corresponds to the rate that has now been reached.

Now, for perhaps the first time in his life on earth, man is obliged to adjust, not simply to changed conditions, but to change itself. In the past he had to give up the old and adapt to the new; now he must adapt, also, to the certain knowledge that the new, with unprecedented rapidity, is being replaced by that which is to follow. Before he becomes fully acquainted with the emerging circumstances of life he is distracted by the moving shadows of their unknown successors. As a modern aircraft may be obsolete by the time it comes off the production line, so the conditions of man's life begin to pass away before he has fairly come to grips with them.

In the last century, to be sure, great changes were encompassed in a single lifetime. Our grandfathers were forced in adult life to adjust to conditions radically different from those of their childhood. Yet the duration of an apparently unchanged culture was greater then than now, and fewer characterological changes were required in a lifetime.

Nowadays no character that is fixed can remain adjusted—unless experience is limited to those conditions under the influence of which character was formed, in which event the dimensions of life shrink rapidly. To be of fixed character and also receptive to the environing culture generates a mounting tension—a circumstance in which psychiatrists become acquainted with a large number of their patients. To remain open to a changing culture and also adapted to it implies the capacity for characterological change. For there is no longer any such thing as an average predictable environment. The only thing that can be predicted with certainty is continued acceleration in the rate of cultural change.

THE LONELY CROWD
David Riesman

More than fifteen years have passed since The Lonely Crowd—*David Riesman's most impressive virtuoso performance—first appeared. By now, and with good reason, it is widely regarded as a classic. Terms first used in that book, by an author with a happy faculty for coining them, have worked their way through several layers of popularization to everyday usage and commonplace abusage. Even the quasi-literate have heard of* inner-directed *and of* other-directed, *which a misplaced sense of symmetry sometimes vulgarizes into "outer-directed." This typology of character alone would guarantee Riesman a certain immortality. He is a gifted phraseologist. Too many people, taken by echoes of his heady language, do not hear the subtle play of ideas that this language was meant to convey. Hedging, qualifying, redressing, forever balancing and thickening his argument, Riesman is no simplifier, as readers of the unbuttoned original text with all its faults are well aware. Of readers there have been many thousands; and today, as with superlative insight it records and counts the human cost of American Progress, the book remains a durable guide to how we have lived and how we live now.*

With The Lonely Crowd, *Riesman demonstrated that he was a brilliant amateur. It took such a man, trained and experienced in the law and otherwise enormously cultivated, to help retrieve sociology from the quantitative trivia and costly*

Source: Reprinted by permission of Yale University Press from *The Lonely Crowd*, by David Riesman, Nathan Glazer, Reuel Denney.

but insignificant research into which a generation or more of professional practitioners had plunged it. Addressing himself to them as much as to the general public, he displayed complete mastery of the classical tradition his work has since done much to revive. In the pages presented here will be found a typical representation of Riesman's intellectual antecedents. Among them are many of the great precursors and founders of sociology. Amateurs, one and all! In this excerpt alone figure Alexis de Tocqueville (1805-1859), the French aristocrat who, after a brief visit to these shores while still in his twenties, told us more about ourselves than we have yet been able to absorb; Georg Simmel (1858-1918), a German philosopher of Jewish ancestry, and therefore academically unacceptable in his homeland, who gave public lectures on human interaction so beautifully wrought that today we sit and ponder them word by word; Max Weber (1864-1920), a legal and economic historian of volcanic genius, wholly acceptable in the German academy, which he nevertheless had to abandon because of ill health; Émile Durkheim (1858-1917), heir of Montesquieu and Auguste Comte, who having heretically opted while a student at the École Normale Supérieure for Comte over Kant, received his doctorate as an agrégé de philosophie *only with the greatest difficulty, spent years teaching philosophy in provincial high schools, finally reached the University of Bordeaux as a professor of both sociology and pedagogy, a combination he was obliged to bear, in later years, even at the Sorbonne; and Thorstein Veblen (1857-1929), the American iconoclast, best known as an economist despite his Ph.D. in philosophy, author of more than one ironic masterpiece about contemporary society, who always lived only on the periphery of our culture and in its interstices.*

The list could be extended, but not much. These men provide Riesman with the rich legacy that he puts to such good use. Most of the rest of us in social science draw on the same capital, but have little to add. If Riesman has done better, it is partly for reasons that are broadly methodological. To test meaningful hypotheses suggested by the masters, he ingeniously culls his data from sources that would not occur to a less imaginative investigator. They include conventional interviews skillfully analyzed, and much, much more. Riesman finds meaning in children's literature, adult novels, cookbooks, movies, radio programs, games and other pastimes, popular biographies, mass-circulation magazines, in short, all those phenomena fashionably classified as mass culture, to whose study he has been a major contributor. All this is abundantly clear in The Lonely Crowd, *a book that fuses familiar and unfamiliar elements in an original synthesis. Because Riesman never suffers from cultural amnesia, he is not limited to any ephemeral moment. He knows the past is central to that understanding of the present without which men cannot prepare themselves for whatever future they may have. Ultimately, it is this historical consciousness that, besides all the rest, accounts for the many shocks of recognition we experience in continuing to read this work with pleasure and profit.*

THE INNER-DIRECTED ROUND OF LIFE

THE ACQUISITIVE CONSUMER

In an era depending on inner-direction men who exhibit the desired arduousness in the sphere of work—as shown by their productivity—can afford a good deal of independence in their moments spared for consumption. One result, in the America of the last century, was the crazy millionaire who, having established his status, save in the most exalted circles, by satisfying society's requirements on the productive front, could do as he pleased on the pleasure front. He could hang the "do not disturb" sign over his play as well as over his work. Once possessed of commanding wealth, he could resist or accept as he chose the ministrations of wives and daughters and even more specialized advisers on consumption, taste, and connoisseurship.

A period when such men live is, therefore, the heyday of conspicuous consumption, when energies identical with those deployed at work are channeled by the rich into their leisure budget. While the producer dynamically creates new networks of transportation in order to exploit resources and distribute the finished and semi-finished product, the consumer of this period begins to act with equal dynamism on the market. The producer pushes; the consumer pulls. The first stage in his consumership is a passionate desire to make things *his*.

Perhaps he lavishes money and energy on a house, to the point where it comes to resemble a department store—recall the wonderful sets and furnishings in the films *Citizen Kane* and *The Ghost Goes West*. Perhaps he gathers the treasures of Europe, including titled sons-in-law. Perhaps he goes in for steam yachts or diamonds or libraries or, united with rich cronies in civic spirit, for theaters, planetariums, and zoos. In most cases the activity is as self-justifying as the search for the North Pole, pursued with hardly more hesitation or boredom than the tasks of the production frontier. There is no need to hesitate because in this period most consumer goods, like work commitments, do not become rapidly obsolete but are good for a lifetime.

The type of acquisitive consumer who is less concerned with building up a private hoard or hobby and more concerned with showing his possessions with fashion seems, at first glance, other-directed in his attention. Yet, if we go back to Veblen's classic work, we can see, I think, that the consumers he describes are other-directed in appearance only. The Veblenese conspicuous consumer is seeking to fit into a role demanded of him by his station, or hoped-for station, in life; whereas the other-directed consumer seeks experiences rather than things and yearns to be guided by others rather than to dazzle them with display. The conspicuous consumer possesses a standard allowing him readily to measure what others have, namely cash.

This standard can penetrate the opacity of objects, even objects unique in their nature, such as a geographical site (so much a front foot) or a beautiful woman (the best money can buy). This gives the consumption of the inner-directed man its relatively impersonal quality—it is as impersonal as his production, of which it is a reflection. Similarly, if he collects old masters, he is taking a standardized step on the consumption gradient for his social class at the same time that he is buying a good investment or at least a good gamble. Moreover, he is, in a way, a "master" himself, a technical man, and he can admire the technique of the Renaissance artist, while few other-directed consumers of today, even though they may know a good deal more about art, dare admire the esoteric technique, or seeming lack of it, of a non-representational artist. The conspicuous consumer is engaged, therefore, in an externalized kind of rivalry, as indicated by Veblen's use of such terms as "ostensible," "emulative," "conspicuous," and the rest of his beautifully ironic thesaurus. The other-directed consumer may compete in what looks like the same way, but only to the degree that the peers impel him to. His desire to outshine, as I have already tried to show, is muted.

To be sure, all these changes are changes in degree, and Veblen's emphasis on leisure and consumption—like, in a very different way, Keynes' emphasis on what we might call relentless spending—are indexes of the social changes paving the way for and accompanying the characterological ones.

AWAY FROM IT ALL

The *acquisitive* consumer brings to the sphere of consumption motivations and ideals similar to those he manifests in the sphere of production. The *escaping* consumer seeks, on the contrary, to dramatize an emotional polarity between work and play.

Because the whole concept of escape is a very slippery one, we must always ask: escape from what and to what? The inner-directed individual can afford a certain kind of escape since his character and situation give him a core of sufficient self-reliance to permit dreaming without disintegration. He learns this as a boy when he escapes by himself a good deal of the time—playing hooky from the dreary and demanding tasks of home and school. Unlike Tootle the engine, he is seldom worried by the fear that, if he gathers primroses by the river's brim, he will not make the grade—though he may be punished, since the right to play has not yet been granted school children. Perhaps he will feel guilt when he escapes, but the guilt will lend savor to the adventure, turning escape into escapade. Like the Victorian father, the stability of whose family life often depended on an occasional visit to a prostitute, the inner-directed person can let himself go in "unsocialized" ways because in the ways that count, the ways of work, he has a definitely socialized self to return to.

To be sure, he may often be too inhibited for that. He may be unable to stop timetabling himself by the internalized pocket watch that he has substituted for the chimes of the Middle Ages. He may be unable to shift his one-price, one-role policy even in dealing with status inferiors, though this, in the explicit class structure of the era, is unusual. Above all, he may feel that, with the reining in and observing of the self on all fronts, he cannot afford to undertake unsanctioned experiments in spontaneity. He may feel his character, covert as well as overt, as a kind of capital that might be dissipated in a catastrophic gamble—all the more dangerous in view of the lifetime goals to which he is committed. We see this complex process rationalized by the puritan in terms of "saving himself." The puritan treats himself as if he were a firm and, at the same time, the firm's auditor.

But we speak in this section of those who, despite internal and external inhibitions, are able to escape in some fashion. Escape as we use it here means a shift of pace and attitude from the nearly all-embracing domain of work. Thus, as we shall see below, it may be escape onto a "higher" level than that of business or professional life, or onto a "lower" level.

Onward and Upward with the Arts / The great events of "escape upward" in leisure time are intermittent: Chautauqua, the traveling theater, the Sunday service complete with one antibusiness preacher per year or per city, the itinerant book peddler. To come into contact with them requires some effort, and making the effort is itself a sign of virtue. There is even a change of dress—Sunday-go-to-meeting dress or top hats—to signify the change of role.

There is, moreover, a good deal of amateur performance. Even more perhaps than plumbing, the piano and the cultivation of amateur musical skills mark the boundary of middle-class aspirations to respectability. At the same time, for the mobile youth from the working class there are the mechanics' institutes and the many traveling lecturers, from prison reformers to single taxers, who analyze the workings of the system for their eager audiences. We need only recall the tremendous mushrooming of discussion clubs that greeted Bellamy's *Looking Backward*.

Obviously the motives of such participants are not purely escapist. There is the desire, often thinly disguised, to move onward and upward in the social hierarchy. Through religious revivalism and Bible reading the individual may seek to escape not from this world but from the dangers of the next. Daily life is hard and drab; leisure is an occasional essay at refinement.

Aspirations for culture make people want to escape into an image of some past heroic period, as inherited from the pre-nineteenth-century upper class. Thus, the cultivated bourgeois of the nineteenth century looks back in his leisure to an earlier and more heroic quasi-bourgeois epoch, in Periclean Athens or Renaissance Italy. Work-driven, chained to routines, he pictures for himself the swagger and versatility of a Benvenuto Cellini or a Leonardo. As the Chautauqua circuit spreads accounts of contemporary travel and discovery, so there exists a semipopular culture about the achievements of the ancient world—note the popularity of *Ben Hur*—and of the Renaissance. Very often the occupational hardness of the era has its obverse side in sentimentality concerning the non-work side of life.

Though fashion, of course, plays a role in the vogue of ancient history, of European travel, and of these other escapist pursuits, it is important, I think, for the security of the inner-directed people that these spheres of interest are remote not only from their work but also from their immediate social concerns. Reading about Greece—even visiting Florence—they are not forced to think about their own epoch or themselves in any realistic sense; such identifications with ancient heroes as there are can be fantastic. We must qualify this only when we arrive at the late Victorian or Edwardian stories of Henry James or E. M. Forster, in which travel in Italy may turn out to be much more emotionally problematic than mere escape upward for Anglo-Saxon ladies and gentlemen. These fictional tourists, concerned with whether they are experiencing to the full the cultural contrasts and sensitivities they seek, find foreshadowed the ambiguities of escape that are typical for other-direction.

Feet on the Rail / The inner-directed person may escape down as well as up. He finds in dime novels, in cock fighting, in trotting races, in barbershop song, a variant from his working role. While some visit Chartres, others visit the hootchy-kootch on the Midway. Despite the efforts of the puritans and womenfolk to drive out of life these recreations that are reminiscent of medieval pastimes, the middle-class men of the nineteenth century make a firm effort to hang on to them.

Sherwood Anderson's work is an epic of men coming into the house after midnight on stocking feet. How much of this lore survives was made plain a few years ago by Allen Funt, on one of the "Candid Microphone" programs. Funt stood on a street corner at three in the morning and pretended he was afraid to go home. He buttonholed passing men and asked them to come home with him, to explain to the wife why he was overfilled and overdue. All the men were sympathetic. Though none wanted the role of go-between, each suggested the dodge that he himself had found workable in the same spot. One wanted him to telephone first. Another would help him get bandaged up. Still another thought that a present might fix matters. Some suggested stories, other courage. Most of the men, judging from their voices, seemed to be of middle age. Perhaps the major point of all this is that in earlier generations the strictness of the American proper-female regime gave a glamour to sin that obscured its inevitable limitations.

In thinking of the meaning of escape for the inner-directed man we must not, however, put too much emphasis on the merely convention-breaking patterns of Victorian amusement, vice, and sinful fantasy. Even where the conventions were absent or fragile, another issue was involved. This was the issue of competence in the enjoyment and judgment of recreation.

On the one hand, the American inner-directed man was committed in every generation to face increasingly the demand that his escape be upward with the arts. Sometimes he sought out this escape on his own. More usually, perhaps, mobility strivings and feminine influence put pressure on the man to go beyond the sphere where he felt competent: the sleepy businessman dragged to the opera sung in a language he could not understand. But on the other hand, he combated becoming merely a passive consumer by protecting, as a rebel in shirt sleeves, his escape downward to the lower arts of drink mixing and drink holding, poker, fancy women, and fancy mummery. Thus he protected in his minor sphere of play, as in his major sphere of work, his feeling of competence in the living of life. The separateness of the play sphere was dramatized precisely because the personal competence involved in these downward escapes could contribute little, or negatively, to his social status in the world of work and family. Because play competence could not be directly geared to the production economy, the inner-directed man was somewhat less likely than other-directed men today to exploit his recreation by telling himself that he owed it to himself to have fun. If he went to baseball games (one of the few sports where the other-directed man's competence, too, rests considerably on having once played the game), it was not part of an act designed to prove himself "one of the boys."

However, we must not exaggerate these distinctions between inner-directed and other-directed escapes. Many inner-directed men worked painfully hard to maintain their showing of recreational competence. The Reverend Endicott Peabody, later founder of Groton, established himself as the hero of a western frontier town in which he held a pastorate by getting up a baseball team. A similar strategy, with its roots in an era depending on tradition-direction, appears in the modern movie characterization of the Catholic priest, brother, or nun who is a good sport—as in Bing Crosby's *Going My Way*. Moreover, many inner-directed American business and professional men exploited, and still exploit, their leisure to make contacts. Their golf game was anything but an escape, and their wives' gardening was often harnessed to the same mobility drives. Such men had a great deal at stake economically, even if they had less at stake psychologically than the other-directed.

But there were often psychological stakes, too. The over-steered men of the period, unable either to throw off or accept their inhibitions, were not always able to guard them by withdrawal into privacy. Where there was pressure to prove oneself a good fellow in tavern or brothel, their bodies sometimes betrayed them into nausea or impotence—in the effort to be competent weakness of the flesh gave away unwillingness of the spirit. On the whole, however, the inner-directed man was much less susceptible than men are today to the requirement that he be liked for his recreations and loved for his vices.

III. The Struggle for Self-Approval

We may sum up much that is significant about inner-direction by saying that, in a society where it is dominant, its tendency is to protect the individual against the others at the price of leaving him vulnerable to himself.

One bit of evidence for this is in the widespread fear of and attack upon apathy which seems to date from the era of inner-direction. The monastic orders had faced the problem of sloth or *accidie* as psychological dangers to their regimen—dangers of which St. Augustine was acutely aware in his own struggle with himself. When puritanism, as Max Weber put it, turned the world into a monastery, the fear of this inner danger began to plague whole social classes and not merely a few select monks. The puritan inner-directed man was made to feel as if he had constantly to hold on to himself; that without ceaseless vigilance he would let go and drift—on the assumption that one can let go if one wills or, rather if one stops willing. It is as if his character, despite its seeming stability, did not feel stable and, indeed, the puritan, in a theological projection of this inner feeling, had constantly to fight against doubts concerning his state of grace or election.

Out of his continuing battle against the Demon of Sloth that sometimes turned into a hypochondria about apathy, he built up a myth, still very much with us, that the tradition-directed person is completely easy going, lacking "get up and go." This attack against others as apathetic—as today, for instance, in the constant complaints over political and civic apathy—sometimes served as a way of fighting against apathy in oneself. In fact, the inner-directed person testifies to his unconscious awareness that his gyroscope is not his but is installed by others through his chronic panic fear that it will stop spinning, that he is really not a self-starter, that life itself is not a process and renewal but an effortful staving off of psychic death.

Moreover, for easier bookkeeping in the control of apathy, the inner-directed person frequently divides his life into sectors, in each of which he can test his psychic defenses against it. Within himself he remains the child, committed early to goals and ideals that may transcend his powers. If these drives are demanding, no amount of contemporary acclaim can drown the feeling of inadequacy: the acclaim of others may in fact be the by-product of efforts to satisfy the self. Within himself he must find justification not only in what he does but in what he is—not by works but by faith is he saved. And while clever bookkeeping can transmute works into faith, self-criticism is seldom completely silenced. *Mere behavioral conformity cannot meet the characterological ideal.*

These internalized standards of the inner-directed man allow him, on the other hand, a certain freedom to fail in the eyes of the others without being convinced by them of his own inadequacy. Like Edison he will try and try again, sustained by his internal judgment of his worth. For while the others cannot protect him against self-criticism, self-criticism can protect him against the others. The inner-directed man can justify his existence not only by what he has done but what he will do. But this holds only up to a point. If repeated failures destroy his hope of future accomplishment, then it is likely that his internal strengths can no longer hold the fort against the external evidence. Overwhelmed with guilt, he will despise himself for his failures and inadequacies. The judgment, though set off by external happenings, is all the more severe for being internalized. Durkheim was right to see comparatively high suicide rates in the advanced industrial countries as symptoms of a psychological malaise uncontrolled by any cultural tradition.

THE OTHER-DIRECTED ROUND OF LIFE: FROM INVISIBLE HAND TO GLAD HAND

Since sociability in its pure form has no ulterior end, no content and no result outside itself, it is oriented completely about personalities. . . . But precisely because all is oriented about them, the personalities must not emphasize themselves too individually.

GEORG SIMMEL, *The Sociology of Sociability*

The inner-directed person is not only chained to the endless demands of the production sphere; he must also spend his entire life in the internal production of his own character. The discomforts of this internal frontier are as inexhaustible as the discomforts of the frontier of work itself. Like the fear of being retired or unemployed in the economic realm, apathy in many sectors of his inner or outer life is felt as underemployment of characterological resources. The inner-directed man has a generalized need to master resource exploitation on all the fronts of which he is conscious. He is job-minded.

The frontiers for the other-directed man are people; he is people-minded. Hence both work and pleasure are felt as activities involving people. Many of the job titles that exist today existed in the earlier era; many recreations likewise. My effort is to see how change of character is connected with change of meaning in the same pursuits as well as with development of new pursuits.

I. The Economic Problem: the Human Element

As the phase of transitional growth drew to an end in America, the "no help wanted" sign was posted on the frontier in 1890, in imagination if not in actual land-grant practice, and the same sign was hung out on our borders in 1924 with the virtual cutting off of immigration from Europe. With these valedictories a great symbol of hope and movement in the western world was destroyed. The combination of curtailed immigration and a falling birth rate eventually altered the population profile of the country; and, in the ways already hinted at, its characterological profile as well. Today it is the "softness" of men rather than the "hardness" of material that calls on talent and opens new channels of social mobility.

Whereas the production frontier, and even the land frontier, may actually be roomy even in the phase of incipient population decline, it nevertheless feels crowded; and certainly the society is no longer felt to be a wilderness or jungle as it often was earlier.

This is particularly true in industry and the professions. Take, for example, the position of the foreman. He no longer stands alone, a straw boss in a clear hierarchy, but is surrounded with people. He is a two-way communication channel between the men under him and a host of experts above and around him: personnel men, safety directors, production engineers, comptroller's representatives, and all the rest of the indirect managerial work force. The plant manager is hardly better off for emotional elbowroom: he is confronted not only with the elaborate intraplant hierarchy but with the public outside: the trade association group, the unions, consumers, suppliers, the government, and public opinion. Likewise, the professional man feels surrounded by a swarm of competitors, turned out by the vastly expanded educational system of a society whose capital plant is in such good shape that it can afford to devote—in fact, can hardly help devoting—a large share of the national income to the service trades and professions and to education for their proper use.

People, therefore, become the central problem of industry. This does not mean that the older revolutions in tooling, the machine process, and factory organization come to a halt. Rather, advances here are increasingly routinized; the continuing increment in productivity becomes a by-product of institutional forms. However, the newer industrial revolution which has reached its greatest force in America (although it is also beginning to be manifest elsewhere, as in England) is concerned with techniques of communication and control, not of tooling or factory layout. It is symbolized by the telephone, the servomechanism, the IBM machine, the electronic calculator, and modern statistical methods of controlling the quality of products; by the Hawthorne counseling experiment and the general preoccupation with industrial morale. The era of economic abundance and incipient population decline calls for the work of men whose tool is symbolism and whose aim is some observable response from people. These manipulators, of course, are not necessarily other-directed in character. Many inner-directed people are successful manipulators of people; often, their very inner-direction makes them unaware of how much they do manipulate and exploit others. Nevertheless, for manipulating others, there is a somewhat greater compatibility between characterological other-direction and sensitivity to others' subtler wants.

This can be explained more clearly by reference to one of our interviews. The man interviewed is the vice-president for sales and advertising of a large west coast machine-tool company, and he is also head of one of the leading trade associations for his industry. In origin he is the son of a Congregationalist preacher in a small midwestern town. His background, his mobility drive, his initial technical orientation are typical for the inner-directed; but his situation calls for the negotiating skill and interpersonal sensitivity more characteristic of the other-directed. This conflict produces strain. Asked about political issues on which he has recently changed his mind, he says:

> I don't think this fits the category you're working on now, but I've become a great deal more tolerant of labor leaders and organizers [then catching himself]—not agitators, necessarily. I've come to appreciate what they're doing. They don't have much choice in taking the particular methods and means sometimes. I need a psychoanalyst.

He also told the interviewer that his principal worry is that he does not get along too well with another top executive of his company. He was troubled when a suggestion of his that was rejected later turned out to be right—and the other chap knew it was right. In such a situation he felt exposed. He cannot eat before going into a board meeting, and wondered to the interviewer whether he might not be better off running his own small company rather than as an official of a large one. For recreation he plays golf, though he does not seem to care for it and, in good inner-directed style, or perhaps simply good American style, does "a little fooling around with tools in the basement."

Material from interviews is, of course, open to a variety

of possible interpretations, and I have no great confidence that those here suggested are correct. It would surely be erroneous to conclude that this executive has doubts about himself because he is not fully other-directed or inner-directed (by the very definition of these terms, no one is fully one or the other). The point is rather that the modern executive, regardless of the blend of the two modes of conformity he displays, is put under constant social pressure, in and out of the office. This executive is perhaps better able than most to verbalize the strain this pressure sets up.

FROM CRAFT SKILL TO MANIPULATIVE SKILL

The pressure toward social competence, with its concurrent playing down of technical competence, suggests another aspect of this executive's history which is typical for the emergence of a new pattern in American business and professional life: *if one is successful in one's craft, one is forced to leave it.* The machine-tool man began in the shop; as V.P. for sales and advertising he has become an uneasy manipulator of people and of himself. Likewise, the newspaperman who rises becomes a columnist or deskman, the doctor becomes the head of a clinic or hospital, the professor becomes a dean, president, or foundation official, the factory superintendent becomes a holding company executive. All these men must bury their craft routines and desert their craft companions. They must work less with things and more with people.

To be sure, business was always work with people. But when the size of enterprises was small, the new head of the enterprise could remain a colleague among other colleagues; he did not cut connections entirely and enter a new milieu. William Allen White's *Autobiography* shows that he was able to maintain all his life the amiable fiction that he was only a working newspaperman. Similarly, the older generation of college presidents was composed largely of men who continued to think of themselves as scholars. So, too, the older generation of business executives kept their hats on in the office, chewed tobacco, and otherwise tried to retain their connections with the shop. Today, however, the familiar organizational concepts of "staff and line" symbolize the cutting off of direct contact between the executive and the working staffs of both staff and line. To sit at his new big desk—or to get there—he has to learn a new personality-oriented specialty and unlearn or at least soft-pedal his old orientation.

To the point is a story of an engineer who is offered the far more lucrative job of sales manager.[1] He loves engineering, but his wife won't let him turn down the promotion. His sponsor in the organization tells him it is now or never: does he want to be wearing a green eyeshade all his life? He reluctantly accepts. That night he has a dream. He has a slide rule in his hands, and he suddenly realizes that he does not know how to use it. He wakes in panic. The dream clearly symbolizes his feeling of impotence in a new job where he is alienated from his craft.

The executive who has moved up from a professional position can hardly help feeling that his work is air conditioned: fine only so long as the machinery below runs smoothly. Those colleagues whom he has left behind will not be slow, in their envy, to remind him that he can no longer consider himself a competent craftsman among his fellow craftsmen, that he does not fool them if, as an editor or by-line columnist, he occasionally attends a presidential press conference; or, as a college administrator, an occasional scholarly convention; or, as a sales manager, occasionally makes a mark on a drawing board.

Indeed, a society increasingly dependent on manipulation of people is almost as destructive of the craft-oriented professional and businessman as a society in the earlier stages of industrialization is destructive of the handicraft-oriented peasant and artisan. The professional of the more recent period is

[1] Professor Everett Hughes of the University of Chicago, who has guided me in the analysis of changing career lines in business and the professions, tells this story.

pushed upstairs into the managerial class while the artisan of the earlier period was pushed into the proletariat; and this testifies to a profound difference in the two historic situations. Yet in both cases the industrial process advances by building into machines and into smooth-flowing organizations the skills that were once built, by a long process of apprenticeship and character-formation, into men.

Despite this pattern, there are many positions in business, and in particular in the older professions, that offer comfortable places to inner-directed types. In medicine and law the ideology of free enterprise is strong. The attempt to apply objective criteria in selecting personnel persists, and is strengthened by the otherwise odious emphasis on grades in the educational and licensing system. In a hospital, a law firm, a university, there is room not only for those who can bring people together but for those who can bring together chemicals, citations, or ideas. There are many niches for the work-minded craftsman who does not care to learn, or cannot learn, to move with the crowd.

Even in big industry some such areas can continue to exist because not all technological problems—problems of the hardness of the material—have been solved or put on a routine problem-solving basis. Moreover, there are certain key spots in big business and big government where at times it is precisely an inner-directed rate-buster who is needed—for instance, a man who can say no without going through an elaborate song and dance. At the same time the values characteristic of other-direction may spread at such a rate as to hit certain sectors of the economy before these sectors have solved their technological problems. In the United States the lure of other-directed work and leisure styles cannot be everywhere modulated to the uneven front of economic advance.

FROM FREE TRADE TO FAIR TRADE

Very soon after the Federal Trade Commission Act of 1914 outlawed unfair competition it became clear that what was unfair was to lower the price of goods, though this view was concealed under attacks against cheating or mislabeling of goods. But in the NRA period this covert attitude received government and public sanction, and it became libelous to call someone a price cutter. With the passage of the Robinson-Patman Act and state fair-trade laws, free trade and fair trade became antithetical terms. Prices come to be set by administration and negotiation or, where this is too likely to bring in the Anti-trust Division, by "price leadership." Relations that were once handled by the price mechanism or fiat are now handled by negotiation.

Price leadership often looks to the economist simply as the manipulation of devices to avoid price wars and divide the field. But price leadership has other aspects as well. It is a means by which the burden of decision is put onto the "others." The so-called price leaders themselves look to the government for clues, since cost—that mythical will-of-the wisp—is no longer, if it ever really was, an unequivocal guide. Follow-the-leader is also played in arriving at the price and working conditions of labor; and unions have profited from their ability to play on the wishes of top management to be in stride with the industry leaders, and to be good fellows to boot. As we shall see later, the other-directed pattern of politics tends to resemble the other-directed pattern of business: leadership is in the same amorphous state. Moreover, both in business and in politics, the other-directed executive prefers to stabilize his situation at a level that does not make too heavy demands on him for performance. Hence, at various points in the decision-making process he will vote for an easier life as against the risks of expansion and free-for-all competition.

Such a business life does not turn out to be the "easy" one. For one thing, the other-directed people do not have things all their own way in business any more than they do in politics. Free trade is still a powerful force, despite the incursions of the fair traders. Many observers, judging the degree of monopoly by looking at the percentage of assets controlled by the large, administered-price corporations, overlook the fact that even a small percentage of companies outside the range of the glad hand can have a leverage quite disproportionate to their assets. Rubber may be a monopoly, but will we always need rubber? Movies may be monopolistic, but what about television? In the small and marginal industries, the monopolies not of today but of tomorrow, there is often no need to be a good fellow. What is more, the dynamics of technological change remain challenging; whole departments within industries, as well as whole industries themselves, can become obsolete, despite their ability to negotiate repeated stays of the death sentence imposed by technological change. Even within the great monopolistic industries there are still many technologically oriented folk as well as many technologically oriented departments; no management planning in any one company can completely smooth out and routinize the pressure resulting from their innovations.

To the extent that the businessman is freed by his character and situation from cost considerations, he must face the problem of finding new motives for his entrepreneurship. He must tune in to the others to see what they are saying about what a proper business ought to be. Thus, a psychological sensitivity that begins with fear of being called a price cutter spreads to fear of being unfashionable in other ways. The businessman is as afraid of pursuing goals that may be obsolete as of living a style of life that may not be stylish. Oriented as he is to others, and to the consumption sphere, *he views his own business as a consumer.*

By and large, business firms until World War I needed only three kinds of professional advice: legal, auditing, and engineering. These were relatively impersonal services, even when, in the case of the lawyers, the services included buying —for cash on the barrelhead—a few legislators or judges. Since the number of available specialists was fairly small in comparison with demand, they could be absorbed into either or both of the two types of prevailing nexus: one, the family-status-connection nexus which persisted from earlier times in the smaller communities and does so even today in these communities and in the South; the other, the cash nexus based on performance, or on "character" in the older sense. Today the buyer is, first of all, not sure which of many services to buy: shall he get a lawyer or a public relations man or a market research agency or call in a management consulting firm to decide; second, he is not sure of his choice among the many potential suppliers of each of these services—none of whom must he accept either for family-status-connection reasons or for obviously superior character and performance. Thus choice will turn on a complex of more or less accidental, whimsical factors: a chance contact or conversation, a story in *Business Week* or a "confidential" newsletter, the luck of a salesman.

We can see the shift in many corporate histories. A business that begins as a small family enterprise, whose founders have their eye on the main chance—with a focus on costs and a "show me" attitude about good will and public relations—often alters its aims in the second generation. *Fortune* is put on the table, a trade association is joined, and the aim becomes not so much dollars as the possession of those appurtenances which an up-to-date company is supposed to have. We see a succession of demi-intellectuals added to the staff: industrial relations directors, training directors, safety directors. A house organ is published; consultants are called in on market research, standard operating procedures, and so on; shop and store front have their faces lifted; and in general status is sought, with profits becoming useful as one among many symbols of status and as the reserve for further moves toward a status-dictated expansion.

In many cases this shift is accompanied by a conflict of the older, more inner-directed with the younger, more other-directed generation. The older men have come up through the shop or through a technical school with no pretensions in the field of human relations. The younger ones are imbued with the new ethic. They seem still to be concerned about making money, and to some extent they are, but they are also concerned with turning their company into the model which they learned at business school. Businessmen recognize this new orientation when they speak of themselves, as they frequently do, as trustees for a variety of publics. And while they try to manipulate these publics and to balance among them, they, like the political leaders, are manipulated by the expectations the public has, or is thought to have, of them.

If one had to set a date for the change, one might say that the old epoch ended with the death of Henry Ford. After his death his firm, a last stronghold of older ways, completed the installation of new labor, accounting, and other managerial techniques and orientations.

The word *fair* in part reflects a carry-over of peer-group values into business life. The peer-grouper is imbued with the idea of fair play; the businessman, of fair trade. Often this means that he must be willing to negotiate matters on which he might stand on his rights. The negotiator, moreover, is expected to bring home not only a specific victory but also friendly feelings toward him and toward his company. Hence, to a degree, the less he knows about the underlying facts, the easier it will be to trade concessions. He is like the street-corner salesman who, reproached for selling for four cents apples that cost him five, said "But think of the turnover!" Here again craft skill, if not an actual drawback, becomes less important than manipulative skill.

Obviously, much of what has been said applies to the trade unions, the professions, and to academic life as well as to the business world. The lawyer, for instance, who moves into top positions inside and outside his profession is no longer necessarily a craftsman who has mastered the intricacies of, let us say, corporate finance, but may be one who has shown himself to be a good contact man. Since contacts need to be made and remade in every generation and cannot be inherited, this creates lucrative opportunities for the mobile other-directed types whose chief ability is smooth negotiation.

FROM THE BANK ACCOUNT TO THE EXPENSE ACCOUNT

In this phrase Professor Paul Lazarsfeld once summed up some recent changes in economic attitudes. The expense account is tied in with today's emphasis on consumption practices as firmly as the bank account in the old days was tied in with production ideals. The expense account gives the glad hand its grip. In doing so it still further breaks down the wall that in the era depending on inner-direction separated the paths of pleasure and of work. The successful other-directed man brings to business the set of attitudes learned in the consumption sphere not only when he appraises his own firm with a customer's eye but also when he is "in conference."

Business is supposed to be fun. As World War II inflation cooled off, the business pages repeatedly carried speeches at conventions on the theme: "Now selling will be fun again!" The inner-directed businessman was not expected to have fun; indeed, it was proper for him to be gloomy and even grim. But the other-directed businessman seems increasingly exposed to the mandate that he enjoy the sociabilities that accompany management. The shortening of hours has had much greater effect on the life of the working class than on that of the middle class: the executive and professional continues to put in long hours, employing America's giant productivity less to leave for home early than to extend his lunch hours, coffee breaks, conventions, and other forms of combining business with pleasure. Likewise, much time in the office itself is also spent in sociability: exchanging office gossip ("conferences"), making good-will tours ("inspection"), talking to salesmen and joshing secretaries ("morale"). In fact, depleting the expense account can serve as an almost limitless occupational therapy for men who, out of a tradition of hard work, a dislike of their wives, a lingering asceticism, and an anxiety about their antagonistic cooperators, still feel that they must put in a good day's work at the office. But, of course, Simmel would not admit, in his brilliant essay from which I quoted [on page 50], that this kind of sociability, carrying so much workaday freight, was either free or sociable.

For the new type of career there must be a new type of education. This is one factor, of course not the only one, behind the increasing vogue of general education and the introduction of the humanities and social studies into technical high school and university programs. The educators who sponsor these programs urge cultivating the "whole man," speak of training citizens for democracy, and denounce narrow specialisms—all valuable themes. Indeed this book grows in part out of the stimulation of teaching in a general social science program. But while it may be doubtful that engineers and businessmen will become either better citizens or better people for having been exposed to these programs, there is little question that they will be more suave. They may be able to demonstrate their edge on the roughnecks from the "tech" schools by trotting out discourse on human relations. Such eloquence may be as necessary for professional and business success today as a knowledge of the classics was to the English politician and high civil servant of the last century.

Meanwhile, I do not wish to exaggerate the emphasis on human relations even in the bureaucratized sectors of the economy. There is much variety still: some companies, such as Sears Roebuck, seem to be run by glad handers, while others like, let us say, Montgomery Ward, are not; some, like Anaconda, are public relations conscious; others, like Kennecott, are less so. Much current progress in distribution, even in selling, tends to reduce the importance of the salesman. This is clear enough in the Automat. Moreover, the personality aspects of selling can be minimized wherever a technician is needed: for instance, salesmen of specialized equipment which requires a reorientation of the customer's work force. Though IBM salesmen have to be go-getters, they also have to know how to wire a tabulating machine and, still more important, how to rationalize the information flow within a company.

Hence, although they are facilitators of the communications revolution, they must be no less craft oriented than the salesmen of the less complex equipment of an earlier era. Within most such industries there is a great need for technically minded people who are, to a considerable degree, protected by their indispensable skills from having to be nice to everybody, with or without an expense account.

II. The Milky Way

. . . The inner-directed man, socialized with reference to an older model, might choose for emulation a star from the heroes of his field. By contrast, the other-directed person does not so often think of his life in terms of an individualized career. He seeks not fame, which represents limited transcendence of a particular peer-group or a particular culture, but the respect and, more than the respect, the affection, of an amorphous and shifting, though contemporary, jury of peers.

To attain this goal he struggles not with the hardness of the material but with the very antagonistic cooperators who are engaged in the same pursuit and to whom he looks at the same time for values and for judgments of value. Instead of referring himself to the great men of the past and matching himself against his stars, the other-directed person moves in the midst of a veritable Milky Way of almost but not quite indistinguishable contemporaries. This is partly a tribute to the size of the educated middle class in the phase of incipient decline of population.

The uncertainty of life in our day is certainly a factor in the refusal of young people to commit themselves to long-term goals. War, depression, military service, are felt today as obstacles to planning a career far more than in the period prior to World War I. But these changes are not the whole story: the type of man who will not commit himself to long-range goals rationalizes his perspective on the future and his deferral of commitment by pointing to the all too evident uncertainties. We can conceive of people living at a time of equal uncertainty who would, out of ignorance and insensitivity as much as out of strength of character, plow ahead in pursuit of extensive aims. Doubtless, many other factors are also in the air: such as the fact, mentioned in a preceding section, that mobility often depends on leaving one's craft skill behind; and this very fork in the road which separates avenues within a craft from those achievable only by leaving the craft, suggests itself at an early stage of occupational life and complicates the planning of the mobile youth's career.

There are certain positive sides to this development. The seemingly sure commitment of many inner-directed youths was based on an unquestioning acceptance of parental orders and parental ranking of occupations. The other-directed youth of today often asks more of a job than that it satisfy conventional status and pecuniary requirements; he is not content with the authoritative rankings of earlier generations. The age of other-direction does open up the possibilities of more individual and satisfying choices of career, once society's pressure for an early decision, and the person's feeling of panic if he can make no decision, can be relaxed.

It follows that the heavens of achievement look quite different to the other-directed youth than they did to his inner-directed predecessor. The latter found security in moving to the periphery of the various frontiers and establishing an isolated and recognizable claim on a new piece of territory—often with quite grandiose and imperialistic trappings. If he founded a firm, this was his lengthened shadow. Today the man is the shadow of the firm. Such long-term aims as exist are built into the firm, the institution; this is also the repository of the imperialistic drives that sometimes take shape as the institution harnesses the mild and tractable wills of many other-directed people who are competing for places of marginal differentiation on the Milky Way.

To outdistance these competitors, to shine alone, seems hopeless, and also dangerous. To be sure, one may try to steal a march—to work harder, for instance, than the propaganda about working would permit—but these are petty thefts, not major stick-ups. They do, however, keep the competition for a position on the major streamlined runs of occupational life from being entirely cooperative. Yet even such behavior that may marginally flout the prevailing concepts of fairness looks to the peer-group for its norms of what is to be desired. And since each projects his own tendencies to unfair play onto the others, this, too, requires living in a state of constant alert as to what the others may be up to.

Hence the Milky Way is not an easy way, though its hardships differ from those of the earlier era. Obliged to conciliate or manipulate a variety of people, the other-directed person handles all men as customers who are always right; but he must do this with the uneasy realization that, as Everett Hughes has put it, some are more right than others. This diversity of roles to be taken with a diversity of customers is not institutionalized or clear cut, and the other-directed person tends to become merely his succession of roles and encounters and hence to doubt who he is or where he is going. Just as the firm gives up the one-price policy for an administered price that is set in secrecy and differs with each class of customer depending on the latter's apparent power and "good will" requirements, so the other-directed person gives up the one-face policy of the inner-directed man for a multiface policy that he sets in secrecy and varies with each class of encounters.

United with others, however, he can seek a modicum of social, economic, and political protection. The peer-group can decide that there are certain outcasts, in class or ethnic terms, to whom the glad hand need not be extended, or who can (like the Negro in the South) be forced to personalize without the privilege of demanding a reciprocal response. A class of customers can be politically created who are by definition wrong. Yet no amount of exclusiveness, though it may make life a bit easier for the insiders, can completely guarantee continuance in a place of visibility and approval in the Milky Way.

THE OTHER-DIRECTED ROUND OF LIFE (CONTINUED): THE NIGHT SHIFT

But it must not be supposed that in the midst of all their toils the people who live in democracies think themselves to be pitied; the contrary is noticed to be the case. No men are fonder of their own condition. Life would have no relish for them if they were delivered from the anxieties which harass them, and they show more attachment to their cares than aristocratic nations to their pleasures.

TOCQUEVILLE, *Democracy in America*

The only thing that has changed since Tocqueville wrote (no small change, it is true) is that the sphere of pleasures has itself become a sphere of cares. Many of the physical hardships of the older frontiers of production and land use have survived in altered, psychological form on the newer one of consumption. Just as we saw in [a previous section] that the day shift of work-mindedness is invaded by glad-hand attitudes and values that stem in part from the sphere of leisure, so the night shift of leisure-mindedness is haunted by the others with whom one works at having a good time.

First of all, however, with the rise of other-direction, we see the passing both of the acquisitive consumers and of the escapists of the earlier era. The passion for acquisition diminishes when property no longer has its old stability and objective validity; escape diminishes by the very fact that work and pleasure are interlaced. We can see these new tendencies, in what is perhaps their most extreme form, the attitudes toward food and sexual experience prevailing among some upper middle-class groups.

I. Changes in the Symbolic Meaning of Food and Sex

FROM THE WHEAT BOWL TO THE SALAD BOWL

Among inner-directed types there is of course great variation as to interest in food. In America—the story is different among the food-loving peoples of the rest of the world—puritans and nonpuritans of the recent past might use food for display, with relatively standardized menus for company and for dining out; what was put on display was a choice cut of meat, an elegant table, and good solid cooking. All this was an affair largely of the women, and in many circles food was not a proper topic for dinner conversation. Having the proper food was something one owed to one's status, one's claim to respectability, and more recently to one's knowledge of hygiene with its calories and vitamins. (This last pattern did not spread to the South, where an older, more gastronomically rugged tradition of ceremonial fondness for food prevailed.) The earlier editions of the *Boston Cooking School Cookbook* breathe this air of solidity, conservatism, and nutrition-mindedness.

The other-directed person of the midtwentieth century in America, on the contrary, puts on display his taste and not directly his wealth, respectability, cubic capacity, or caloric soundness. Indeed we [have seen] how the radio begins the other-directed person's training in food taste even before the child goes to school and how seriously he takes his lessons. While well-educated upper middle-class parents are becoming hesitant to tell children to eat something because it is good for them—lest they create oral complexes—they join the radio in discussion of what is "good" as a matter of taste. Often, in fact, this merely disguises the emotion focused on the child's eating habits, almost as much emotion as their parents concentrated on the regimen of no-nonsense plate cleaning. The other-directed person is thus prepared for the search for marginal differentiation not only in what he sets before his guests but in how it is talked about with them.

Earlier there existed a small coterie of gourmets; fastidious enjoyment of food was one hobby, among others, that inner-directed people might choose. Today, in wide circles, many people are and many more feel that they must be gourmets. The abundance of America in the phase of incipient population decline is perhaps the most important factor in this development; it has made the good foods available to nearly everybody. The seasonal and geographic limitations that in the earlier period narrowed food variations for all but the very rich have now been largely done away with by the network of distribution and the techniques of preserving food—both being legacies from the phase of transitional population growth. The consumer's choice among foods need therefore no longer be made on the basis either of tradition or of Malthusian limits.

As a result, both the setting of the meal and its content are affected. Informality breaks down the puritan inhibition against talking about food and drink, just as Mexican casseroles and copper kettles replace the white napery and classic decor of the nineteenth-century middle-class table. More important still, the housewife can no longer blame the preferential and limited cuisine offered by a kitchen servant for her failure to personalize her own tastes in food. In the period of incipient population decline servants disappear from the middle-class home, and where they do not, they lack any traditional pattern of prerogatives that allows them, rather than the host and hostess, to control the menu and its stylized serving. No walls of privacy, status, or asceticism remain to protect or prevent one from displaying personalized taste in food and decor as an element in one's competition with others. The diner has the power, unlike Jiggs, to decide that corned beef and cabbage is an amusing dish; he can ransack immigrant cookeries or follow the lead of food columnist Clementine Paddleford toward exoticism. Only at the conventional conventions can one still find the uniform menu of steak or chicken, potatoes, and marbled peas. And at home, in place of the staple menu, the hostess today is encouraged to substitute her own specialty, such as lasagna or rüstoffel. Men are involved almost as much as women, and in the kitchen as well as at the back-yard grill.

The most popular cookbook today is said to be *The Joy of Cooking,* and the number of specialized cookbooks—ethnic, chatty, and atmospheric—constantly increases to meet the demand for marginal differentiation. The very change in titles —from the *Boston Cooking School Cookbook* to *How to Cook a Wolf* or *Food Is a Four Letter Word*—reveals the changing attitude. For the other-directed person cannot lean on such objective standards of success as those which guided the inner-directed person: he may be haunted by a feeling that he misses the joy in food or drink which he is supposed to feel. Meal-time must now be "pleasurable"; the new *Fireside Cookbook* is offered to "people who are not content to regard food just as something one transfers periodically from plate to mouth." And if one still fails to get much joy out of the recipes given there, he may search in books like *Spécialité de la Maison* to see what "others" are eating—to get the "favorite recipes" of such people as Noel Coward and Lucius Beebe. Fred Mac-Murray and Claudette Colbert testify to the delights of new concoctions such as "The Egg and I Julep"; and "There is nothing," writes MacMurray in a little collection of his favorite egg recipes, "so appealing as a pair of fried eggs with their limpid golden eyes gazing fondly at you from the center of a breakfast plate, festooned with strips of crisp bacon or little-pig sausage. Or poached, gaily riding a raft of toast." The most popular translation of an old French cookbook, *Tante Marie*, is also extremely chatty, and *The Joy of Cooking* explains its chattiness by saying that originally the recipes were collected and written down for the author's daughter, who in turn thought "other daughters" might like them. (As there is today less teaching of daughters by mothers, the daughter must rely on the instruction of an outsider, if she is to cook at all.) In short, the other-directed person in his approach to food, as in his sexual encounters, is constantly looking for a qualitative element that may elude him. He suffers from what Martha Wolfenstein and Nathan Leites call "fun-morality."[2]

Of course, putting matters this way exaggerates the disadvantages of the shift: undeniably, many more people today

[2] In *Movies* (Glencoe, Illinois, Free Press, 1950).

really enjoy food and enjoy talk about food than they did when the monotony of the American diet was notorious.

Many people, to be sure, follow the new fashions in food without being other-directed in character, just as many personnel directors in industry are zealous inner-directed believers in the glad hand. Even so, if we wanted to demarcate the boundaries of other-direction in America, we might find in the analysis of menus a not too inaccurate index. As tossed salads and garlic, elaborate sauces, dishes en casserole, *Gourmet* magazine, wine and liqueurs, spread west from New York and east from San Francisco, as men take two-hour lunch periods and exhibit their taste in food and wine, as the personalized cookbook tends to replace the Boston Cooking School type—in all these signs of the times we see indications of the new type of character. Recently, Russell Lynes, in his article, "Highbrow, Lowbrow, Middlebrow,"[3] sought to delineate the contemporary urban American social system in terms of similar consumption indexes. Thus, the tossed salad is the sign of the high-brow, who may also be tagged by his taste in cars, clothes, and posture. What we really see emerging is an embryonic social system whose criteria of status are inconsistent with the criteria of the more traditional class system. This has been seen by Lloyd Warner, who actually defines class less in terms of wealth or power and more in terms of who is sociable with whom, and of styles of consumer behavior. These observers, however, are exceptional; . . . most Americans continue to see their social structure in terms of an older one based on wealth, occupation, and position in the society-page sense. But beneath these older rubrics, I believe that a much more amorphous structure is emerging in which opinion leadership is increasingly important, and in which the "brow" hierarchy competes for recognition with the traditional hierarchies based on wealth and occupational position.

[3] *Harper's, 198* (1949), 19.

SEX: THE LAST FRONTIER

In the era depending on inner-direction sex might be inhibited, as in classes and areas affected strongly by the Reformation and Counter Reformation. Or its gratification might be taken for granted among men and within given limits, as in Italy, Spain, and the non-respectable elements, such as the "riverbottom people," in every population. In both cases there was a certain simplification of sex, in the one instance by taboos, in the other by tradition. The related problems of livelihood and of power, problems of mere existence or of "amounting to something," were uppermost; and sex was relegated to its "proper" time and place: night, the wife or whore, occasional rough speech, and daydreams. Only in the upper classes, precursors of modern other-directed types, did the making of love take precedence over the making of goods (as alleged in France) and reach the status of a daytime agenda. In these circles sex was almost totally separated from production and reproduction.

This separation, when it goes beyond the upper class and spreads over almost the whole society, is a sign that a society, through birth control and all that it implies, has entered the population phase of incipient decline by the route of industrialization. In this phase there is not only a growth of leisure, but work itself becomes both less interesting and less demanding for many; increased supervision and subdivision of tasks routinize the industrial process even beyond what was accomplished in the phase of transitional growth of population. More than before, as job-mindedness declines, sex permeates the daytime as well as the playtime consciousness. It is viewed as a consumption good not only by the old leisure classes but by the modern leisure masses.

The other-directed person, who often suffers from low responsiveness, may pursue what looks like a "cult of effortlessness" in many spheres of life. He may welcome the routinization of his economic role and of his domestic life; the auto companies may tempt him by self-opening windows and self-shifting gears; he may withdraw all emotion from politics. Yet he cannot handle his sex life in this way. Though there is tremendous insecurity about *how* the game of sex should be played, there is little doubt as to *whether* it should be played or not. Even when we are consciously bored with sex, we must still obey its drive. Sex, therefore, provides a kind of defense against the threat of total apathy. This is one of the reasons why so much excitement is channeled into sex by the other-directed person. He looks to it for reassurance that he is alive. The inner-directed person, driven by his internal gyroscope and oriented toward the more external problems of production, did not need this evidence.

While the inner-directed acquisitive consumer could pursue the ever receding frontiers of material acquisition, these frontiers have lost much of their lure for the other-directed person. . . . The latter begins as a very young child to know his way around among available consumer goods. He travels widely, to camp or with his family. He knows that the rich man's car is only marginally, if at all, different from his own—a matter at best of a few additional horsepower. He knows anyway that next year's model will be better than this year's. Even if he has not been there, he knows what the night clubs are like; and he has seen television. Whereas the deprived inner-directed person often lusted for possessions as a goal whose glamour a wealthy adulthood could not dim, the other-directed person can scarcely conceive of a consumer good that can maintain for any length of time undisputed dominance over his imagination. Except perhaps sex.

For the consumption of love, despite all the efforts of the mass media, does remain hidden from public view. If someone else has a new Cadillac, the other-directed person knows what that is, and that he can duplicate the experience, more or less. But if someone else has a new lover, he cannot know what that means. Cadillacs have been democratized. So has sexual glamour, to a degree: without the mass production of good-looking, well-groomed youth, the American pattern of sexual competition could not exist. But there is a difference between Cadillacs and sexual partners in the degree of mystery. And with the loss of submergence of moral shame and inhibitions, but not completely of a certain unconscious innocence, the other-directed person has no defenses against his own envy. He is not ambitious to break the quantitative records of the acquisitive consumers of sex like Don Juan, but he does not want to miss, day in day out, the qualities of experience he tells himself the others are having.

In a way this development is paradoxical. For while cook-books have become more glamorous with the era of other-direction, sex books have become less so. The older marriage manuals, such as that of Van der Velde (still popular, however), breathe an ecstatic tone; they are travelogues of the joy of love. The newer ones, including some high school sex manuals, are matter of fact, toneless, and hygienic—Boston Cooking School style. Nevertheless, much as young people may appear to take sex in stride along with their vitamins, it remains an era of competition and a locus of the search, never completely suppressed, for meaning and emotional response in life. The other-directed person looks to sex not for display but for a test of his or her ability to attract, his or her place in the "rating-dating" scale—and beyond that, in order to experience life and love.

One reason for the change is that women are no longer objects for the acquisitive consumer but are peer-groupers themselves. The relatively unemancipated wife and socially inferior mistresses of the inner-directed man could not seriously challenge the quality of his sexual performance. Today, millions of women, freed by technology from many household tasks, given by technology many "aids to romance," have become pioneers, with men, on the frontier of sex. As they become knowing consumers, the anxiety of men lest they fail to satisfy the women also grows—but at the same time this is another test that attracts men who, in their character, want to be judged by others. The very ability of women to respond in a way that only courtesans were supposed to in an earlier age means, moreover, that qualitative differences of sex experience —the impenetrable mystery—can be sought for night after night, and not only in periodic visits to a mistress or brothel. Whereas the pattern of an earlier era was often to make fun of sex, whether on the level of the music hall or of Balzac's *Droll Stories*, sex today carries too much psychic freight to be really funny for the other-directed person. By a disguised asceticism it becomes at the same time too anxious a business and too sacred an illusion.

This anxious competitiveness in the realm of sex has very little in common with older patterns of social climbing. To be sure, women still use sex as a means to status in spheres controlled by men. But they can do this chiefly in industries that are still competitive in the pre-monopolistic patterns. Thus until recently the theater and the movies were controlled by *novi homines* who remind us of those early nineteenth-century British mill owners who, before the Factory Acts, relied on their mills as a harem.[4] And Warner, Havighurst, and Loeb in *Who Shall Be Educated?*[5] describe how women schoolteachers may still cabin-date their way up the relatively unbureaucratized hierarchies of local school systems. These, however, are exceptional cases; the search for experience on the frontier of sex is, in the other-directed era, generally without ulterior motives.

II. Changes in the Mode of Consumption of Popular Culture

ENTERTAINMENT AS ADJUSTMENT TO THE GROUP

. . . The inner-directed youth is made ready to leave home and go far both by directly didactic literature and by novels

[4] See G. M. Young, *Portrait of an Age* (London, Oxford University Press, 1936), p. 16, n. 1.

[5] W. Lloyd Warner, Robert J. Havighurst, and Martin Loeb, *Who Shall Be Educated?* (New York, Harper, 1944), e.g., p. 103.

and biographies that gave him a sense of possible roles on the frontiers of production. In contrast to this, the other-directed person has recourse to a large literature that is intended to orient him in the noneconomic side of life. This orientation is needed because, with the virtually complete disappearance of tradition-direction, no possibility remains of learning the art of life in the primary group—a possibility that persisted even in the mobile families of the era dependent on inner-direction. The child must look early to his mass-media tutors for instruction in the techniques of getting directions for one's life as well as for specific tricks of the trade.

We can trace an edifying sequence that runs from the success biography of the Samuel Smiles or the Horatio Alger sort to the contemporary books and periodicals that deal with peace of mind. The earlier books are directly concerned with social and economic advance, dealt with as achievable by the virtues of thrift, hard work, and so on. Then we find in the first years of this century the development in America of the now almost forgotten "New Thought" movement. As described by A. Whitney Griswold, the movement's motto was: "Think Your Way to Wealth."[6] That is, wealth was to be achieved no longer by activity in the real world but by self-manipulation, a kind of economic Couéism. But wealth itself as a goal was unquestioned.

From then on, inspirational literature becomes less and less exclusively concerned with social and economic mobility. Dale Carnegie's *How to Win Friends and Influence People*, written in 1937, recommends self-manipulative exercises for the sake not only of business success but of such vaguer, nonwork goals as popularity. Perhaps it is not only the change from depression to full employment that led Carnegie to write *How to Stop Worrying and Start Living* in 1948, in which self-manipulation is no longer oriented toward some social achievement but is used in a solipsistic way to adjust one to one's fate and social state. The same tendencies can be found in a large

[6] "The American Cult of Success" (Doctor's thesis, Yale University, 1933); abstracted in *American Journal of Sociology*, XL (1934), 309–318.

group of periodicals, with an interlocking directorate of authors and with titles such as *Journal of Living, Your Personality, Your Life,* which testified to the alteration of paths to upward mobility and to the increase of anxiety as a spur to seeking expert help. The *New York Times Book Review* of April 24, 1949, advertises *Calm Yourself* and *How to Be Happy While Single;* the latter deals according to the advertisement with such problems as "how to handle the men in your life (heavy dates, office companions, friends, drunks) . . . making conversation . . . liquor, boredom—just about every problem you'll encounter on your own." Certainly, there are many positive sides to a development that substitutes for the older, external, and often pointless goals such as wealth and power, the newer, internal goals of happiness and peace of mind, though of course, one must always ask whether, in changing oneself, one is simply adapting to the world as it is without protest or criticism.

Here, however, I am not evaluating these trends but am interested in showing how popular culture is exploited for group-adjustment purposes not only in the form of manifestly didactic literature and services but also in fictional guise. There is nothing new in the observation that people who would rather not admit their need for help, or who prefer to spice it with fun, look to the movies and other popular media as the sources of enlightenment. In the studies of the movies made under the Payne Fund twenty years ago, much evidence was gathered concerning use of the movies by young people who wanted to learn how to look, dress, and make love.[7] The combination of learning and excitement was clear in these cases, especially among children of lower-class origin suddenly brought face to face with sex and splendor. Today, however, as audiences have become more sophisticated, the mixture of messages has become more subtle.

From a sample of a group of women's magazines, *Ladies'*

[7] See, for example, Herbert Blumer and Philip Hauser, *Movies, Delinquency, and Crime* (New York, Macmillan, 1933), pp. 102 *et seq.*

Home Journal, American, Good Housekeeping, and *Mademoiselle,* for October, 1948, I concluded that a good many stories and features and, of course, far less subtly, many ads, dealt largely with modes of manipulating the self in order to manipulate others, primarily for the attainment of intangible assets such as affection. Two stories will illustrate: "The Rebellion of Willy Kepper" by Willard Temple in *Ladies' Home Journal* and "Let's Go Out Tonight" by Lorna Slocombe in the *American* magazine.

Handling the Office / "The Rebellion of Willy Kepper" is unusual in that it deals with a work situation rather than one of domestic and leisure life. It is the story of a paint salesman, Willy, a shy young man who has worked himself up through the factory. There is a pretty file clerk whom Willy wants to know better but does not know how to approach. At this point the stockholder's son enters the business, gets the promotion Willy hoped for, and makes time with the file clerk. Willy, previously so mild, loses his temper and becomes gruff and rasping with people in the office and shop. This is his "rebellion." This change of mood is of course noticed at once.

Willy, however, has built up an enormous capital of good will by his previous good temper, so that plant people, instead of turning on him, try to find out what the trouble is; it cannot be Willy's fault. They discover that the stockholder's son is to blame, and they set out to hex him—he trips into paint, gets orders mixed up, and rapidly learns how dependent he is on others' liking him if he is to do his job. Willy, in fact, saves him from his worst jam with a customer, and after a few knocks of this sort the son decides to start at the bottom in the factory, in order to earn his own capital of good will. Thus the road to Willy's promotion is reopened. At the end Willy asks the stockholder's son what techniques he used with the file clerk. He tells Willy to compliment her on her eyes; he does so and succeeds in making a date.

There are some fairly obvious things to be said about this

story. In the first place, though it is set in the sphere of production, it deals with the sales end of a factory which is a net of interpersonal relations that will deliver paint to the customer only against a bill of lading marked "good will." The work situation is seen in terms of its human element and its noneconomic incentives. There are no problems about paint, but only about people. In the second place, the stockholder's son was able to date the girl not because of his wealth and position but because of his line, his skill in the leisure arts of language. Language is presented as a free consumers' good; one, moreover, of which the consumer is also a producer; there is no patent or monopoly on lines. Finally, we have a picture of the "antagonistic cooperators" of the same sex—Willy and the son—whose rivalry for job and girl is so muted that they can exchange advice on how to win both; in a way, they are more interested in each other's approval than in victory. In the end Willy has regained his lost good temper and his rival has given up his early arrogance.

Handling the Home / "Let's Go Out Tonight" pictures the consumption frontier of a young, college-bred suburban matron. Her husband is a good provider and faithful; her two children are healthy; she has everything—except enough attention from her tired businessman spouse. The latter comes home, reads a paper, goes to bed, and his wife complains to her friend in their morning telephone chat that they never go places and do things any more. She looks back nostalgically on her college days when he was courting her and when life seemed glamorous. Suddenly she decides to go back to her college to see just what the magic was in those days.

When she gets to her old room she realizes that only in retrospect was her college dating effortless. Actually, she recalls, she slaved to arrange parties for her future husband, to manipulate him into kissing her and finally into proposing. She concludes that she just has been loafing on her job as a housewife, and returns full of tolerant understanding for her husband and enthusiasm for new and improved manipulation. By buying a new dress, arranging with a sitter to have the children taken care of, and similar measures, she inveigles her husband into a theater date and is able to report success to her friend on the telephone.

In the era of inner-direction, stories of a similarly orientational cast often encouraged the reader to aspire to distant horizons, to play for big stakes; many such stories today strike us as escapist and sentimental. In contrast, the type of "realism" in modern magazine fiction is neither uplifting nor escapist. There is an all too sensible refusal, in a story like "Let's Go Out Tonight," to admit that there can be decisively better marriages than this one, with its continuous petty deception. The reader of these stories will by no means always find his ideals and ways of life approved—it is a mistake to suppose that such magazines as *Ladies' Home Journal* are edited by a formula of giving "the public what it wants"—but he is seldom stimulated to make great demands on life and on himself. In both of the stories I have used here as illustration, the assumption is made that a solution of conflict is available that involves neither risk nor hardship but only the commodities—interpersonal effort and tolerance—that the other-directed person is already prepared to furnish.

"Conspiracy" theories of popular culture are quite old, summed up as they are in the concept of "bread and circuses." In "The Breadline and the Movies" Thorstein Veblen presented a more sophisticated concept, namely, that the modern American masses paid the ruling class for the privilege of the very entertainments that helped to keep them under laughing gas. Such views assume the culture to be more of a piece than it is. Group adjustment and orientational influence in contemporary popular culture do not serve the interest of any particular class. In fact, pressures for other-directed conformity appear strongest in the better educated strata. The form these pressures take may be illustrated by a few examples.

Heavy Harmony / The head of a progressive boarding school in the East recently addressed the parents of its children as follows:

> The music department at X School wishes to provide for every child as rich a musical experience as possible.
>
> We believe that music is a necessary part of life and its influence is felt in every phase of living. Singing and playing together can bring understanding and good-will and it seems to me that this world needs more of this kind of harmony.
>
> At X, we try to provide some kind of music participation for every child and wish to encourage more musical activity, especially that of playing with a group in an orchestra.

This letter does not betray much interest in music as such. It sees music primarily as a way of bringing people together locally and internationally too. Music as a way of escape into one's individual creative life—a private refuge—would strike many such school authorities today as selfish.

A similar theme appears in more refined form in Helen Howe's novel of Harvard academic life, *We Happy Few*.[8] The heroine Dorothea is viewed by Miss Howe as a selfish woman who, during the war, escapes from her social duties by having a love affair and by playing Bach and Mozart to herself on the piano. She is taken in the novel through a series of group-adjustment experiences that deflate what Miss Howe regards as her intellectual snobbery. Becoming a nurse's aid, she meets other nurse's aids socially; they are fine and dull. Traveling to Coeur d'Alene to be near her son in training, she "sees" America: in the stench of the ladies' room, the sadness of platform partings, the good-heartedness of midwesterners. The townsfolk of Coeur d'Alene are another group-adjusting experience; they, too, are fine and dull. At the end Dorothea returns to Cambridge a sadder and wiser woman: her pride is

[8] I have dealt with the implications of this book in more detail in "The Ethics of We Happy Few," *University Observer*, I (1947), 19; I draw on this article in what follows.

gone, and she has learned humbly to admire the great open spaces and the open sentiments usually associated with them in song and story.

As a symbol of the learning process, Miss Howe writes that Dorothea, while a nurse's aid staggering through agonizing days at the hospital, learns in her few off hours to enjoy Schumann as well as her beloved Bach and Mozart: "Her aesthetic as well as her human taste was stretching, too—cruder, possibly, but warmer and more inclusive."

This quotation hardly needs comment. Instead of permitting the heroine to escape either up or down from the exasperating human contacts of a nurse's workday, Dorothea must move sideways. She must acquire warmer, group-adjusted musical tastes—she would be forgiven even more, doubtless, if she learned to like Ethelbert Nevin.[9]

Yet granting Dorothea should learn this interpersonal art as a benefit to her work as a nurse's aid—perhaps the sick are a special case and do need warmth of this sort—it is striking that she must bring the identical attitude into her leisure time: no change of roles is permitted. Leisure and work must, like Dorothea herself, be stretched (assuming, falsely, that Schumann's sentimentality is "warmer") until they completely overlap. The theme of both is group adjustment.

What I have said is not to be understood as a polemic for coldness as against warmth or as a criticism of the genuine elements in the other-directed person's concern for warmth, in himself and in others. Certainly it is an advance from the compulsory emotional constriction, the frightening coldness, of many inner-directed Americans to open up sociability to a wider and more outgoing responsiveness.

[9] The reference to warmth is especially significant in the analysis of peer-group preferences in people. In a very interesting set of experiments, Solomon E. Asch has shown that the warm-cold axis is for his student subjects the controlling dimension of personality: people who are said to be warm are positively valued no matter what other traits they have, while people who are cold are distrusted no matter how honorable and brave they may be. See Solomon E. Asch, "A Test for Personality," *Journal of Abnormal and Social Psychology, 41* (1946), 258–290.

Lonely Successes / In our discussion of the comics, of *Tootle,* and of "Willy Kepper," we saw how modern popular culture stresses the dangers of aloneness and, by contrast, the virtues of group-mindedness. In a thoughtful article, "The Gangster as Tragic Hero," Robert Warshow deals with a number of recent gangster films from this perspective.[10] He notes that, inevitably, the gangster's success spells his undoing. For it cuts him off from the group—not only the law-abiding community but also his own gang. At the peak of success he is therefore miserable and frightened, waiting to be cut down from the heights.

We can interpret this as a cautionary tale about what happens if one goes off on one's own pursuits. Success is fatal. According to the code of the movies one is not permitted to identify with the lonely escapist; his lot is pictured, like that of Dorothea in the novel, as a set of miseries and penances. The movie *Body and Soul* points a similar moral. The hero is a Jewish boy from the East Side who gets to be boxing champion and proceeds to alienate all surrounding groups: his family circle and faithful girl; his unambitious, devoted retinue; the East Side Jews who see him as a hero. He agrees for a large sum to throw his last fight and bets against himself; his losing will complete his alienation from these groups. En route to the fight he is told that the Jews see him as a hero, a champion in the fight against Hitler. Recalled to "himself," he double-crosses his gangster backers by winning the fight; and, poor again, he is restored to the primary group of family, girl, and Jews.

A movie or book occasionally comes along that departs from this formula. *The Fountainhead,* by Ayn Rand, a popular book and movie, pictures its architect hero as standing out, in violent integrity, against the pressure for group adjustment and, in the end, successfully bringing the jury of his peers along with him. He *does* take all: the heights of fame, his rival's wife, the death of his rival. What is most striking

[10] *Partisan Review, XV* (1948), 240.

in all this, however, is the unintended caricature, both of group adjustment and of group resistance. The group is made out not tolerant but mean, inartistic, and corrupt. And group resistance is seen in terms of nobility on the part of the sadistic hero, who wants to deny any ties to humanity, any dependency. This superman for adults is the very apotheosis of the lonely success, to be admired perhaps by the reader but too stagey to be imitated.

In all likelihood, moreover, the Ayn Rand audience that applauds fiery denunciations of group-mindedness and submission to others is quite unaware of its own tendencies to submission in the small, undramatic situations of daily life. In that sense *The Fountainhead* is escapist.

GOOD-BYE TO ESCAPE?

So far, in these illustrations, we have seen little that would correspond to the unambiguous escapes of the inner-directed. Rather, we have seen popular culture used, often quite desperately, for training in group adjustment. In the same way, we may find popular culture used as training in the orientation of consumers, which is hardly a less serious problem (in many ways it is the same problem) for the other-directed person. Despite appearances, the other-directed person seems often unable to get away from himself or to waste time with any gestures of abundance or abandon. (Of course, if we compared patterns of alcoholic escape, we might come up with somewhat different results.)

The inner-directed person, if influenced by Protestantism, is of course also unable to waste time. The mobile youth from the lower classes shows his commitment to inner-direction by cutting himself off from hard-drinking horse-play-indulging pals: he continues the production of an inner-directed character through practicing a kind of mental bookkeeping by which the demons of Waste and Sloth are ruthlessly driven out. Such a person has little leisure, unless he can justify it as self-improving, and a life that has never an idle moment must have many a tense one. On the face of it the other-directed person is no puritan; he seems much less preoccupied with waste; his furnishings, manners, and morals are more casual. But an attenuated puritanism survives in his exploitation of leisure. He may say, when he takes a vacation or stretches a weekend, "I owe it to myself"—but the self in question is viewed like a car or house whose upkeep must be carefully maintained for resale purposes. The other-directed person has no clear core of self to escape from; no clear line between production and consumption; between adjusting to the group and serving private interests; between work and play.

One interesting index of this is the decline of evening dress, especially among men, and conversely, the invasion of the office by sport clothes. This looks like an offshoot of the cult of effortlessness, and of course men say "it's too much trouble" in explaining why they don't change for dinner or the evening. But the explanation lies rather in the fact that most men today simply do not know how to change roles, let alone mark the change by proper costuming. Another reason may be the fear of being thought high-hat; one can wear gaudy shirts but not stiff ones. Thus the sport shirt and casual dress show that one is a good fellow not only on the golf course or on vacation but in the office and at dinner too.

Women are still permitted to dress for the evening, a sign, perhaps, of their laggard response to changing modes. They are more involved than men in the dying patterns of conspicuous consumption. However, they probably make more of an actual shift from housework and babies to dinner party than many men do, who exchange office gossip both at work and play: moreover, they really like the shift, dragging the men, who would just as soon be in the office, along with them. I have observed that women's shop talk of children and domestic matters is often—though certainly not always!—conducted with more skill, interest, and realism than that of men since the change of role refreshes both work and play.

What is it that drives men who have been surrounded

with people and their problems on the day shift to seek often exactly the same company (or its reflection in popular culture) on the night shift? Perhaps in part it is the terror of loneliness that the gangster movies symbolize. But certainly it makes for strain. Though popular culture on one level "fills in" between people so as to avoid any demand for conversational or sexual gambits, on another level the popular-culture performance is not simply a way of killing time: in the peer-group situation, it makes a demand that it be appraised. The other-directed girl who goes in company to the movies need not talk to the others during the picture but is sometimes faced with the problem: should she cry at the sad places or not? What is the proper reaction, the sophisticated line about what is going on? Observing movie audiences coming out of a "little" or "art" theater, it is sometimes apparent that people feel they ought to react, but how?

In contrast to this, the inner-directed person, reading a book alone, is less aware of the others looking on; moreover, he has time to return at his own pace from being transported by his reading—to return and put on whatever mask he cares to. The poker game in the back room, with its praise of masks, fits his habituation to social distance, even loneliness. His successor, dreading loneliness, tries to assuage it not only in his crowd but in those fantasies that, like a mirror, only return his own concerns to him.

III. The Two Types Compared

We have completed our direct confrontation of the two types; and it now becomes necessary to redress the balance against other-direction, which, I know, has come off a bad second in these pages. It is hard for us to be quite fair to the other-directed. The term itself suggests shallowness and superficiality as compared to the inner-directed, even though direction in *both* cases comes from outside and is simply internalized at an early point in the life cycle of the inner-directed.

There are factors outside of terminology that may lead

readers to conclude that inner-direction is better. Academic and professional people are frequently only too pleased to be told that those horrid businessmen, those glad-handing advertisers, are manipulative. And, as we all know, the businessmen and advertisers themselves flock to plays and movies that tell them what miserable sinners they are. Of course it is especially gratifying to look down one's nose at Hollywood, soap opera, and other phenomena of mass culture.

Inner-directed persons of high status, moreover, are associated with the Anglo-Saxon tradition and with the reverence we pay to those among the aged who are still powerful. Furthermore, since the inner-directed face problems that are not the problems of the other-directed, they seem to be made of sterner and more intrepid stuff. As we already find the Victorians charming, so we can patronize the inner-directed, especially if we did not personally suffer from their limitations, and view the era depending on inner-direction with understandable nostalgia.

Furthermore I do not want to be understood as saying it is wrong to be concerned with the "others," with human relations. That we can afford to be concerned with such problems is one of the important abundances of a society of advanced technological accomplishment. We must ask anyone who opposes the manipulation of men in modern industry whether he prefers to return to their brutalization, as in the early days of the industrial revolution. In my scheme of values, persuasion, even manipulative persuasion, is to be preferred to force. There is the danger, in fact, when one speaks of the "softness of the personnel," that one will be understood to prefer hardness. On the contrary, one of the main contentions of this book is that the other-directed person, as things are, is already too hard on himself in certain ways and that his anxieties, as child consumer-trainee, as parent, as worker and player, are very great. He is often torn between the illusion that life should be easy, if he could only find the ways of proper adjustment to the group, and the half-buried feeling that it is not easy for him. Under these conditions it would only complicate his life still further to hold up the opposite illusion of stern inner-direction as an ideal, though this is just what many people propose. In fact, just because he is other-directed he is often overready to take some intransigent and seemingly convinced person as a model of what he himself ought to be like; his very sympathy and sensitivity may undo him.

It is easy to score verbal triumphs over American personnel practices and popular culture, for age-old snobberies converge here. Thus, a critique of the glad hand can be made from many points of view, radical or reactionary. The context out of which I have written is, however, somewhat different—it is an effort to develop a view of society which accepts rather than rejects new potentialities for leisure, human sympathy, and abundance. Both the glad hand and the search for lessons of adjustment in popular culture are themselves often poignant testimonials to these potentialities. The values of the era of the invisible hand accompanied scarcity, and thus require reinterpretation before they become relevant to an era of abundance. The promising alternative to other-direction . . . is not inner-direction, but autonomy.

WHITE COLLAR

C. Wright Mills

The late C. Wright Mills (1916-1962) described himself as "a Texas bull." He had resolved to thresh about in the china shop of American sociology, destroying fragile vessels that too many naïve laymen might otherwise buy and cherish. Those who knew him realized that he also had a gentler side, but it was in his self-appointed task of creative destruction that Mills shone most brightly. If "bull" was too strong, then "maverick" was not, and that word with all its rich Texan connotations should be warmly attached to his memory.

Even when he was a graduate student at the University of Wisconsin, there must have been a roar in his voice. Young Mills cannot always have pleased his professors, not at least with the kind of action he once reported to us. He had submitted a term paper for John Gillen's seminar in social disorganization of which his mentor thought so little that he graded it "C." Nevertheless, Mills sent his paper to The American Journal of Sociology, *after having appended to it a title destined soon to become famous: "The Professional Ideology of Social Pathologists." Like all the articles of his novitiate, this one, while professionally acceptable, revealed a mind that would not be contained within the usual disciplinary limits. From the beginning he challenged the views of even those who taught him most. It was almost as if the unreconstructed Texan could be heard to sing, "Don't Fence Me In."*

No one ever did fence him in; he looked out and broke loose. Regaining for social analysis the audience most of his col-

Source: Chapters 2 and 3 of *White Collar: The American Middle Classes* by C. Wright Mills. Copyright by Oxford University Press, Inc. Reprinted by permission.

leagues had long since relinquished, Mills became a national figure, and alas—for it nearly ruined him—with The Causes of World War III *and* Listen Yankee: The Cuban Revolution, *Mills was transformed into a culture hero. At the end, during a period of personal disorganization and political aberration, when he found authoritarianism attractive, a state from which he seemed to be recovering only months or weeks before his premature death, C. Wright Mills was an international celebrity. Despised by a host of narrow American academics who belittled the solid achievement of his middle years, he was celebrated by young and rebellious people everywhere in the world, not for that achievement but for a momentary political stance that ill became him.*

In the American grain and against it, Mills left his mark. Spiritually he was a Wobbly—and nothing else tells us so much about a book like White Collar, *in which bureaucracy is seen as a force that envelops and smothers free men, that fences them in beyond endurance. Who else would have called a chapter (included below) on so prosaic a subject as the executive class, "The Managerial Demiurge"?* The Oxford English Dictionary *defines* demiurge *first in the Platonic sense to mean "Maker of the Cosmos," and then, "in the Gnostic system, conceived as a being subordinate to the Supreme Being, and sometimes as the author of evil." Both descriptively and normatively, "demiurge" is Mills's* mot juste. *It stands for the destructive element, intolerable to such a man as Mills.*

Like his The New Men of Power *and* The Power Elite, *Mills's* White Collar *captures a large part of contemporary reality. We keep going back to the text, which has not dated since 1951, because something lifts it above ordinary analysis. For one thing, a lively sensibility is at work; for another, the anarchist streak is never wholly subdued; for yet another, the author is endlessly resourceful in his use of empirical data. Mills had a broad vision of society, but he did not disdain facts and figures; his work was a demonstration to the squeamish among sociologists, showing them how "objective" material could be appropriated in addressing precisely those big issues from which they habitually recoiled. The generalist can go to historical records, mine fragmentary studies, cross the usual boundaries, and tell us something. All this Mills in his prime did with remarkable skill.*

In White Collar, *he was at the peak of his powers. He had absorbed much by then, perhaps most from a great teacher and collaborator, Hans Gerth, of the University of Wisconsin. Tremendously learned, his gifts not fully appreciated, Gerth has already taught more than one generation of students. The best of them have become scholar-artist-sociologists—none more so than C. Wright Mills, who learned of Weber and Marx and Freud from Gerth, and of George Herbert Mead from others at Wisconsin. Balzac may have been Mills's own discovery. How he drew upon* The Human Comedy *is evident in our excerpt. Indeed, Mills wished most of his life to be an American Balzac, to treat every major aspect of American life with as much thoroughness as the French master had achieved in his time. Balzac was a sociologist* malgré lui; *just so, Mills the sociologist was an artist: "trained" to do one thing, he was scorned or praised for constantly transcending it. More's the pity that he could not have lived to complete his worthiest mission. In his beginning was his end, but that beginning deserves our closest attention.*

THE NEW MIDDLE CLASS, I

In the early nineteenth century, although there are no exact figures, probably four-fifths of the occupied population were self-employed enterprisers; by 1870, only about one-third, and in 1940, only about one-fifth, were still in this old middle class. Many of the remaining four-fifths of the people who now earn a living do so by working for the 2 or 3 per cent of the population who now own 40 or 50 per cent of the private property in the United States. Among these workers are the members of the new middle class, white-collar people on salary. For them, as for wage-workers, America has become a nation of employees for whom independent property is out of range. Labor markets, not control of property, determine their chances to receive income, exercise power, enjoy prestige, learn and use skills.

1. Occupational Change

Of the three broad strata composing modern society, only the new middle class has steadily grown in proportion to the whole. Eighty years ago, there were three-quarters of a million middle-class employees; by 1940, there were over twelve and a half million. In that period the old middle class increased 135 per cent; wage-workers, 225 per cent; new middle class, 1600 per cent.[1]

The employees composing the new middle class do not make up one single compact stratum. They have not emerged on a single horizontal level, but have been shuffled out simultaneously on the several levels of modern society; they now form, as it were, a new pyramid within the old pyramid of society at large, rather than a horizontal layer. The great bulk of the new middle class are of the lower middle-income brackets, but regardless of how social stature is measured, types of white-collar men and women range from almost the top to almost the bottom of modern society.

THE LABOR FORCE	1870	1940
Old Middle Class	33%	20%
New Middle Class	6	25
Wage-Workers	61	55
TOTAL	100%	100%

The managerial stratum, subject to minor variations during these decades, has dropped slightly, from 14 to 10 per cent; the salaried professionals, displaying the same minor

[1] In the tables in this section, figures for the intermediate years are appropriately graded; the change has been more or less steady.

ups and downs, have dropped from 30 to 25 per cent of the new middle class. The major shifts in over-all composition have been in the relative decline of the sales group, occurring most sharply around 1900, from 44 to 25 per cent of the total new middle class; and the steady rise of the office workers, from 12 to 40 per cent. Today the three largest occupational groups in the white-collar stratum are schoolteachers, salespeople in and out of stores, and assorted office workers. These three form the white-collar mass.

NEW MIDDLE CLASS	1870	1940
Managers	14%	10%
Salaried Professionals	30	25
Salespeople	44	25
Office Workers	12	40
TOTAL	100%	100%

White-collar occupations now engage well over half the members of the American middle class as a whole. Between 1870 and 1940, white-collar workers rose from 15 to 56 per cent of the middle brackets, while the old middle class declined from 85 to 44 per cent:

THE MIDDLE CLASSES	1870	1940
Old Middle Class	*85%*	*44%*
Farmers	62	23
Businessmen	21	19
Free Professionals	2	2
New Middle Class	*15%*	*56%*
Managers	2	6
Salaried Professionals	4	14
Salespeople	7	14
Office Workers	2	22
TOTAL MIDDLE CLASSES	100%	100%

Negatively, the transformation of the middle class is a shift from property to no-property; positively, it is a shift from property to a new axis of stratification, occupation. The nature and well-being of the old middle class can best be sought in the condition of entrepreneurial property; of the new middle class, in the economics and sociology of occupations. The numerical decline of the older, independent sectors of the middle class is an incident in the centralization of property; the numerical rise of the newer salaried employees is due to the industrial mechanics by which the occupations composing the new middle class have arisen.

2. *Industrial Mechanics*

In modern society, occupations are specific functions within a social division of labor, as well as skills sold for income on a labor market. Contemporary divisions of labor involve a hitherto unknown specialization of skill: from arranging abstract symbols, at $1,000 an hour, to working a shovel, for $1,000 a year. The major shifts in occupations since the Civil War have assumed this industrial trend: as a proportion of the labor force, fewer individuals manipulate *things*, more handle *people* and *symbols*.

This shift in needed skills is another way of describing the rise of the white-collar workers, for their characteristic skills involve the handling of paper and money and people. They are expert at dealing with people transiently and impersonally; they are masters of the commercial, professional, and technical relationship. The one thing they do not do is live by making things; rather, they live off the social machineries that organize and co-ordinate the people who do make things. White-collar people help turn what someone else has made into profit for still another; some of them are closer to the means of production, supervising the work of actual manufacture and recording what is done. They are the people who keep track; they man the paper routines involved in distributing what is produced. They provide technical and personal services, and they teach others the skills which they themselves practice, as well as all other skills transmitted by teaching.

As the proportion of workers needed for the extraction and production of things declines, the proportion needed for servicing, distributing, and co-ordinating rises. In 1870, over three-fourths, and in 1940, slightly less than one-half of the total employed were engaged in producing things.

	1870	1940
Producing	77%	46%
Servicing	13	20
Distributing	7	23
Co-ordinating	3	11
TOTAL EMPLOYED	100%	100%

By 1940, the proportion of white-collar workers of those employed in industries primarily involved in the production of things was 11 per cent; in service industries, 32 per cent; in distribution, 44 per cent; and in co-ordination, 60 per cent. The white-collar industries themselves have grown, and within each industry the white-collar occupations have grown. Three trends lie back of the fact that the white-collar ranks have thus been the most rapidly growing of modern occupations: the increasing productivity of machinery used in manufacturing; the magnification of distribution; and the increasing scale of co-ordination.

The immense productivity of mass-production technique and the increased application of technologic rationality are the first open secrets of modern occupational change: fewer men turn out more things in less time. In the middle of the nineteenth century, as J. F. Dewhurst and his associates have calculated, some 17.6 billion horsepower hours were expended in American industry, only 6 per cent by mechanical energy; by the middle of the twentieth century, 410.4 billion horse-power hours will be expended, 94 per cent by mechanical energy. This industrial revolution seems to be permanent, seems to go on through war and boom and slump; thus 'a decline in production results in a more than proportional decline in employment; and an increase in production results in a less than proportional increase in employment.'

Technology has thus narrowed the stratum of workers needed for given volumes of output; it has also altered the types and proportions of skill needed in the production process. Know-how, once an attribute of the mass of workers, is now in the machine and the engineering elite who design it. Machines displace unskilled workmen, make craft skills unnecessary, push up front the automatic motions of the machine-operative. Workers composing the new lower class are predominantly semi-skilled: their proportion in the urban wage-worker stratum has risen from 31 per cent in 1910 to 41 per cent in 1940.

The manpower economies brought about by machinery and the large-scale rationalization of labor forces, so apparent in production and extraction, have not, as yet, been applied so extensively in distribution—transportation, communication, finance, and trade. Yet without an elaboration of these means of distribution, the wide-flung operations of multi-plant producers could not be integrated nor their products distributed. Therefore, the proportion of people engaged in distribution has enormously increased so that today about one-fourth of the labor force is so engaged. Distribution has expanded more than production because of the lag in technological application in this field, and because of the persistence of individual and small-scale entrepreneurial units at the same time that the market has been enlarged and the need to market has been enlarged and the need to market has been deepened.

Behind this expansion of the distributive occupations lies the central problem of modern capitalism: to whom can the available goods be sold? As volume swells, the intensified search for markets draws more workers into the distributive occupations of trade, promotion, advertising. As far-flung and intricate markets come into being, and as the need to find and create even more markets becomes urgent, 'middle men' who move, store, finance, promote, and sell goods are knit into a vast network of enterprises and occupations.

The physical aspect of distribution involves wide and fast transportation networks; the co-ordination of marketing involves communication; the search for markets and the selling of goods involves trade, including wholesale and retail outlets as well as financial agencies for commodity and capital markets. Each of these activities engage more people, but the manual jobs among them do not increase so fast as the white-collar tasks.

Transportation, growing rapidly after the Civil War, began to decline in point of the numbers of people involved before 1930; but this decline took place among wage-workers; the proportion of white-collar workers employed in transportation continued to rise. By 1940, some 23 per cent of the people in transportation were white-collar employees. As a new industrial segment of the U.S. economy, the communication industry has never been run by large numbers of free enterprisers; at the outset it needed large numbers of technical and other white-collar workers. By 1940, some 77 per cent of its people were in new middle-class occupations.

Trade is now the third largest segment of the occupational structure, exceeded only by farming and manufacturing. A few years after the Civil War less than 5 out of every 100 workers were engaged in trade; by 1940 almost 12 out of every 100 workers were so employed. But, while 70 per cent of those in wholesaling and retailing were free enterprisers in 1870, and less than 3 per cent were white-collar, by 1940, of the people engaged in retail trade 27 per cent were free enterprisers; 41 per cent white-collar employees.

Newer methods of merchandising, such as credit financing, have resulted in an even greater percentage increase in the 'financial' than in the 'commercial' agents of distribution. Branch banking has lowered the status of many banking employees to the clerical level, and reduced the number of executive positions. By 1940, of all employees in finance and real estate 70 per cent were white-collar workers of the new middle class.

The organizational reason for the expansion of the white-collar occupations is the rise of big business and big government, and the consequent trend of modern social structure, the steady growth of bureaucracy. In every branch of the economy, as firms merge and corporations become dominant, free entrepreneurs become employees, and the calculations of accountant, statistician, bookkeeper, and clerk in these corporations replace the free 'movement of prices' as the co-ordinating agent of the economic system. The rise of thousands of big and little bureaucracies and the elaborate specialization of the system as a whole create the need for many men and women to plan, co-ordinate, and administer new routines for others. In moving from smaller to larger and more elaborate units of economic activity, increased proportions of employees are drawn into co-ordinating and managing. Managerial and professional employees and office workers of varied sorts—floorwalkers, foremen, office managers—are needed; people to whom subordinates report, and who in turn report to superiors, are links in chains of power and obedience, co-ordinating and supervising other occupational experiences, functions, and skills. And all over the economy, the proportion of clerks of all sorts has increased: from 1 or 2 per cent in 1870 to 10 or 11 per cent of all gainful workers in 1940.

As the worlds of business undergo these changes, the increased tasks of government on all fronts draw still more people into occupations that regulate and service property and men. In response to the largeness and predatory complications of business, the crises of slump, the nationalization of the rural economy and small-town markets, the flood of immigrants, the urgencies of war and the march of technology disrupting social life, government increases its co-ordinating and regulating tasks. Public regulations, social services, and business taxes require more people to make mass records and to integrate people, firms, and goods, both within government and in the various segments of business and private life. All branches of government have grown, although the most startling increases are found in the executive branch of the Federal Government, where the needs for co-ordinating the economy have been most prevalent.

As marketable activities, occupations change (1) with shifts in the skills required, as technology and rationalization are unevenly applied across the economy; (2) with the enlargement and intensification of marketing operations in both the commodity and capital markets; and (3) with shifts in the organization of the division of work, as expanded organizations require co-ordination, management, and recording. The mechanics involved within and between these three trends have led to the numerical expansion of white-collar employees.

There are other less obvious ways in which the occupational structure is shaped: high agricultural tariffs, for example, delay the decline of farming as an occupation; were Argentine beef allowed to enter duty-free, the number of meat producers here might diminish. City ordinances and zoning laws abolish peddlers and affect the types of construction workers that prevail. Most states have bureaus of standards which limit entrance into professions and semi-professions; at the same time members of these occupations form associations in the attempt to control entrance into 'their' market. More successful than most trade unions, such professional associations as the American Medical Association have managed for several decades to level off the proportion of physicians and surgeons. Every phase of the slump-war-boom cycle influences the numerical importance of various occupations; for instance, the movement back and forth between 'construction worker' and small 'contractor' is geared to slumps and booms in building.

The pressures from these loosely organized parts of the occupational world draw conscious managerial agencies into the picture. The effects of attempts to manage occupational change, directly and indirectly, are not yet great, except of course during wars, when government freezes men in their jobs or offers incentives and compulsions to remain in old occupations or shift to new ones. Yet, increasingly the class levels and occupational composition of the nation are managed; the occupational structure of the United States is being slowly reshaped as a gigantic corporate group. It is subject not only to the pulling of autonomous markets and the pushing of technology but to an 'allocation of personnel' from central points of control. Occupational change thus becomes more conscious, at least to those who are coming to be in charge of it.

3. *White-Collar Pyramids*

Occupations, in terms of which we circumscribe the new middle class, involve several ways of ranking people. As specific activities, they entail various types and levels of *skill*, and their exercise fulfils certain *functions* within an industrial division of labor. These are the skills and functions we have been examining statistically. As sources of income, occupations are connected with *class* position; and since they normally carry an expected quota of prestige, on and off the job, they are relevant to *status* position. They also involve certain degrees of *power* over other people, directly in terms of the job, and indirectly in other social areas. Occupations are thus tied to class, status, and power as well as to skill and function; to understand the occupations composing the new middle class, we must consider them in terms of each of these dimensions.[2]

'Class situation' in its simplest objective sense has to do with the amount and source of income. Today, occupation rather than property is the source of income for most of those who receive any direct income: the possibilities of selling their services in the labor market, rather than of profitably buying and selling their property and its yields, now determine the life-chances of most of the middle class. All things money can buy and many that men dream about are theirs by virtue of occupational income. In new middle-class occupations men work for someone else on someone else's property. This is the clue to many differences between the old and new middle classes, as well as to the contrast between the older world of the small propertied entrepreneur and the occupational structure of the new society. If the old middle class once fought big property structures in the name of small, free properties, the new middle class, like the wage-workers in latter-day capitalism, has been, from the beginning, dependent upon large properties for job security.

Wage-workers in the factory and on the farm are on the propertyless bottom of the occupational structure, depending upon the equipment owned by others, earning wages for the time they spend at work. In terms of property, the white-collar people are *not* 'in between Capital and Labor'; they are in exactly the same property-class position as the wage-workers. They have no direct financial tie to the means of production, no prime claim upon the proceeds from property. Like factory workers—and day laborers, for that matter—they work for those who do own such means of livelihood.

[2] The following pages are not intended as a detailed discussion of the class, prestige, and power of the white-collar occupations, but as preliminary and definitional.

Yet if bookkeepers and coal miners, insurance agents and farm laborers, doctors in a clinic and crane operators in an open pit have this condition in common, certainly their class situations are not the same. To understand their class positions, we must go beyond the common fact of source of income and consider as well the amount of income.

In 1890, the average income of white-collar occupational groups was about double that of wage-workers. Before World War I, salaries were not so adversely affected by slumps as wages were but, on the contrary, they rather steadily advanced. Since World War I, however, salaries have been reacting to turns in the economic cycles more and more like wages, although still to a lesser extent. If wars help wages more because of the greater flexibility of wages, slumps help salaries because of their greater inflexibility. Yet after each war era, salaries have never regained their previous advantage over wages. Each phase of the cycle, as well as the progressive rise of all income groups, has resulted in a narrowing of the income gap between wage-workers and white-collar employees.

In the middle 'thirties the three urban strata, entrepreneurs, white-collar, and wage-workers, formed a distinct scale with respect to median family income: the white-collar employees had a median income of $1,896; the entrepreneurs, $1,464; the urban wage-workers, $1,175. Although the median income of white-collar workers was higher than that of the entrepreneurs, larger proportions of the entrepreneurs received both high-level and low-level incomes. The distribution of their income was spread more than that of the white collar.

The wartime boom in incomes, in fact, spread the incomes of all occupational groups, but not evenly. The spread occurred mainly among urban entrepreneurs. As an income level, the old middle class in the city is becoming less an evenly graded income group, and more a collection of different strata, with a large proportion of lumpen-bourgeoisie who receive very low incomes, and a small, prosperous bourgeoisie with very high incomes.

In the late 'forties (1948, median family income) the income of all white-collar workers was $4000, that of all urban wage-workers, $3300. These averages, however, should not obscure the overlap of specific groups within each stratum: the lower white-collar people—sales-employees and office workers—earned almost the same as skilled workers and foremen,[3] but more than semi-skilled urban wage-workers.

In terms of property, white-collar people are in the same position as wage-workers; in terms of occupational income, they are 'somewhere in the middle.' Once they were considerably above the wage-workers; they have become less so; in the middle of the century they still have an edge but the over-all rise in incomes is making the new middle class a more homogeneous income group.

As with income, so with prestige: white-collar groups are differentiated socially, perhaps more decisively than wage-workers and entrepreneurs. Wage earners certainly do form an income pyramid and a prestige gradation, as do entrepreneurs and rentiers; but the new middle class, in terms of income and prestige, is a superimposed pyramid, reaching from almost the bottom of the first to almost the top of the second.

People in white-collar occupations claim higher prestige than wage-workers, and, as a general rule, can cash in their claims with wage-workers as well as with the anonymous public. This fact has been seized upon, with much justification, as the defining characteristic of the white-collar strata, and although there are definite indications in the United States of a decline in their prestige, still, on a nation-wide basis, the majority of even the lower white-collar employees—office workers and salespeople—enjoy a middling prestige.

[3] It is impossible to isolate the salaried foremen from the skilled urban wage-workers in these figures. If we could do so, the income of lower white-collar workers would be closer to that of semi-skilled workers.

The historic bases of the white-collar employees' prestige, apart from superior income, have included the similarity of their place and type of work to those of the old middle-classes' which has permitted them to borrow prestige. As their relations with entrepreneur and with esteemed customer have become more impersonal, they have borrowed prestige from the firm itself. The stylization of their appearance, in particular the fact that most white-collar jobs have permitted the wearing of street clothes on the job, has also figured in their prestige claims, as have the skills required in most white-collar jobs, and in many of them the variety of operations performed and the degree of autonomy exercised in deciding work procedures. Furthermore, the time taken to learn these skills and the way in which they have been acquired by formal education and by close contact with the higher-ups in charge has been important. White-collar employees have monopolized high school education—even in 1940 they had completed 12 grades to the 8 grades for wage-workers and entrepreneurs. They have also enjoyed status by descent: in terms of race, Negro white-collar employees exist only in isolated instances —and, more importantly, in terms of nativity, in 1930 only about 9 per cent of white-collar workers, but 16 per cent of free enterprisers and 21 per cent of wage-workers, were foreign born. Finally, as an underlying fact, the limited size of the white-collar group, compared to wage-workers, has led to successful claims to greater prestige.

The power position of groups and of individuals typically depends upon factors of class, status, and occupation, often in intricate interrelation. Given occupations involve specific powers over other people in the actual course of work; but also outside the job area, by virtue of their relations to institutions of property as well as the typical income they afford, occupations lend power. Some white-collar occupations require the direct exercise of supervision over other white-collar and wage-workers, and many more are closely attached to this managerial cadre. White-collar employees are the assistants of authority; the power they exercise is a derived power, but they do exercise it.

Moreover, within the white-collar pyramids there is a characteristic pattern of authority involving age and sex. The white-collar ranks contain a good many women: some 41 per cent of all white-collar employees, as compared with 10 per cent of free enterprisers, and 21 per cent of wage-workers, are women.[4] As with sex, so with age: free enterprisers average (median) about 45 years of age, white-collar and wage-workers, about 34; but among free enterprisers and wage-workers, men are about 2 or 3 years older than women; among white-collar workers, there is a 6- or 7-year difference. In the white-collar pyramids, authority is roughly graded by age and sex: younger women tend to be subordinated to older men.

The occupational groups forming the white-collar pyramids, different as they may be from one another, have certain common characteristics, which are central to the character of the new middle class as a general pyramid overlapping the entrepreneurs and wage-workers. White-collar people cannot be adequately defined along any one possible dimension of stratification—skill, function, class, status, or power. They are generally in the middle ranges on each of these dimensions and on every descriptive attribute. Their position is more definable in terms of their relative differences from other strata than in any absolute terms.

On all points of definition, it must be remembered that white-collar people are not one compact horizontal stratum. They do not fulfil one central, positive *function* that can define them, although in general their functions are similar to those of the old middle class. They deal with symbols and with

[4] According to our calculations, the proportions of women, 1940, in these groups are: farmers, 2.9%; businessmen, 20%; free professionals, 5.9%; managers, 7.1%; salaried professionals, 51.7%; salespeople, 27.5%; office workers, 51%; skilled workers, 3.2%; semi-skilled and unskilled, 29.8%; rural workers, 9.1%.

other people, co-ordinating, recording, and distributing; but they fulfil these functions as dependent employees, and the skills they thus employ are sometimes similar in form and required mentality to those of many wage-workers.

In terms of property, they are equal to wage-workers and different from the old middle class. Originating as propertyless dependents, they have no serious expectations of propertied independence. In terms of income, their class position is, on the average, somewhat higher than that of wage-workers. The overlap is large and the trend has been definitely toward less difference, but even today the differences are significant.

Perhaps of more psychological importance is the fact that white-collar groups have successfully claimed more prestige than wage-workers and still generally continue to do so. The bases of their prestige may not be solid today, and certainly they show no signs of being permanent; but, however vague and fragile, they continue to mark off white-collar people from wage-workers.

Members of white-collar occupations exercise a derived authority in the course of their work; moreover, compared to older hierarchies, the white-collar pyramids are youthful and feminine bureaucracies, within which youth, education, and American birth are emphasized at the wide base, where millions of office workers most clearly typify these differences between the new middle class and other occupational groups. White-collar masses, in turn, are managed by people who are more like the old middle class, having many of the social characteristics, if not the independence, of free enterprisers.

THE MANAGERIAL DEMIURGE

As the means of administration are enlarged and centralized, there are more managers in every sphere of modern society, and the managerial type of man becomes more important in the total social structure.

These new men at the top, products of a hundred-year shift in the upper brackets, operate within the new bureaucracies, which select them for their positions and then shape their characters. Their role within these bureaucracies, and the role of the bureaucracies within the social structure, set the scope and pace of the managerial demiurge. So pervasive and weighty are these bureaucratic forms of life that, in due course, older types of upper-bracket men shift their character and performance to join the managerial trend, or sink beneath the upper-bracket men.

In their common attempt to deal with the underlying population, the managers of business and government have become interlaced by committee and pressure group, by political party and trade association. Very slowly, reluctantly, the labor leader in his curious way, during certain phases of the business cycle and union history, joins them. The managerial demiurge means more than an increased proportion of people who work and live by the rules of business, government, and labor bureaucracy; it means that, at the top, society becomes an uneasy interlocking of private and public hierarchies, and at the bottom, more and more areas become objects of management and manipulation. Bureaucratization in the United States is by no means total; its spread is partial and segmental, and the individual is caught up in several structures at once. Yet, over-all, the loose-jointed integration of liberal society is being replaced, especially in its war phases, by the more managed integration of a corporate-like society.

1. *The Bureaucracies*

As an epithet for governmental waste and red tape, the word 'bureaucracy' is a carry-over from the heroic age of capitalism, when the middle-class entrepreneur was in revolt against mercantile company and monarchist dynasty. That time is now long past, but the epithet persists in the service of different aims.

In its present common meaning, 'bureaucracy' is inaccurate and misleading for three major reasons: (1) When the corporation official objects to 'bureaucracy' he means of course the programs of the Federal Government, and then only in so far as they seem to be against the interests of his own private business bureaucracy. (2) Most of the waste and inefficiency associated in popular imagery with 'bureaucracy' is, in fact, a lack of strict and complete bureaucratization. The 'mess,' and certainly the graft, of the U.S. Army, are more often a result of a persistence of the entrepreneurial outlook among its personnel than of any bureaucratic tendencies as such. Descriptively, bureaucracy refers to a hierarchy of offices or bureaus, each with an assigned area of operation, each employing a staff having specialized qualifications. So defined, bureaucracy is the most efficient type of social organization yet devised. (3) Government bureaucracies are, in large part, a public consequence of private bureaucratic developments, which by centralizing property and equipment have been the pace setter of the bureaucratic trend. The very size of modern business, housing the technological motors and financial say-so, compels the rise of centralizing organizations of formal rule and rational subdivisions in all sectors of society, most especially in government.

In business, as the manufacturing plant expands in size, it draws more people into its administrative scope. A smaller proportion of plants employ a larger proportion of manufacturing wage earners. Even before World War II concentration, 1 per cent of all the plants employed over half the workers. These enlarged plants are knit together in central-office or multi-plant enterprises. Less than 6000 such enterprises control the plants that employ about half of the workers; they have an output valued 760 per cent higher, and a production per wage-worker 19.5 per cent higher, than independent plants. Multi-plant as well as independent-plant enterprises merge together in various forms of corporation: by the time of the Great Depression, the 200 largest industrial corporations owned about half of the total industrial wealth of the country. These large corporations are linked by their directorships and by trade associations. Administrative decisions merge into the check and balance of the interlocking directorships; in the middle 'thirties some 400 men held a full third of the 3,544 top seats of the 250 largest corporations. Supra-corporate trade associations, as Robert Brady has observed, become 'funnels for the new monopoly,' stabilizing and rationalizing competing managements economically, and serving as the political apparatus for the whole managerial demiurge of private wealth.

The slump-war-boom rhythm makes business bureaucracy grow. During the crises, the single business concern becomes tied to an intercorporate world which manages the relations of large business and government. The larger and more bureaucratic business becomes, the more the Federal Government elaborates itself for purposes of attempted control, and the more business responds with more rational organization. The bureaucracies of business tend to duplicate the regulatory agencies of the federal hierarchy, to place their members within the governmental commissions and agencies, to hire officials away from government, and to develop elaborate mazes within which are hidden the official secrets of business operations. Across the bargaining tables of power, the bureaucracies of business and government face one another, and under the tables their myriad feet are interlocked in wonderfully complex ways.

The American governing apparatus has been enlarged, centralized, and professionalized both in its means of administration and the staff required. Presidents and governors, mayors and city managers have gathered into their hands the means of administration and the power to appoint and supervise. These officials, no longer simply political figures who deal mainly with legislatures, have become general managerial chieftains who deal mainly with the subordinates of a bureaucratic hierarchy. The executive branch of modern government has become dynamic, increasing its functions and enlarging its staff at the expense of the legislative and the judicial. In 1929, of all civilian governmental employees 18 per cent were employed in the executive branch of the Federal Government; in 1947, after the peak of World War II, the proportion was 37 per cent.

Who are the managers behind the managerial demiurge?

Seen from below, the management is not a Who but a series of Theys and even Its. Management is something one reports to in some office, maybe in all offices including that of the union; it is a printed instruction and a sign on a bulletin board; it is the voice coming through the loudspeakers; it is the name in the newspaper; it is the signature you can never make out, except it is printed underneath; it is a system that issues orders superior to anybody you know close-up; it blueprints, specifying in detail, your work-life and the boss-life of your foreman. Management is the centralized say-so.

Seen from the middle ranks, management is one-part people who give you the nod, one-part system, one-part yourself. White-collar people may be part of management, like they say, but management is a lot of things, not all of them managing. You carry authority, but you are not its source. As one of the managed, you are on view from above, and perhaps you are seen as a threat; as one of the managers, you are seen from below, perhaps as a tool. You are the cog and the beltline of the bureaucratic machinery itself; you are a link in the chains of commands, persuasions, notices, bills, which bind together the men who make decisions and the men who make things; without you the managerial demiurge could not be. But your authority is confined strictly within a prescribed orbit of occupational actions, and such power as you wield is a borrowed thing. Yours is the subordinate's mark, yours the canned talk. The money you handle is somebody else's money; the papers you sort and shuffle already bear somebody else's marks. You are the servant of decision, the assistant of authority, the minion of management. You are closer to management than the wage-workers are, but yours is seldom the last decision.

Seen from close to the top, management is the ethos of the higher circle: concentrate power, but enlarge your staff. Down the line, make them feel a part of what you are a part. Set up a school for managers and manage what managers learn; open a channel of two-way communication: commands go down, information comes up. Keep a firm grip but don't boss them, boss their experience; don't let them learn what you don't tell them. Between decision and execution, between command and obedience, let there be reflex. Be calm, judicious, rational; groom your personality and control your appearance; make business a profession. Develop yourself. Write a memo; hold a conference with men like you. And in all this be yourself and be human: nod gravely to the girls in the office; say hello to the men; and always listen carefully to the ones above: 'Over last week end, I gave much thought to the information you kindly tendered me on Friday, especially . . .'

2. *From the Top to the Bottom*

According to Edwin G. Nourse, recently head of the President's Council of Economic Advisers, 'Responsibility for determining the direction of the nation's economic life today and of furnishing both opportunity and incentive to the masses centers upon some one or two per cent of the gainfully employed.' The managers, as the cadre of the enterprise, form a hierarchy, graded according to their authority to initiate tasks, to plan and execute their own work and freely to plan and order the work of others. Each level in the cadre's hierarchy is beholden to the levels above. Manager talks with manager and each manager talks with his assistant managers and to the employees, that is, those who do not plan work or make decisions, but perform assigned work. Contact with non-managerial employees probably increases down the managerial hierarchy: the top men rarely talk to anyone but secretaries and other managers; the bottom men may have 90 per cent of their contacts with managed employees. In employee parlance, The Boss is frequently the man who actually gives orders; the top men are The Higher Ups who are typically unapproachable except by the narrow circle directly around them.

Down the line, managers are typically split into two types: those who have to do with business decisions and those who have to do with the industrial run of work. Both are further subdivided into various grades of importance, often according to the number of people under them; both have assigned duties and fixed requirements; both as groups have been rationalized. The business managers range from top executives who hold power of attorney for the entire firm and act in its behalf, to the department managers and their assistants under whom the clerks and machine operators and others work. The industrial managers range from the production engineer and designer at the top of the foremen immediately above the workmen at the bottom. The engineering manager and technician are typically subordinated to the business and financial manager: in so far as technical and human skills are used in the modern corporation they serve the needs of the business side of the corporation as judged by the business manager. The engineering manager, recruited from upper middle-income groups, via the universities, is assisted by lower middle-income people with some technical training and long experience.

The men at the top of the managerial cadre in business are formally responsible to the stockholders; in government, to the elected politicians and through them to the people. But neither are responsible to any other officials or managers; that is what being at the managerial top means. Often they are the least specialized men among the bosses; the 'general manager' is well named. Many a business firm is run by men whose knowledge is financial, and who could not hold down a job as factory superintendent, much less chief engineer.

Going from problem to problem and always deciding, like Tolstoy's generals, when there really is no basis for decision but only the machine's need for command, the need for no subordinate even to dream the chief is in doubt—that is different from working out some problem alone to its completion. For one thing, an appointment schedule, set more or less by the operation of the machine, determines the content and rhythm of the manager's time, and in fact of his life. For another, he hires and so must feel that the brains of others belong to him, because he knows how to use them. So Monroe Stahr, Scott Fitzgerald's hero in *The Last Tycoon*, first wanted to be chief clerk of the works, 'the one who knows where everything was,' but when he was chief, 'found out that no one knew where anything was.'

Relations between men in charge of the administrative branches of government and men who run the expanded corporations and unions are often close. Their collaboration may occur while each is an official of his respective hierarchy, or by means of personal shiftings of positions; the labor leader accepts a government job or becomes the personnel man of a corporation; the big-business official becomes a dollar-a-year man; the government expert accepts a position with the corporation his agency is attempting to regulate. Just how close the resemblance between governmental and business officials may be is shown by the ease and frequency with which men pass from one hierarchy to another. While such changes may seem mere incidents in an individual career, the meaning of such interpenetration of managerial elite goes beyond this, modifying the meaning of the upper brackets and the objective functions of the several big organizations.

Higher government officials, as Reinhard Bendix has suggested, probably come mostly from rural areas and medium-size towns, from middle-class and lower middle-class families; they have worked their way through college and often to higher educational degrees. Their occupational experience prior to government work is usually law, business, journalism, or college teaching. In line with general occupational shifts, the tendency over the last generation has been for fewer officials to come from farms and more from professional circles. Except perhaps on the very highest levels, these men do not suffer from lack of incentive, as compared with business officials. They do, however, tend to suffer from lack of those privileges of income, prestige, and security, which many of them believe comparable officials in large businesses enjoy.

The officials of business corporations are somewhat older than comparable government officials. The big companies do not yet have what experts in efficient bureaucracy would call an adequate system of recruiting for management. There may be even more 'politics' in appointments in the corporate hierarchies than in Federal Government bureaus. Among bureau heads in Washington, for instance, by 1938 only about 10 percent were simple political appointees.

Seniority, of course, often plays a large part in promotions to managerial posts in both hierarchies. The tenure of one representative group of business bureaucrats was about 20 years; turnover among top executives of large corporations is typically small. But the average tenure for bureau heads in the federal service, as A. W. MacMahon and J. D. Millet have observed, is about 11 years. On the next level up the federal hierarchies, of course, the Secretaries and Undersecretaries of Departments average only from three to five years.

The upper management of U.S. business may be recruited from among (1) insiders in the administrative hierarchy: (2) insiders in the firm's financial or clique structure; (3) outsiders who have proved themselves able at managing firms and are thus viewed as promising men on the management market; or (4) younger outsiders, fresh from technical or business training, who are usually taken in at lower levels with the expectation that their promotion will be unencumbered and rapid.

To the extent that the last three methods of recruitment

are followed, the advancement chances of the upper middle brackets of the cadre are diminished; thus they typically desire the first alternative as a policy, in which they are joined by most personnel advisers. The upper middle brackets would further individual security and advancement in a collective way, by fair and equal chances' being guaranteed, which is to say by the strict bureaucratization of the management field.

Symptomatic of the shift from entrepreneurship to bureaucratic enterprise in business is the manner of executive compensation. In the world of the small entrepreneur, where owner and manager were one, net profit was the mode of compensation. In the white-collar worlds, the top manager is a salaried employee receiving $25,000 to $500,000 a year. With increasing bureaucratization, annuities, pensions, and retirement plans come into the picture and bonuses based on profit shares fade out.

In between the entrepreneurial and the bureaucratic mode of payment there are various intermediary forms, many of them designed to maximize incentive and to beat the federal tax. Over the last quarter of a century taxes have become big: in 1947, for instance, the $25,000-a-year-man took home about $17,000; the $50,000-a-year-man about $26,000, the $150,000-a-year-man about $45,000—this from salary, not counting returns from property. Above certain levels, money as such loses incentive value; its prestige value and the experience of success for which it is a token gain as incentives. The more one makes the more one needs, and if one did not continue to make money, one would experience failure. There is no limit to the game, and there is no way out. And its insecurities are unlimited. So heightened can they become on the upper income levels that one management consultant, after diligent research, has plainly stated that the high-paid executive, like the wage-worker and salaried employee, has security at the center of his dream-life. To the manager, according to an Elmo Roper survey, security means (1) a position with dignity; (2) a rich and prompt recognition of accomplishments; (3) a free hand to do as he wants with his job and company; and (4) plenty of leisure. These are the security contents of the Big Money, which combine, as is appropriate in the transition era of corporate business, entrepreneurial freedom with riskless bureaucratic tenure.

The recruitment of a loyal managerial staff is now a major concern of the larger businesses, which tend toward the development of 'civil service' systems for single large corporations and even for large parts of entire industries. The lag in putting such bureaucratic procedures into effect occasions much urging from more 'progressive' corporation officials.

The big management shortage, the consequent load of managerial work during the Second World War, and the boom led to many formal recruitment and training plans. Selected men are sent to courses in management at graduate schools of Business Administration. Rotation training systems for key managerial personnel are also frequently employed: by allowing managers to take up various tasks for scheduled brief periods of time, the system fits them for over-all as well as delimited spheres of management. In this way the managerial cadre rationally enlarges its opportunity for a secure chance by seeing the whole operation in detail; by definite schedules, the experience of individual members of the cadre can be guided and the grooming of men for advancement controlled. The management cadre itself is being rationalized into military-like shape; in fact, some of the very best ideas for business management have come from men of high military experience —the 'bureaucrats' about whom businessmen complained so during the war.

Yet this increased bureaucratic training, recruitment, and promotion does not extend to the very bottom or to the very top of the business hierarchies. At the top, especially, those who run corporations and governments are the least bureaucratic of personnel, for above a certain point 'political,' 'property,' and 'character' qualifications set in and determine who shapes policy for the entire hierarchy. It is in the middle brackets of managers that bureaucratic procedures and styles are most in evidence.

These middle managers can plan only limited spheres of work; they transmit orders from above, executing some with their staffs and passing on others to those below them for execution.

Although the middle management often contains the most technically specialized men in the enterprise, their skills have become less and less material techniques and more and more the management of people. This is true even though supervision has been both intensified and diversified, and has lost many of its tasks to newer specialists in personnel work. While engineers take over the maintenance of the plant's new machinery, the middle managers and foremen take on more 'personnel' controls over the workers, looking more often to the personnel office than to the engineering headquarters.

The existence of middle managers indicates a further separation of worker from owner or top manager. But even as their functions have been created, the middle managers have had their authority stripped from them. It is lost, from the one side, as management itself becomes rationalized and, from the other side, as lower-management men, such as foremen, take over more specialized, less authoritative roles.

The middle managers do not count for very much in the larger world beyond their individual bureaucracies. In so far as power in connection with social and economic change is concerned, the important group within the managerial strata is the top managers; in so far as numbers are concerned, the important group is the foremen, who are about half of all managers (although less than 1 per cent of the total labor force). As with any 'middle' group, what happens to the middle managers is largely dependent upon what happens to those above and below them—to top executives and to foremen. The pace and character of work in the middle management are coming increasingly to resemble those in the lower ranks of the management hierarchy.

3. *The Case of the Foreman*

Once the foreman, representing the bottom stratum of management, was everything to the worker, the holder of his 'life and future.' Industrial disputes often seemed disputes between disgruntled workmen and rawhiding foremen; and yet the foreman's position was aspired to by the workman. The close relations, favored by the smaller plant and town, helped make for contentment, even though the foreman held the first line of defense for management. Having a monopoly on job gratification, he often took for himself any feeling of achievement to which his gang's labor might lead; he solved problems and overcame obstacles for the men laboring below him. He was the master craftsman: he knew more about the work processes than any of the men he bossed. Before mass production, the foreman was works manager and supervisor, production planner and personnel executive, all in one.

He is still all of that in many small plants and in certain industries that have no technical staff and few office workers. But such plants may be seen historically as lags and their foremen as precursors of modern technical and supervisory personnel.

Of all occupational strata, in fact, none has been so grievously affected by the rationalization of equipment and organization as the industrial foreman. With the coming of the big industry, the foreman's functions have been diminished from above by the new technical and human agents and dictates of higher management; from below, his authority has been undermined by the growth of powerful labor unions.

Along with the host of supervisory assistants and new kinds of superiors there has been developed in many industries semi-automatic machinery that may require the service of highly trained technicians, but not master craftsmen. With such machinery, Hans Speier has observed, the foreman's sphere of technical competence diminishes and his skills become more those of the personnel agent and human whip than of the master craftsman and work guide. As engineers and college-trained technicians slowly took over, the foreman, up from the ranks, had to learn to take orders in technical matters. In many industries the man who could nurse semi-automatic machines, rather than boss gangs of workmen, became the big man in the shop.

The experience originally earned and carried by the foreman stratum is systematized, then centralized and rationally redistributed. The old functions of the foreman are no longer embodied in any one man's experience but in a team and in a rule book. Each staff innovation, of personnel specialist, safety expert, time-study engineer, diminishes the foreman's authority and weakens the respect and discipline of his subordinates. The foreman is no longer the only link between worker and higher management, although, in the eyes of both, he is still the most apparent link in the elaborate hierarchy of command and technique between front office and workshop.

Authority, Ernest Dale remarks, 'can now be exercised by many foremen only in consultation with numerous other authorities, and the resulting interrelationships are often ill-defined and disturbing.' The foremen exercise authority at the point of production but they are not its final source. Often they exercise an authority of social dominance without superior technical competence. Their sharing of authority, and thus being shorn of it, has gone far: in only 10 per cent of the companies in one sample study do foremen have the complete right to discharge; in only 14 per cent, the absolute right to make promotions within their departments; in only 10 per cent the complete right to discipline. Only 20 per cent of the companies hold foremen's meetings or practice any form of active consultation. 'The foreman,' concludes the Slichter panel of the National War Labor Board, 'is more managed than managing, more and more an executor of other men's decisions, less and less a maker of decisions himself.'

From below, the foreman has lost authority with the men, who are themselves often powerful in their union. Men who used to go to their foremen with grievances now go to their union. Foremen complain about union stewards, who frequently accomplish more for the subordinate than the foreman can. Stewards are said by foremen to be independent: 'We are unable to make the stewards do anything. . . They challenge even our limited authority.' The unions can do something about the rank-and-file's problems; in fact, the unions have in some shops got benefits for the men once enjoyed only by foremen, including increased security of the job. Originating typically in the working ranks, the foreman is no longer of them, socially or politically. He may be jealous of union picnics and parties, and he is socially isolated from higher management.

The foreman's anxiety springs from the fact that the union looks after the workmen; the employer is able to look after himself; but who will look after the foreman?

Having arisen from the ranks of labor, he often cannot expect to go higher because he is not college-trained. By 1910 it was being pointed out in management literature that if the manager, in his search for dependable subordinates, turns to a 'former subordinate or fellow worker, he finds that they are attached too much to the old regime and can't do the job well. In this dilemma, he will turn to the technically educated young man. The employer [not technically educated] sneers at and yet respects this man.' Today, only 21 per cent of the foremen under 40 years of age, and 17 per cent over 40, believe they will ever get above the foreman level. No longer belonging to labor, not 'one of the boys in the union,' the foreman is not secure in management either, not of it socially and educationally. 'The snobbery of executive management is his pet peeve and the chief cause of his complaining.' Foremen are older than the run-of-the-mill workers under them; they are more often settled and have larger families. These facts limit their mobility and perhaps to some extent their courage. Hans Speier has even asserted, on the basis of such factors, that 'political opportunism' is 'the outstanding characteristic of the foreman.'

During the later 'thirties and the war, standing thus in the middle, a traffic cop of industrial relations, with each side expecting him to give its signals, the foreman became the object of both union and management propaganda. Even though foremen are no longer master craftsmen and work-guides as of old, they are still seen by management as key men, not so much in their technical roles in the work process as in their roles in the social organization of the factory. It is in keeping with the managerial demiurge and the changed nature of the foreman's role that he is led into the ways of manipulation. He is to develop discipline and loyalty among the workers by using his own personality as the main tool of persuasion.

He must be trained as a loyal leader embodying managerially approved opinions. 'Under present-day techniques the foreman is chosen for his skillfulness in handling personnel—rather than because of length-of-service or mastery of the particular operation in his charge. . . Getting along with people is 80 per cent of the modern foreman's job.' Recruitment officers and personnel directors are advised to consider the prospective foreman's family and social life along with his formal education and shop ability. The prime requisite is a rounded, well-adjusted personality; foremen must 'always be the same' in their relations with people—which means 'leaving your personal troubles at home, and being just as approachable and amiable on a "bad day" as on a good one.'

All manner of personal traits and behaviors are blandly suggested to foremen as indispensable. 'The essential quality of friendliness is *sincerity*. . . They should memorize, from the personnel records, the following about all the members of their department: first name; if married, whether husband or wife works in the plant; approximate ages and school grades of children . . . etc.' From local newspapers 'he will learn such valuable items as: accidents; births; deaths; children's activities; participation in Red Cross, YMCA . . . wedding anniversaries; parties; recitals.' 'The orientation of new recruits offers a real opportunity to win the friendship and loyalty of the new worker.' 'The manner of speech of the foreman during even a minor conversation is perhaps more important than what he says. . . Good listening habits are a must. . . He should fine himself 10 cents for every fall from grace. . . He needs a pleasant, clear voice [test recordings are recommended]. . . The words "definitely" and "absolutely" are taboo. . . His own prejudices must be "parked" outside the plant.' Higher managers who cannot yet grasp the point should recognize that such human engineering is capable of reducing the 'hourly cost of 1.2 hours of direct labor cost per pound of fabricated aircraft to .7 hour per pound within an 18 month period.'

To secure the foreman's allegiance, management has showered attention upon him. In return, management has written into its rule book for foremen: 'Solidarity with his class, which is of course the middle management group, is owed to his fellows by every foreman.' 'What needs to be demonstrated is that executive and supervisory management are one. Their interests must not be divided and their only difference is that of function within management.'

Realizing management's exploitation of their developing insecurities, younger union-conscious foremen have attempted to rejoin the men, have tried to form unions. The unions that began under the Wagner Act, in the 'forties, soon found themselves caught between the antagonism of organized labor and the indifference of management. Probably not more than 100,000 foremen were directly committed to unions under the Wagner Act. During the Second World War, foreman unionization took on impetus, for foremen who had to train some 8 million green workers began to feel their mettle and to search for a means of asserting it. Yet out of an estimated one to one-and-a-half million foremen in the United States, the

Foreman's Association, founded in Detroit in 1941, had at its peak only 50,000 or 5 per cent. Even these small beginnings were beset by legal confusion, and have certainly proved no solution.

4. The New Entrepreneur

Balzac called bureaucracy 'the giant power wielded by pygmies,' but actually not all the men who wield bureaucratic control are appropriately so termed. Modern observers without first-hand or sensitive experience in bureaucracies tend, first, to infer types of bureaucrats from the ideal-type definition of bureaucracy, rather than to examine the various executive adaptations to the enlarged enterprise and centralized bureau; and, second, to assume that big businesses are strictly bureaucratic in form. Such businesses are, in fact, usually mixtures, especially as regards personnel, of bureaucratic, patrimonial, and entrepreneurial forms of organization. This means, in brief, that 'politics' (as well as administration) is very much at work in selecting and forming types of managers.

There are in the modern enterprise men who fulfil the bureaucratic formula; in brief, here is how they look and act:

They follow clearly defined lines of authority, each of which is related to other lines, and all related to the understood purposes of the enterprise as a going concern. Their activities and feelings are within delimited spheres of action, set by the obligations and requirements of their own 'expertise.' Their power is neatly seated in the office they occupy and derived only from that office; all their relations within the enterprise are thus impersonal and set by the formal hierarchical structure. Their expectations are on a thoroughly calculable basis, and are enforced by the going rules and explicit sanctions; their appointment is by examination, or, at least, on the basis of trained-for competencies; and they are vocationally secure, with expected life tenure, and a regularized promotion scheme.

Such a description is, of course, a rational caricature, although useful as a guide to observation. There are, in fact, two sorts of managers whose personal adaptations most closely approximate the 'bureaucratic' type. At the top of some hierarchies, one often notices personalities who are calm and sober and unhurried, but who betray a lack of confidence. They are often glum men who display a great importance of manner, seemingly have little to do, and act with slow deliberation. They reduce the hazards of personal decision by carefully following the rules, and are heavily burdened by anxiety if decisions not covered by previous rule are forced upon them. They are carefully protected from the world-to-be-impressed by subordinates and secretaries who are working around them; they are men who have things done for them. Liking the accoutrements of authority, they are always in line with the aims of the employer or other higher ups; the ends of the organization become their private ends. For they are selected by and act for the owners or the political boss, as safe and sound men with moderate ambitions, carefully held within the feasible and calculable lines of the laid-out career. That is why they are at the top and that is the point to be made about them: they are cautiously selected to represent the formal interest of the enterprise and its organizational integrity: they serve that organization and, in doing so, they serve their own personal interests. Among all the apparatus, they sit cautiously, and after giving the appearance of weighty pondering usually say No.

Often identical with this bureaucratic type, but usually lower down the hierarchy of safety, are 'the old veterans.' They are men who say they started in the business when it was small, or in some other small business now a division of the big one. They follow instructions, feeling insecure outside the bounds of explicit orders, keeping out of the limelight and passing the buck. Usually they feel a disproportion between their abilities and their experience, and having come to feel that competition is without yield, often become pedantic in order to get a much-craved deference. Carefully attending to formalities with their co-workers and with the public, they strive for additional deference by obedience to rule. They sentimentalize the formal aspects of their office and feel that their personal security is threatened by anything that would detach them from their present setting.

But there are other types of managers who are adapted to bureaucratic life, but who are by no means bureaucrats in the accepted image. The bureaucratic ethos is not the only content of managerial personalities. In particular, bureaucracies today in America are vanguard forms of life in a culture still dominated by a more entrepreneurial ethos and ideology. Among the younger managers, two types display a blend of entrepreneurial and bureaucratic traits. One is the 'live-wire' who usually comes up from the sales or promotion side of the business, and who represents a threat to those above him in the hierarchy, especially the old veterans, although sometimes also to the glum men. It may be that in due course the live-wire will settle down; occasionally one does settle down, becomes somebody's 'bright boy,' somebody else's live-wire who is then liked and favored by those whom he serves. If his loyalty is unquestionable, and he is careful not to arouse anxieties by his brightness, he is on the road to the top.

Some live-wires, however, do not readily become somebody's bright boy: they become what we may call New Entrepreneurs, a type that deserves detailed discussion.

The dominating fact of the new business setting is the business bureaucracy and the managerial supplementation, or even replacement, of the owner-operator. But bureaucratization has not completely replaced the spirit of competition. While the agents of the new style of competition are not exactly old-fashioned heroes, neither are conditions old-fashioned. Initiative is being put to an unexampled test.

In a society so recently emerged from the small-entrepreneur epoch, still influenced by models of success congruent with that epoch's ideology, it is not likely that the sober-bureaucratic type can readily become dominant. Yet the structure of the society will not permit the traditional way of amassing personal wealth. The nineteenth-century scene of competition was one of relatively equal powers and the competition was between individual businessmen or firms. The twentieth-century scene contains huge and powerful units which compete not so much with one another but as a totality with the consuming public and sometimes with certain segments of the government. The new entrepreneur represents the old go-getting competition in the new setting.

The general milieu of this new species of entrepreneur is those areas that are still uncertain and unroutinized. The new entrepreneur is very much at home in the less tangible of the 'business services'—commercial research and public relations, advertising agencies, labor relations, and the mass communication and entertainment industries. His titles are likely to be 'special assistant to the president,' 'counsel for the general manager,' 'management counsellor and engineering adviser.' For the bright, young, educated man, these fields offer limitless opportunities, if he only has the initiative and the know-how, and if only the anxieties of the bureaucratic chieftains hold up. The new entrepreneur may in time routinize these fields, but, in the process of doing so, he operates in them.

The areas open to the new entrepreneur, usually overlapping in various ways, are those of great uncertainties and new beginnings: (1) adjustments between various business bureaucracies, and between business and government; (2) public relations, the interpretative justification of the new powers to the underlying outsiders; and (3) new industries that have arisen in the last quarter-century, especially those—for example, advertising—which involve selling somewhat intangible services.

The old entrepreneur succeeded by founding a new concern and expanding it. The bureaucrat gets a forward-looking job and climbs up the ladder within a pre-arranged hierarchy.

The new entrepreneur makes a zig-zag pattern upward within and between established bureaucracies. In contrast to the classic small businessman, who operated in a world opening up like a row of oysters under steam, the new entrepreneur must operate in a world in which all the pearls have already been grabbed up and are carefully guarded. The only way in which he can express his initiative is by servicing the powers that be, in the hope of getting his cut. He serves them by 'fixing things,' between one big business and another, and between business as a whole and the public.

He gets ahead because (1) men in power do not expect that things can be done legitimately; (2) these men know fear and guilt; and (3) they are often personally not very bright. It is often hard to say, with any sureness, whether the new entrepreneur lives on his own wits, or upon the lack of wits in others. As for anxiety, however, it is certain that, although he may be prodded by his own, he could get nowhere without its ample presence in his powerful clients.

Like Balzac's des Lupeaulx, thrown up by the tide of political events in France in the first quarter of the nineteenth century, who had discovered that 'authority stood in need of a charwoman,' the American new entrepreneur is an 'adroit climber . . . to his professions of useful help and go-between he added a third—he gave gratuitous advice on the internal diseases of power. . . He bore the brunt of the first explosion of despair or anger; he laughed and mourned with his chief . . . It was his duty to flatter and advise, to give advice in the guise of flattery, and flattery in the form of advice.'

The talent and intelligence that go with the new entrepreneurship are often dangerous in the new society. He who has them but lacks power must act as if those in power have the same capacities. He must give credit for good ideas to his superiors and take the rap himself for bad ones. The split between the executive who judges and the intelligence that creates is sharp and finds a ready justification: 'So I write a show? Or produce one?' asks an account executive in one of the recent tales of unhappiness among the new entrepreneurs. 'And I take it down to [the] sponsor. And he asks me, in your judgment should I spend a million dollars a year on this show you've created? See, Artie? Actually, I'd have no judgment. I wouldn't be in a position to criticize. In short, I wouldn't be an executive.'

As a competitor, the new entrepreneur is an agent of the bureaucracy he serves, and what he competes for is the good will and favor of those who run the system; his chance exists because there are *several* bureaucracies, private and public, in complicated entanglements. Unlike the little white-collar man, he does not often stay within any one corporate bureaucracy; his path is within and between bureaucracies, in a kind of uneasy but calculated rhythm. He makes a well-worn path between big business and the regulatory agencies of the Federal Government, especially its military establishment and political parties.

On the higher managerial levels there is a delicate balance of power, security, and advancement resting upon a sensitive blend of loyalty to one's firm and knowledge of its intimately valuable secrets—secrets which other firms or governments would like to know. Not 'secrets' in any hush-hush sense, although there have been simple sell-outs, but secrets in the sense of what is inaccessible to those who have not operated in the context. In a bureaucratic world, the individual's experience is usually controlled; the clever executive squashes entrepreneurial tendencies by using his formal power position to monopolize contacts with important clients. It is a characteristic of the new entrepreneur that he manages to gain experience without being controlled.

There are many instances of men who learn the secrets and procedures of a regulatory agency of government to which they are not loyal in a career sense. Their loyalties are rather to the business hierarchy to which they intend to return. This is the structure of one type of twentieth-century opportunity. The curriculum of such 'businessmen in government' is familiar: they have been in and out of Washington since the NIRA days, serving on advisory boards, in commerce department committees and war production boards, retaining contact with a middle or large-scale business enterprise. In this interlinked world, there has been genuine opportunity for big success over the last fifteen years.

The openings have been on all levels. On the lower levels, a chief clerk of an OPA board may set up a business service —an OPA buffer—for firms dealing with OPA, and slowly grow into a management counselling service. At the center, however, operations have gone on in a big way during and after the war. Surplus-property disposal, for example, became so complicated that 'the government' wasn't sure just what it was doing. The surface has only been scratched, but evidence has been published of millions being made from investments of thousands; of expediters buying surplus tools from the government and selling them back again; of buying from the Navy and immediately selling to the Army, et cetera. A few smaller fry have been caught; the big fixers probably never will be, for they were only carrying on business as usual during wartime and with the government.

Perhaps the Number One figure in the short history of the new entrepreneur has been Thomas Gardner ('Tommy-the-Cork') Corcoran, who for two terms was one of President Roosevelt's 'principal advisers and . . . trouble shooters. . . He possessed that rare asset, either inside or outside of the Federal Government, of knowing the whole, intricate mechanism of the Washington establishment.' A free-ranging talent scout for the administration, he was, as John H. Crider of the *New York Times* puts it, 'personally responsible for putting literally scores of men in key positions throughout the Federal organization. . . He has more pipelines into the Government than probably any other individual on the outside. . . He always operated for the President behind the scenes, having had several titles during his government employment, including counsel . . . assistant . . . special assistant.' Leaving the government service which paid him only $10,000 a year, he earned as lawyer and expeditor $100,000 plus.

For the 'fixer,' who lives on the expectation that in the bureaucratic world things cannot be accomplished quickly through legitimate channels, bargaining power and sources of income consist of intangible contacts and 'pipe-lines' rather than tangible assets. Yet he is no less an entrepreneur in spirit and style of operation than the man of small property; he is using his own initiative, wile, and cunning to create something where nothing was before. Of course, he does not have the security that property ownership once provided; that is one thing that makes Sammy run. Yet, for the successful, the risks are not incommensurate with the returns.

Sometimes, of course, the new entrepreneur does become a member of the propertied rich. He can scatter his property in various stocks in a sensible attempt to spread risks and concentrate chances of success. If he does not invest capital, his success is all the greater measure of his inherent worth, for this means that he is genuinely creative. Like the more heroic businessmen of old, he manages to get something for very little or nothing. And like them, he is a man who never misses a bet.

The power of the old captain of industry purportedly rested upon his engineering ability and his financial sharp dealing. The power of the ideal bureaucrat is derived from the authority vested in the office he occupies. The power of the managerial chieftain rests upon his control of the wealth piled up by the old captain and is increased by a rational system of guaranteed tributes. The power of the new entrepreneur, in the first instance at least, rests upon his personality and upon his skill in using it to manipulate the anxieties of the chieftain. The concentration of power has thus modified the character and the larger meaning of competition. The new entrepreneur's success or failure is decided not so much by the 'supply and demand' of the impersonal market as by the personal anxieties and decisions of intimately known chieftains of monopoly.

The careers of both the new entrepreneur and the ordinary white-collar workers are administered by powerful others. But there is this difference: the toadying of the white-collar employee is small-scale and unimaginative; he is a member of the stable corps of the bureaucracy, and initiative is regimented out of his life. The new ulcered entrepreneur operates on the guileful edges of the several bureaucracies.

With his lavish expense account, the new entrepreneur sometimes gets into the public eye as a fixer—along with the respectable businessman whose work he does—or even as an upstart and a crook: for the same public that idolizes initiative becomes incensed when it finds a grand model of success based simply and purely upon it. For one Murray Garsson caught how many others were there? The Garssons ran a letterhead corporation title into a profit of 78 million dollars out of war contracts, and the same public that honors pluck and success and the Horatio Alger story became angry. In an expanding system, profits seem to coincide with the welfare of all; in a system already closed, profits are made by doing somebody in. The line between the legitimate and the illegitimate is difficult to draw because no one has set up the rules for the new situation. Moreover, such moral questions are decisively influenced by the size of the business and the firmness and reliability of contacts.

Part of the new entrepreneur's frenzy perhaps is due to apprehension that his function may disappear. Many of the jobs he has been doing for the chieftains are now a standardized part of business enterprise, no longer requiring the entrepreneurial flair, and can be handled by cheaper and more dependable white-collar men. Increasingly, big firms hire their own talent for those fields in which the new entrepreneurs pioneered. In so far as this is so, the new entrepreneurs become bright boys and, as salaried employees, are stable members of the managerial cadre.

In the more strictly bureaucratic setting, the value of contacts a given manager has and the secrets he learns are definitely lessened. Rationalization of the managerial hierarchy decreases the chance for any one man down the line to get a view of the whole. It is the Tommy Corcoran *without* a definite bureaucratic role who learns the whole, and serves his chief—and in due course himself—by telling selected others about it. In the General Somervell type of managership, the executive's control section monopolizes the chance to see things whole, and tells what it will once each month to all executives.

Rationalization prohibits a total view: by rationalizing the organization via rotation systems and control sections, top bureaucrats can guide the vision of underlings. The 'entrepreneurial type' who does not play ball can be excluded from inside information. Like the commodity market before it, the top level of the personality market may well become an object to be administered, rather than a play of free forces of crafty wile and unexampled initiative.

5. The Power of the Managers

There is no doubt that managers of big business have replaced captains of industry as the ostensibly central figures in modern capitalism. They are the economic elite of the new society; they are the men who have the most of whatever there is to have; the men in charge of things and of other men, who make the large-scale plans. They are the high bosses, the big money, the great say-so. But, in fact, the 'top' of modern business is complicated: alongside top corporation executives are scattered throngs of owners and, below them, the upper hierarchies of managerial employees.

As modern businesses have become larger, the ownership of any given enterprise has expanded and the power of 'the owners' in direct operation has declined.[5] The power of property within plant, firm, and political economy has often

[5] *Owners* are people who legally claim a share of profits and expect that those who operate the enterprise will act for their best interests. *Managers* are people who have operating control over the enterprise, the ones who run it.

become indirect, and works through a host of new agents. The owners of property do not themselves give commands to their workmen: there are too many workmen and not enough concentrated owners. Moreover, even if personal command were technically possible, it is more convenient to hire others for this purpose. Adam Smith, writing even before the 'proprietor's liability' was limited, asserted: 'The greater part of the proprietors seldom pretend to understand anything of the business of the company . . . give themselves no trouble about it, but receive contentedly each half-yearly or yearly dividend as the directors think proper to make them.'

The facts of the split of manager and owner, and the indirect power of the owner, have long been known. Such facts, however, since at least the beginning of this century, have been widely and erroneously taken to mean that 'a managerial revolution' has been and is under way and that big management, replacing big property, is slated to be the next ruling class.

While owner and manager are no longer the same person, the manager has not expropriated the owner, nor has the power of the propertied enterprise over workers and markets declined. Power has not been split from property; rather the power of property is more concentrated than is its ownership. If this seems undemocratic, the lack of democracy is within the propertied classes. If the Van Sweringen brothers controlled 8 railroads worth $2 billion with only $20 million, still there was the $20 million, and the power they exercised was power made possible by the $2 billion.

The powers of property ownership are depersonalized, intermediate, and concealed. But they have not been minimized nor have they declined. Much less has any revolution occurred, managerial or otherwise, involving the legitimations of the institution of private property. Under the owners of property a huge and complex bureaucracy of business and industry has come into existence. But the right to this chain of command, the legitimate access to the position of authority from which these bureaucracies are directed, is the right of property ownership. The stockholder is neither willing nor able to exercise operating control of his ownership. That is true. And the power of the managers is not dependent upon their own personal ownership. That is also true. But it cannot be concluded that there is no functional relation between ownership and control of large corporations. Such an inference focuses upon personnel issues instead of legitimations and institutions.

Property as a going concern means that the owner may, if necessary, employ violent coercion against those who do not own but would use. With legal ownership, one may borrow the police force to oust and to punish anyone, including former owners and all their managers as well as non-owners, who tries to seize control of property. Even if it were true that the power of 'the owners' had been expropriated by the managers, this would not mean that their property has been expropriated. Any owner who can prove any case of 'expropriation' of property by any manager can have the managers prosecuted and put in jail.

Such changes in the distribution of power as have occurred between owners and their managers have certainly neither destroyed the propertied class nor diminished its power. All the structural changes upon which the notion of 'a managerial revolution' presumably rests are more accurately understood (1) as a modification of the distribution of operating power within the propertied class as a whole; and (2) as a general bureaucratization of property relations.

Changes have occurred within the industrial propertied class in such a way that the actual wielding of power is delegated to hierarchies; the entrepreneurial function has been bureaucratized. But the top man in the bureaucracy *is* a powerful member of the propertied class. He derives his right to act from the institution of property; he does act in so far as he possibly can a manner he believes is to the interests of the private-property system; he does feel in unity, politically and status-wise as well as economically, with his class and its source of wealth.

Observers who are shocked by recognition of the fact that the immediate power which property gives may be delegated or, under certain circumstances, usurped by higher employees and cliques of minority owners, often overlook the source of power and the meaning of property, while looking at the huge and intricate form of bureaucratic big business. The division between 'ownership' and 'control' of property does not diminish the power of property: on the contrary, it may even increase it. It does, however, change the personnel, the apparatus, and the property status of the more immediate wielders of that power.

If the powerful officials of U.S. corporations do not act as old-fashioned owners within the plants and do not derive their power from personal ownership, their power is nevertheless contingent upon their control of property. They are managers *of* private properties, and if private property were 'abolished,' their power, if any, would rest upon some other basis, and they would have to look to other sources of authority. Many of these same men might continue as managers of factories and mines, but that is a new political question.

To say that managers are managers of private property means, first, that the principles they attempt to follow are not the budgetary considerations of those who manage public property, but rather that they use their power in the interest of maximizing profits. Secondly, it means that property institutions determine whom the managers are responsible to; 'they are responsible to the effective clique of owners,' conclude TNEC economists, and to the 'large property class in general.' Managers have not been known to act intentionally against the property interests of the large owners. Their actions are in the interests of property as they see them. This is the case whether they act in relation to the workman in the plant, toward competing firms, toward the government, or toward the consumers of their company's product. Of course many men who own stocks and bonds and other promises do now own enough productive facilities to make a difference in the distribution of power. But this only means that the managers are agents of big property owners and not of small ones. Managers of corporations are the agents of those owners who own the concentrated most; they derive such power as they have from the organizations which are based upon property as a going system.

'The Managers' are often thought of as scientific technologists or administrative experts having some autonomous aim. But they are not experts in charge of technology; they are executors of property. Their chief attention is to finance and profits, which are the major interests of owners. The managers who are supposed to have usurped the owners' function actually fulfil it with as much or more devotion as any owner could. The personal relations between big owners and their big managers are of course not necessarily 'authoritative,' except in so far as the owners and their boards of directors are interested in the profitable balance sheet, and accordingly judge their managers as, in fact, the managers judge themselves. External authority is not necessary when the agent has internalized it.

That the activities of the managers of industry and finance are in line with property interests, rather than with 'independent' aims, is revealed by the motives for the merging and building up of huge businesses. By the end of the nineteenth century, industrial consolidation in the United States had in many lines gone far enough to realize the major technical advantages of large-scale production. The pre-World War I trust movement was not primarily motivated by a desire for technical efficiency, but by 'financial and strategic advantages.' Creating size in business has often permitted the manipulation of funds and power by business insiders and financial outsiders for their own enrichment—and, of course, the suppression of competition and the gaining of promotional and underwriting profits. The kind of combinations of functions in industry which increases productivity occurs primarily within a physical plant, rather than between various plants.

The question is whether or not the managers fulfil the entrepreneurial function in such a way as to modify the way in which the owners would fulfil it. But how could they do so, when the institution of private property, the power of property, and the function of the entrepreneur remain? The manager, as Edwin Nourse observes, is still rated 'on evidence of the profitableness of the company's operations while under his management. . .' It is true that managers do not personally own the property they manage. But we may not jump from this fact to the assertion that they are not personally of the propertied class. On the contrary, compared to the population at large, they definitely form a segment of the small, much-propertied circle. At least two-thirds of the $75,000 a year and up incomes of corporation managers are derived from property holdings. Top-level managers (presumably the most 'powerful') are socially and politically in tune with other large property holders. Their image of ascent involves moving further into the big propertied circles. The old road to property was starting a firm and building it up, rising in class position with its expansion; that road is now closed to nearly all. The way into propertied circles, via management posts and/or suitable marriages, is more likely to be *within* the large propertied bureaucracies.

Intercorporate investments and multiple directorships among 'managers' give further unity to the propertied classes as a stratum. The handful of officers and directors of the A T & T who hold 171 directorships or offices in other enterprises are not simply holding 'honorary degrees'; where the corporations whose directors interlock also have interlocking business, these men pay attention; in such ways a community of property interest, a resolution of sharp competitive conflicts, can arise. Consolidations have given further 'unity to the ownership, but not to the productive processes of subsidiary plants.' The aim has been further monopoly of national markets and the profitable consolidation of property.

The image of the big businessman as master-builder and profit-maker, as already noted of the old captain of industry, no longer holds. The top manager's relation to productive work and engineering is a financial one. His relations with the industrial manager, in terms of power, are not unlike those of the politician with the government official, or the elected labor leader with his appointed staff expert. The corporation official has the final say-so; for in the bureaucratization of the powers of property, he represents the big money and in his relations with major owners is treated as a status equal, belonging to their clubs, and acting in their behalf.

In the political sphere, no American manager has taken a stand that is against the interests of private property as an institution. As its chief defender, rhetorically and practically, the manager has a political mind similar to that of any large owner, from whom he derives his power; and in his present form he will last no longer than property as an institution. Thus, although the bureaucratization of property involves a distribution of power among large subordinate staffs, the executives of the modern corporation in America form an utterly reliable committee for managing the affairs and pushing for the common interests of the entire big-property class.

So far as men may do as they will with the property that they own or that they manage for owners, they have power over other men. Changes in the size and the distribution of property have brought with them an increased power for some and a corresponding powerlessness for many. The shift is from widespread entrepreneurial property to narrowed class property. The ownership of property now means much more than power over the things that are owned; it means power over men who do not own these things; it selects those who may command and those who must obey.

THE ORGANIZATION MAN

William H. Whyte, Jr.

Published in 1956, The Organization Man *immediately struck a responsive chord in thoughtful readers. The times were tense. An amiable man of modest intellectual resources presided in the White House, loving peace but unable to keep the Cold War from heating up, committed to decency but vacillating over the spirit of McCarthyism, which put a quietus on politics. The young showed no great disposition to protest. Virtually a whole generation was struck dumb, receding into prudent silence, quietly calculating, playing the game or "disaffiliating," joining up as "beat" Bohemians addicted to cool jazz and depressant drugs. They were flailed by some of their elders, especially by those who felt nostalgic for the radical thirties, when for many, adolescence meant rebellion. These same elders nodded in agreement as Irving Howe stigmatized the times in a famous article entitled "This Age of Conformity." But such misgivings seemed to carry no weight with the vast majority. Most intellectuals overestimated the general state of material well-being, and many confounded it with spiritual well-being. Daniel Bell prematurely proclaimed the end of ideology; self-satisfaction mounted to self-congratulation; the American celebration was in full swing.*

To recall history enacted so recently is to conjure up another world, another Zeitgeist. *Given a constantly accelerated pattern of social change, the familiar becomes unfamiliar overnight, and "well-adjusted" men are transformed into old fogies. Thus the sixties are radically different from the fifties. A domestic war, so far resulting only in minor skirmishes, has suddenly been declared against poverty — whose very existence, outside certain small "pockets," was vigorously denied but a few years ago. Now there are assumed to be from thirty to fifty million Americans living in poverty. One hears much less about affluent America and much more about* The Other America *described by Michael Harrington. All along, during the period of complacency and quiescence, there were those who stood off and took a deeper view of things. With the wisdom of hindsight, we know that irreverent ideas were making headway, and that a bit later they really caught fire.*

If in the Eisenhower era most Americans could find very little fault with their way of life, there were also a few far-sighted men who saw trouble all about them and the seeds of more evil just ahead. Some were muckrakers bent on fixing up evanescent evils. A smaller group brought unusual breadth and scope to their analyses. William H. Whyte, Jr., belongs to that select group. He addressed himself to a deplorable tendency, which all of us, having absorbed his message, are the better equipped to combat. If The Organization Man *should finally come to be obsolete—and no such prospect is as yet in sight—that will be, in part, a triumph for the book.*

The sociological critic of his own age always runs the risk of romanticizing an earlier age. Like the other authors represented in this book, Whyte had to beware of prettifying the past while seeking to establish its contrasts with the mercurial present. It was a difficult undertaking—in which Whyte, like Riesman and Wheelis, may fairly be said to have succeeded. Whyte charts "the decline of the Protestant ethic," making clear that if individualism has been thrown into jeopardy, so has the old ruthlessness that was part and parcel of early American capitalism. There are virtues in the new dispensation as in the old—and there are the defects of those virtues.

The brilliance of the chapters we have anthologized consists in their explanation of a big change, without which countless little changes would be unintelligible. The big change, from one ethic to another, is systematically related to pragmatism, progressivism, and scientism as they culminate in the philosophy of "togetherness" and "belongingness." This distillation of elements has led to a public ideology, both flexible and unified, which at its worst serves to undermine our humanity and to make corporate robots of us all. As anatomized by Whyte, the organization man is instantly recognizable to all those millions employed in large impersonal establishments where the individual's freedom and spontaneity are threatened with extinction.

The outlines of this situation were already apparent to Tocqueville and to Max Weber. Whyte's delineation of the crisis simply brings theirs up to date. Tocqueville warned that civilization might not only be torn from men's grasp but that men might trample it underfoot and noiselessly forsake their freedom. How like Tocqueville is the Whyte who exclaims, "The danger, to put it another way, is not man being dominated but man surrendering."

Whyte was serving as an editor of Fortune *magazine when he wrote* The Organization Man. *This journalist, who consulted academic sociologists in putting his book together, succeeded in eclipsing most of them at their own game. Now they, and the reader, can only feel thankful for his contribution.*

Let us go back a moment to the turn of the century. If we pick up the Protestant Ethic as it was then expressed we will find it apparently in full flower. We will also find, however, an ethic that already had been strained by reality. The country had changed. The ethic had not.

Here, in the words of banker Henry Clews as he gave some fatherly advice to Yale students in 1908, is the Protestant Ethic in purest form:

Survival of Fittest: You may start in business, or the professions, with your feet on the bottom rung of the ladder; it rests with you to acquire the strength to climb to the top. You can do so if you have the will and the force to back you. There is always plenty of room at the top. . . . Success comes to the man who tries to compel success to yield to him. Cassius spoke well to Brutus when he said, "The Fault is not in our stars, dear Brutus, that we are underlings, but in our natures."

Thrift: Form the habit as soon as you become a money-earner, or money-maker, of saving a part of your salary, or profits. Put away one dollar out of every ten you earn. The time will come in your lives when, if you have a little money, you can control circumstances; otherwise circumstances will control you. . . .

Note the use of such active words as *climb, force, compel, control.* As stringently as ever before, the Protestant Ethic still counseled struggle against one's environment—the kind of practical, here and now struggle that paid off in material rewards. And spiritually too. The hard-boiled part of the Protestant Ethic was incomplete, of course, without the companion assurance that such success was moral as well as practical. To continue with Mr. Clews:

Under this free system of government, whereby individuals are free to get a living or to pursue wealth as each chooses, the usual result is competition. Obviously, then, competition means industrial freedom. Thus, anyone may choose his own trade or profession, or, if he does not like it, he may change. He is free to work hard or not; he may make his own bargains and set his price upon his labor or his products. He is free to acquire property to any extent, or to part with it. By dint of greater effort or superior skill, or by intelligence, if he can make better wages, he is free to live better, just as his neighbor is free to follow his example and to learn to excel him in turn. If anyone has a genius for making and managing money, he is free to exercise his genius, just as another is free to handle his tools. . . . If an individual enjoys his money, gained by energy and successful effort, his neighbors are urged to work the harder, that they and their children may have the same enjoyment.

It was an exuberantly optimistic ethic. If everyone could believe that seeking his self-interest automatically improves the lot of all, then the application of hard work should eventually produce a heaven on earth. Some, like the garrulous Mr. Clews, felt it already had.

America is the true field for the human race. It is the hope and the asylum for the oppressed and downtrodden of every clime. It is the inspiring example of America—peerless among the nations of the earth, the brightest star in the political firmament—that is leavening the hard lump of aristocracy and promoting a democratic spirit throughout the world. It is indeed the gem of the ocean to which the world may well offer homage. Here merit is the sole test. Birth is nothing. The fittest survive. Merit is the supreme and only qualification essential to success. Intelligence rules worlds and systems of worlds. It is the dread monarch of illimitable space, and in human society, especially in America, it shines as a diadem on the foreheads of those who stand in the foremost ranks of human enterprise. Here only a natural order of nobility is recognized, and its motto, without coat of arms or boast of heraldry, is "Intelligence and integrity."[1]

Without this ethic capitalism would have been impossible Whether the Protestant Ethic preceded capitalism, as Max Weber argued, or whether it grew up as a consequence, in either event it provided a degree of unity between the way people wanted to behave and the way they thought they *ought* to behave, and without this ideology, society would have been hostile to the entrepreneur. Without the comfort of the Protestant Ethic, he couldn't have gotten away with his acquisitions—not merely because other people wouldn't have allowed him, but because his own conscience would not have. But now he was fortified by the assurance that he was pursuing his obligation to God, and before long, what for centuries had been looked on as the meanest greed, a rising middle class would interpret as the earthly manifestation of God's will.

But the very industrial revolution which this highly serviceable ethic begot in time began to confound it. The in-

[1] Henry Clews, *Fifty Years in Wall Street* (New York: Irving Publishing Company, 1908).

consistencies were a long while in making themselves apparent. The nineteenth-century inheritors of the ethic were creating an increasingly collective society but steadfastly they denied the implications of it. In current retrospect the turn of the century seems a golden age of individualism, yet by the 1880s the corporation had already shown the eventual bureaucratic direction it was going to take. As institutions grew in size and became more stratified, they made all too apparent inconsistencies which formerly could be ignored. One of the key assumptions of the Protestant Ethic had been that success was due neither to luck nor to the environment but only to one's natural qualities—if men grew rich it was because they deserved to. But the big organization became a standing taunt to this dream of individual success. Quite obviously to anyone who worked in a big organization, those who survived best were not necessarily the fittest but, in more cases than not, those who by birth and personal connections had the breaks.

As organizations continued to expand, the Protestant Ethic became more and more divergent from the reality The Organization was itself creating. The managers steadfastly denied the change, but they, as much as those they led, were affected by it. Today, some still deny the inconsistency or blame it on creeping socialism; for the younger generation of managers however, the inconsistencies have become importuning.

Thrift, for example. How can the organization man be thrifty? Other people are thrifty *for* him. He still buys most of his own life insurance, but for the bulk of his rainy-day saving, he gives his proxy to the financial and personnel departments of his organization. In his professional capacity also thrift is becoming a little un-American. The same man who will quote from Benjamin Franklin on thrift for the house organ would be horrified if consumers took these maxims to heart and started putting more money into savings and less into installment purchases. No longer can he afford the luxury of damning the profligacy of the public; not in public, at any rate. He not only has to persuade people to buy more but persuade them out of any guilt feelings they might have for following his advise. Few talents are more commercially sought today than the knack of describing departures from the Protestant Ethic as reaffirmations of it.[2]

In an advertisement that should go down in social history, the J. Walter Thompson agency has hit the problem of absolution head-on. It quotes Benjamin Franklin on the benefits of spending. "Is not the hope of being one day able to purchase and enjoy luxuries a great spur to labor and industry? . . . May not luxury therefore produce more than it consumes, if, without such a spur, people would be, as they are naturally enough inclined to be, lazy and indolent?" This thought, the ad says, in a meaningful aside, "appears to be a mature afterthought, qualifying his earlier and more familiar writings on the importance of thrift."

"Hard work?" What price capitalism, the question is now so frequently asked, unless we turn our productivity into more leisure, more of the good life? To the organization man this makes abundant sense, and he is as sensitive to the bogy of overwork and ulcers as his forebears were to the bogy of slothfulness. But he is split. He believes in leisure, but so does he believe in the Puritan insistence on hard, self-denying work—and there are, alas, only twenty-four hours a day. How, then, to be "broad gauge"? The "broad-gauge" model we hear so much about these days is the man who keeps his work separate from leisure and the rest of his life. Any organization man

[2] Helping in this task is what a good part of "motivation research" is all about. Motivation researcher Dr. Ernest Dichter, in a bulletin to business, says, "We are now confronted with the problem of permitting the average American to feel moral even when he is flirting, even when he is spending, even when he is not saving, even when he is taking two vacations a year and buying a second or third car. One of the basic problems of this prosperity, then, is to give people the sanction and justification to enjoy it and to demonstrate that the hedonistic approach to his life is a moral, not an immoral one."

who managed to accomplish this feat wouldn't get very far. He still works hard, in short, but now he has to feel somewhat guilty about it.

Self-reliance? The corporation estates have been expanding so dynamically of late that until about now the management man could suppress the thought that he was a bureaucrat—bureaucrats, as every businessman knew, were those people down in Washington who preferred safety to adventure. Just when the recognition began to dawn, no one can say, but since the war the younger generation of management haven't been talking of self-reliance and adventure with quite the straight face of their elders.

That upward path toward the rainbow of achievement leads smack through the conference room. No matter what name the process is called—permissive management, multiple management, the art of administration—the committee way simply can't be equated with the "rugged" individualism that is supposed to be the business of business. Not for lack of ambition do the younger men dream so moderately; what they lack is the illusion that they will carry on in the great entrepreneurial spirit. Although they cannot bring themselves to use the word bureaucrat, the approved term—the "administrator"—is not signally different in its implications. The man of the future, as junior executives see him, is not the individualist but the man who works through others for others.

Let me pause for a moment to emphasize a necessary distinction. Within business there are still many who cling resolutely to the Protestant Ethic, and some with as much rapacity as drove any nineteenth-century buccaneer. But only rarely are they of The Organization. Save for a small, and spectacular, group of financial operators, most who adhere to the old creed are small businessmen, and to group them as part of the "business community," while convenient, implies a degree of ideological kinship with big business that does not exist.

Out of inertia, the small business is praised as the acorn

from which a great oak may grow, the shadow of one man that may lengthen into a large enterprise. Examine businesses with fifty or less employees, however, and it becomes apparent the sentimentality obscures some profound differences. You will find some entrepreneurs in the classic sense—men who develop new products, new appetites, or new systems of distribution—and some of these enterprises may mature into self-perpetuating institutions. But very few.

The great majority of small business firms cannot be placed on any continuum with the corporation. For one thing, they are the laundries, the insurance agencies, the restaurants, the drugstores, the bottling plants, the lumber yards, the automobile dealers. They are vital, to be sure, but essentially they service an economy; they do not create new money within their area and they are dependent ultimately on the business and agriculture that does.

In this dependency they react more as antagonists than allies with the corporation. The corporation, it has become clear, is expansionist—a force for change that is forever a threat to the economics of the small businessman. By instinct he inclines to the monopolistic and the restrictive. When the druggists got the "Fair Trade" laws passed it was not only the manufacturers (and customers) they were rebelling against but the whole mass economy movement of the twentieth century.

The tail wagged the dog in this case and it still often does. That it can, in the face of the growing power of the corporation, illustrates again the dominance mythology can have over reality. Economically, many a small businessman is a counterrevolutionist and the revolution he is fighting is that of the corporation as much as the New or Fair Deal. But the corporation man still clings to the idea that the two are firm allies, and on some particulars, such as fair trade, he often makes policy on this basis when in fact it is against the corporation's interests to do so.

But the revolution is not to be stopped by sentiment. Many anachronisms do remain; in personal income, for example, the corporation man who runs a branch plant on which a whole town depends is lucky to make half the income of the local car dealer or the man with the Coca-Cola franchise. The economy has a way of attending to these discrepancies, however, and the local businessman can smell the future as well as anyone else. The bland young man The Organization sent to town to manage the plant is almost damnably inoffensive; he didn't rent the old place on the hill but a smaller house, he drives an Olds instead of a Caddy, and when he comes to the Thursday luncheons he listens more than he talks. But he's the future just the same.

I have been talking of the impact of organization on the Protestant Ethic; just as important, however, was the intellectual assault. In the great revolt against traditionalism that began around the turn of the century, William James, John Dewey, Charles Beard, Thorstein Veblen, the muckrakers and a host of reformers brought the anachronisms of the Protestant Ethic under relentless fire, and in so doing helped lay the groundwork for the Social Ethic. It would be a long time before organization men would grasp the relevance of these new ideas, and to this day many of the most thoroughgoing pragmatists in business would recoil at being grouped with the intellectuals. (And vice versa.) But the two movements were intimately related. To what degree the intellectuals were a cause of change, or a manifestation, no one can say for certain, but more presciently than those in organization they grasped the antithesis between the old concept of the rational unbeholden individual and the world one had to live in. They were not rebels against society; what they fought was the denial of society's power, and they provided an intellectual framework that would complement, rather than inhibit, the further growth of big organization.

It is not in the province of this book to go into a diagnosis of the ideas of Dewey and James and the other pragmatists. But there is one point of history I think very much needs making at this time. Many people still look on the decline of the Protestant Ethic as our fall from grace, a detour from Americanism for which we can blame pragmatism, ethical relativism, Freudianism and other such developments. These movements have contributed much to the Social Ethic, and many of their presuppositions are as shaky as those they replaced. To criticize them on this score is in order; to criticize them as having subverted the American temper, however, is highly misleading.

Critics of pragmatism, and followers too, should remember the context of the times in which the pragmatists made their case. The pragmatists' emphasis on social utility may be redundant for today's needs, but when they made their case it was not a time when psychology or adjustment or social living were popular topics but at a time when the weight of conservative opinion denied that there was anything much that needed adjusting. Quite clearly, revolt was in order. The growth of the organization society did demand a recognition that man was not entirely a product of his free will; the country did need an educational plant more responsive to the need of the people. It did need a new breeze, and if there had been no James or no Dewey, some form of pragmatism would probably have been invented anyway. Nonphilosophical Americans sensed that changes were in order too; what the philosophers of pragmatism did was to give them guidance and tell them in intellectually responsible terms that they were right in feeling that way.

Pragmatism's emphasis on the social and the practical, furthermore, was thoroughly in the American tradition. From the beginning, Americans had always been impatient with doctrines and systems; like the Puritans, many came here because of a doctrine, but what they came to was a new environment that required some powerful adapting to, and whenever the doctrine got in the way of practicality, the doctrine lost out. Few people have had such a genius for bending ideals to the demands of the times, and the construction of fundamental theory, theological or scientific, has never excited Americans overmuch. Long before James, *Does it work?* was a respectable question to ask. If impatience at abstract thought was a defect, it was the defect of a virtue, and the virtue, call it what you will, has always been very close to pragmatism as Dewey and James defined it. By defining it they gave it coherence and power at a time when it needed assertion, but the inclination to the practical antedated the philosophy; it was not the product of it.

Reform was everywhere in the air. By the time of the First World War the Protestant Ethic had taken a shellacking from which it would not recover; rugged individualism and hard work had done wonders for the people to whom God in his infinite wisdom, as one put it, had given control of society. But it hadn't done so well for everybody else and now they, as well as the intellectuals, were all too aware of the fact.

The ground, in short, was ready, and though the conservative opinion that drew the fire of the rebels seemed entrenched, the basic temper of the country was so inclined in the other direction that emphasis on the social became the dominant current of U.S. thought. In a great outburst of curiosity, people became fascinated with the discovering of all the environmental pressures on the individual that previous philosophies had denied. As with Freud's discoveries, the findings of such inquiries were deeply disillusioning at first, but with characteristic exuberance Americans found a rainbow. Man might not be perfectible after all, but there was another dream and now at last it seemed practical: the perfectibility of *society.*

SCIENTISM

Just how these currents of reforms congealed into an orthodoxy is a problem in intellectual history I must duck. Trying to weigh whose ideas were most responsible is in any event somewhat fruitless, for it is what people want to believe that is important, and those whose ideas they so frequently misinterpret should not be whipped for the bowdlerization. Freud, for example, who once remarked that he was not a Freudian, never maintained that man was forever a hostage to childhood traumata; with resolution and intelligence, he believed, the individual could, by understanding these factors, perhaps surmount them. Nor did James or Dewey ever say that the convenience of society was the key test of morality, and they most certainly did not believe that man was totally the product of those around him.

The popular ideology I am describing is highly elastic but it has a remarkable unity nonetheless. Most believers in the many subbranches of American organization life are still unaware of the interlocking nature of their separate credos, and it is partly for this reason they so often feel themselves missionaries in the midst of the unbelieving. Change a word here and there, however, and what many an educator is prescribing is exactly what many a personnel man is prescribing, and many a research director, and so on through the roster of our institutions.

In these next three [sections] I am going to outline three principal denominators which bind them. While each is important in its own right, it is their interrelationship that I wish to illuminate. Until this unity is discerned, to attack the fallacies of technique in each separate field is as futile as hacking away at the hydra; it is the central, nourishing vision that we must address ourselves to.

The first denominator is scientism. This is the practical

part of the Social Ethic, for it is the promise that with the same techniques that have worked in the physical sciences we can eventually create an exact science of man.[3] In one form or another, it has had a long and dismal record of achievement; even its proponents readily admit that the bugs are appalling. But this has not shaken the faith in scientism, for it is essentially a utopian rather than a technical idea.

The preamble of the believers is always the same. We are in a terrible fix and it is almost too late. We have applied science to things, and only now have we begun applying it to man himself. Already we have learned some useful social techniques; we can measure personality, can spot the obstacles to good group dynamics, and predict communication response. But these are merely the beginning; if only we provide the time and money, before long we can unwrap the whole enigma with a unified science of man.

Here, extracted from the proceedings of several conferences, is a fair composite of the message:

> If we draw into our group increasing numbers of hard-headed students, some of whom are not afraid of mathematics, and if we have faith and daring, we can build a science of man. . . . The conditions which determine human happiness are discoverable scientific methods and are to a major extent capable of realization. . . . More than ever, the world's greatest need is a science of human relation-

[3] N.B.: This is a very rough definition, and most people who have used the term have a different way of analyzing its bases. Hayek describes it as based on three fallacies: objectivism, collectivism, and historicism. By this he means the attempt to dispense with subjective knowledge; to treat abstract wholes—such as "society"—as definite objectives, like biological organisms; the attempt to make history a science, and the only one, of social phenomena. (F. A. Hayek, *The Counter-Revolution of Science: Studies on the Abuse of Reason.* Glencoe, Illinois: The Free Press, 1952.) Another critic of scientism, Eric Voegelin, also divides scientism into three components: "(1) the assumption that the mathematized science of natural phenomena is a model science to which all other sciences ought to conform; (2) that all realms of being are accessible to the methods of the sciences of phenomena; and (3) that all reality which is not accessible to sciences of phenomena is either irrelevant or, in the more radical form of the dogma, illusionary." (*Social Research,* December 1948.)

ships and an art of human engineering based upon the laws of such science. We should, to put it brutally, pay more attention, first to the scientific aspects of our problems rather than to the philosophical ones. . . . Although human relationship problems are extremely complicated, science is gradually reducing them to simple fundamentals through which these complexities are reduced to factors that respond to direct and simple treatment.

Inevitably, there is the atom-bomb analogy:

It is trite but true to say that if social science had been given early enough the four billion dollars that have been spent on the atomic bomb and on chemical and germ warfare—say, half for research and the other half for popular education—perhaps then the first release of atomic energy would have been for peaceful purposes.

And how very ancient it all is! Most of the people who hearken to the vision of a unified science of man believe theirs is a fresh new vision, but in reality it is a cliché that has been kicked around for centuries.[4] Ever since Newton, scores of natural scientists have stepped out of their area of competence to suggest the possibilities of a science of man, and Erasmus's *Praise of Folly* suggests that even before this some savants had much the same idea. It was an understandable dream for a natural scientist to have. Even Descartes himself was seized with the idea that the discipline of mathematics could be extended to the affairs of man. Eventually, he thought, a "Universal Mathematical Science" would solve the problem of society—if only there were sufficient funds and time for the job.

Later others tried the geometric tack: Thomas Hobbes worked out a complete set of algebraic equations to explain ethics. As Laurence Sterne remarked, his equations "plussed or minussed you to heaven or hell . . . so that none but the expert mathematician would ever be able to settle his accounts with Saint Peter." In 1725 one Francis Hutchison

[4] For an excellent summary of early attempts at scientism, see "The Invention of the Ethical Calculus," by Louis I. Bredvold in *The Seventeenth Century: Studies in the History of English Thought and Literature from Bacon to Pope*, Richard F. Jones *et al.* (Stanford University Press, 1951.)

devised an even more elaborate mathematical calculation on morality, and without the advantages of modern technocracy, he was able to produce formulas fully as intricate as any being worked out today.

With the founding of the École Polytechnique in Paris at the end of the eighteenth century scientism was given another forward push; Saint-Simon and Auguste Comte energized a formidable school with the promise of positivism. If man would only apply the discipline of the natural sciences to the study of man, then only a sufficient expenditure of time, money, and thought would separate him from the good society.

If only . . . In a hundred variations, this promise has been phrased and rephrased. Yet one would gather from current exhortations that we are just about starting from scratch just the same. Current literature is full of dawn-of-discovery analogies—Balboa discovering the Pacific, Newton and the apple, etc. But it is precisely this figure of thought, this sense of being on the frontier that gives scientism so tremendous an appeal.

And for people in the commercial as well as the academic world. "'SECOND INDUSTRIAL REVOLUTION' TO FORCE MAJOR CHANGES IN PRODUCTION, MERCHANDISING, AND SELLING" headlined *Advertising Age* (October 5, 1953). E. B. Weiss, perhaps the best-known consultant in the merchandising field, explained to readers that it isn't simply that such advances as electronic calculators and automatic factories are going to make for more efficiency. A whole new science, he says, is abuilding, and with the confusion between control of the physical and control of the mental which is characteristic of believers in scientism, he proclaims that "The Second Industrial Revolution will substitute the machine for the common, and for some fairly uncommon functions of the human *mind.*" It is not his contention, he says in qualification, "that the robot will replace *all* human endeavor." But almost all. After initial successes, such as cutting out the personal element in retail selling, making inventory-taking automatic, the machine will advance into hitherto sacrosanct areas, and with what seems unwonted relish, he cites a scientist's prophecy that in time the machine will replace man in the realm of reasoning and logical deduction. "NEXT WEEK: No. 2 in this series—How Cybernetic Principles Are Being and Will Be Applied in Factory, Office, and Warehouse."

The field of public relations is particularly susceptible. Here, for example, the *Public Relations Journal* editorializes on the subject:

> Now, whether he knows it or not, every practicing public-relations man is an engineer too—a social engineer. He developes new relationships and operations in society, designs new organizations and institutions, sets up and lubricates the human machinery for getting things done. The challenge of social engineering in our time is like the challenge of technical engineering fifty years ago. If the first half of the twentieth century was the era of the technical engineers, the second half may well be the era of the social engineers.

Dip into personnel journals, advertising trade journals, and you will find the same refrain. A lot of it is sheer malarkey, of course, but I think most of it is evidence of a genuine longing to be related to a faith.

We talk much about the alienation of the worker from the satisfaction of the whole job, but the same longing for a sense of continuity and purpose affects managerial people every bit as much. As our organizations have grown larger and more bureaucratic, they have created great layers of staff functions and the people in them often feel neither fish nor fowl—intellectuals, yet not of the intellectual world; managerial, yet without authority or prestige. Scientism, with its implications of the specialist as eventual savior, can give the frustrated a sense of purpose that cuts across organization and occupational lines. I do not believe I read into scientism a coherence that they themslves do not feel. No matter what branch of social engineering a man is engaged in—"mass" communication, "the engineering of consent," public relations, advertising, personnel counseling—he can feel himself part of a larger movement.

Their good will is overpowering. Thoreau once said if you see a man approach you with the obvious intent of doing you good, you should run for your life; it is hard to restrain the impulse in talking with social engineers. Theirs is not a mere limited desire to help out a bit with the scientific method; the vision that energizes them is total—and exclusive. Science is not merely a tool; it is the only path to salvation in a world where the laymen have gone mad. There is no justification, one angry social engineer writes, "in inflicting wounds on social scientists who might conceivably be blazing trails toward solutions of an otherwise hopeless crisis in civilization." If the techniques are faulty, and this they admit, that is a matter of unfinished detail and insufficient funds, not principles, and no one should criticize until he offers a counter-utopia himself.

One should not fall into the trap of equating social engineering with social science. Some social scientists do believe in social engineering but a great many do not, and the claims some make in the name of social science are a serious embarrassment to them. A pretty good case could be made that the field would be more productive were it now called social *studies*. The study of man and society is quite worthy enough an occupation without being saddled with the task of hammering out a finite, embracing science, and the ultimate test of a social scientist's particular way of looking at people cannot be absolute truth; only the arrogant—or the stupid—can so aspire.

Part of the trouble lies in our new-found ability to measure more precisely, and the idea that the successes of natural science were due in large measure to the objectiveness of the phenomena studied eludes social engineers. There are, of course, aspects of man's behavior that we can properly measure and we learn much by doing so. But how fascinating, alas, it all is! Here, it would seem, we can at last be rid of the bugbear of values. The median income level of a hundred selected families in an urban industrial universe correlates .76 with population density—not .78 or .61 but .76, and that's a fact. The next step beckons: having measured this far, it seems that there is nothing that can't be measured. We are purged of bias, and somehow by the sheer accumulation of such bias-free findings, we will have the basis of a theoretical formula that describes all. Just like physics.

In pure example of scientism, psychologist James G. Miller has described how an institute could make this final integration.

> In constructing theory, we can employ models from the physical sciences. All psychological phenomena are essentially naturalistic—that is, ultimately they can be translated into principles of physics. . . . By having individuals from different disciplines working closely together on both theory and research, communication between disciplines can be greatly improved. . . . If there are general principles running through them all, these are more likely to be discovered by groups from different fields working together, and in close communication, than by individuals working alone. . . . Another related possibility is the use throughout all theoretical work of what Bertalanffy has called "general system theory." This is the contention, developing from the unity of science movement, that every system —whether it be a strictly physical system like a dry cell, or an automobile; a biological system like a single nerve cell or organ; a total organism; or a society—has certain formal characteristics which make possible comparison of it with all others. Hence, generalizations about all systems are feasible. . . . Perhaps an over-all theory of behavior is too near the end of the rainbow to be reached; perhaps it is a will-o'-the-wisp. If so, our efforts may still be rewarded by the salvage of microtheories about limited areas.

Let us assume, for the moment, that a precise science of man is not a will-o'-the-wisp and that we are on our way to achieving it. We are left with a knotty problem. What do we do about good and evil, right and wrong? Believers in scientism confess that the question requires hard thinking. They are glad that ethical relativism has freed us from the narrow view that our own group's given values are the only correct ones. Obviously, then, a science of man could not freeze on one scheme of ethics. If we are to be governed by it, however, it would need some sort of ethics. How are we to determine just what they should be?

Social engineers have emboldened themselves to seek the final solution. Now, they say, we will *scientifically determine ethics.* This is to be done, in part, through the concept of "equilibrium." "How can we hope . . . to fix with assurity a particular class of behavior as right or good?" asks anthropologist Elliot Chapple. "From our point of view, this can be done by the use of the concept of equilibrium . . . hence good or bad, right or wrong, are comparable to the concept of health and medicine."

I have read definitions of many equilibrium concepts but I am still not sure just what they mean and I am not sure their creators do either; as far as can be determined, it is one of those mushy words so serviceable to obscuring contradictions. As Gunnar Myrdal, in explaining his own theoretical model in *An American Dilemma,* has pointed out, in borrowing the equilibrium notion from physics most social scientists have thought of only one kind of equilibrium, the *stable* equilibrium. This generally can lead to an acceptance of social harmony—either that of the status quo or some future one—and the companion terms such as disharmony, disequilibrium, maladjustment, disorganization, are by implication "bad" things.

This helps explain the bias against conflict that is so prevalent in most social-science literature. Where the by-products of harmony are the good things, the by-products of conflict—such as tension, frustration—are the bad things. Without taking the equally wrong position of saying that tension and frustration per se are good, one can point out that it takes a rather firm set of values to classify them as bad. Few social engineers would state categorically that they classify conflict as bad; nevertheless the practical gist of the ethics-of-equilibrium notion is that good values are values that allow groups to interact benevolently on one another and the individuals in them.

If we grant the concept of equilibrium we are still left with a formidable task in getting down to cases. How do we find what an organization's equilibrium is? If it isn't in it, how is it to be gotten there? If ethics is to be scientized, some specific people will have to do it, and some specific people are going to have to see to it the ethics are applied to society. Who, then, is to be in charge?

Being most of them democratically inclined, the new utopians take this question very seriously. If manipulating people is bad—and manipulation is one of the dirtiest words in the new lexicon—how can one justify the manipulation of people for good ends? At every convocation of believers the matter is dialectically treated, and the result of this soul-searching has been a new enrichment of the vocabulary. Though social engineers love to analyze semantic folly, no group has searched more arduously for the magic term which will combine manipulation with moral sanction. Thus we hear that the wielder of the new social techniques will be a "peace planner," a "group therapist," an "integrative leader," a "social diagnostician"—a person empowered to dominate society, but disciplined by a scientific code of ethics from using his knowledge in any but good ways.

In spelling this out social engineers characteristically shield themselves from the implication of their doctrine by describing how social engineering could be applied to a worthy cause. In a typical example, psychiatrist William Borberg explains how social engineering would be applied to the United Nations.

> Now, the knowledge accumulated in the social sciences and the understanding of its possible value to the United Nations must of necessity be greater among the scientists themselves than among policy-making leaders and diplomats. I therefore wonder whether the social scientists might not consider the desirability of creating

themselves an organ for the purpose of that relationship. . . . This would be one of the means by which we may gradually introduce into the thinking of policy-making leaders more and more scientific knowledge, scientific methods, and scientific mentality, and thus gradually substitute the present, essentially emotional basis for peace by a much better and much more reliable one, the scientific view of peace.[5]

As in other such suggested projects, the scientific elite is not supposed to give orders. Yet there runs through all of them a clear notion that questions of policy can be made somewhat nonpartisan by the application of science. There seems little recognition that the contributions of social science to policy-making can never go beyond staff work. Policy can never be scientific, and any social scientist who has risen to an administrative position has learned this quickly enough. Opinion, values, and debate are the heart of policy, and while fact can narrow down the realm of debate, it can do no more.

And what a terrible world it would be! Hell is no less hell for being antiseptic. In the 1984 of Big Brother one would at least know who the enemy was—a bunch of bad men who wanted power because they liked power. But in the other kind of 1984 one would be disarmed for not knowing who the enemy was, and when the day of reckoning came the people on the other side of the table wouldn't be Big Brother's bad henchmen; they would be a mild-looking group of therapists who, like the Grand Inquisitor, would be doing what they did to help you.

But such a specter is not the consequence of scientism that should preoccupy us. It's not merely that social engineers have no such vision in mind—they don't; the point is that they couldn't pull it off if they did. Curiously, many who have warned most urgently of the horrors of a scientific utopia are

[5] William Borberg, "On Methods of the Social Sciences in Their Approach to International Problems," *American Journal of Psychiatry*, Vol. 107, No. 9, March 1951.

themselves awed by scientism; their fears are based on the premise that it can work. Science-fiction writers, perhaps our most vigorous moralists, often seem to say that what would be wrong would be *too much* scientism, and even those dead set against it appear impressed with the possibility of its dominance. Some European critics of America have gone them one better. They say it has already happened. If anybody wants to see man crushed by science and mechanization, it appears he has only to take a trip to the U.S. The latest such critic, Robert Jungk, draws a picture of white-coated men around UNIVAC, and docile robots listening to piped music. *Tomorrow,* he warns, *is already here.*

That kind of tomorrow isn't here and it probably never will be. The implied choice between science and humanity is a false one. The danger is not in science dominating man, and the fears of this rest on a false personalization of the inanimate, not to mention a romantic, if retrograde, longing for a past utopia. Nor need the specter of a scientific elite worry us. It need not worry us because a "science of man" cannot work in the way its believers think it can, and in subsequent chapters I hope to demonstrate how naïve some of the current techniques are.

But the gospel of scientism is no less important for that reason. To stretch a point, the trouble is not so much that these techniques work, but that they *do not* work. Schemes that don't work can have as much effect on society as schemes that do. Machiavellian rules ask one to compromise, in this case, on one's ethics. But at least they can work, and if we sell our souls we get some satisfying sin in recompense. Scientism asks that we make a compromise, but it can't deliver anything really in return. The scientific formulas for "mass communication," for example: using them we manage to debase our prose, assault our instincts, and insult our listeners—but never do we get that sure-fire communion promised for our surrender. A poor bargain.

What I am arguing is that the real impact of scientism

is upon our values. The danger, to put it another way, is not man being dominated but man surrendering. At the present writing there is not one section of American life that has not drunk deeply of the promise of scientism. It appears in many forms—pedagogy, aptitude tests, that monstrous nonentity called "mass communication"—and there are few readers who have not had a personal collision with it.

BELONGINGNESS

What kind of society is to be engineered? Some critics of social engineering are sure that what is being cooked up for us is a socialistic paradise, a radically new, if not brave, world, alien to every tradition of man. This is wrong. Lump together the social engineers' prescriptions for the new society and you find they are anything but radical. Boiled down, what they ask for is an environment in which everyone is tightly knit into a belongingness with one another; one in which there is no restless wandering but rather the deep emotional security that comes from total integration with the group. Radical? It is like nothing so much as the Middle Ages.

And what, some have been asking, was so wrong with the Middle Ages anyway? They had excellent human relations. They didn't have the self-consciousness about their society to make them rationalize it or the scientific approach with which to do it. But belongingness they had. They knew where they stood—peasant and noble alike. They saw the fruit of their labor, and the tiny world about them protected as well as demanded. Psychologically, they had a home.

Not that we should go back to all this, mind you. The job, to paraphrase, is to *re-create* the belongingness of the Middle Ages. What with the Enlightenment, the Industrial Revolution, and other calamities, the job is immensely more difficult than it was in those simpler days. But with new scientific techniques we can solve the problem. What we must do is to learn consciously to achieve what once came naturally. We must form an elite of skilled leaders who will guide men back, benevolently, to group belongingness.

An unfair paraphrase? The young men who enthuse so unqualifiedly about human relations as the last best hope would be shocked to be accused of holding so reactionary a view. The people who have been the intellectual founders of the human-relations gospel, however, have not been so muddy-minded. They were not the cheery optimists their latter-day followers seem to be; they were rather pessimistic about the capacities of man, and the society they prescribed was by no means a utopia which would be all things to all men. A man would have to make sacrifices to enjoy it, and the prophets of belongingness stated this with admirable toughness of mind.

The father of the human-relations school is Elton Mayo. Mayo, professor of industrial research at the Harvard Business School, was concerned with the anomie, or rootlessness, of the industrial worker. Ever since he first started studying industry in Australia in 1903 he had been looking for a way to reconcile the worker's need for belongingness with the conflicting allegiances of the complex world he now finds himself in.

For Mayo, and his colleagues, the great turning point came as the result of what started to be a very modest experiment. In 1927 some of Mayo's colleagues began the now celebrated study at the Hawthorne, Illinois, plant of Western Electric.[6] The company had a challenging problem for them. For several years it had been trying to measure how much more telephone equipment the workers would produce as lighting was improved in the rooms they worked in. The researchers chose three rooms and progressively increased the illumination in each, at the same time keeping a careful record of the work output. To

[6] For a full account of this experiment, see *Management and the Worker,* by F. S. Roethlisberger and William J. Dickson (Cambridge, Massachusetts: Harvard University Press, 1939). A good summary is to be found in Stuart Chase's *The Proper Study of Mankind* (New York: Harper & Brothers, 1948).

their surprise, there seemed no clear relation between production and better illumination. They tried a more careful experiment: this time they would use only two rooms, one a "control" group where conditions would be left the same and the experimental room where the changes would be introduced. Again, mixed results: output went up in the experimental room —but so did it go up in the control room.

At this point the Harvard group entered the picture and collaborated with the company on a more elaborate experiment: in a "relay assembly" test room they isolated a group of women operators from others doing the same work and one by one introduced changes—not only lighting, but changes in rest periods, hours, and economic incentives. According to the commonly accepted "scientific management principles" earlier advanced by Frederick Taylor, these changes in physical conditions and, most particularly, incentives would make the test group more productive than the other. But they didn't. As experiment followed experiment (the research was to continue until 1932) it became abundantly clear that physical changes were not the key. As in the earlier experiments, output did shoot ahead where conditions were changed, but so did output shoot ahead where no changes had been made.

How come? The researchers came to the conclusion that output shot up in both groups because in both groups the workers' participation had been solicited and this involvement, clearly, was more important than physical perquisites. The workers were a social system; the system was informal but it was what really determined the worker's attitude toward his job. This social system could work against management, but if the managers troubled themselves to understand the system and its functions for the worker, the system could work for management.

In the literature of human relations the Hawthorne experiment is customarily regarded as a discovery. In large part it was; more than any other event, it dramatized the inadequacy of the purely economic view of man. The conclusions that flowed from the experiment, however, were a good bit more than a statement of objective fact, for Mayo and his group were evangelists as well as researchers. He had come to quite similar conclusions many years before, and for him the Hawthorne experiment did not reveal so much as confirm.

The two slim books Mayo published since Hawthorne have proved to be an immensely powerful manifesto. Mayo never pretended that he was free from values and he frankly presents an argument as well as a diagnosis. In *The Social Problems of an Industrial Civilization,* he opens his case by picturing man's happiness in more primitive times. "Historically and traditionally our fathers worked for social co-operation—and achieved it. This is true also of any primitive society. But we, for at least a century of the most amazing scientific and material progress, have abandoned the effort—by inadvertence, it is true—and we are now reaping the consequences."

In the Middle Ages people had been disciplined by social codes into working well together. The Industrial Revolution, as Mayo described the conesquences, had split society into a whole host of conflicting groups. Part of a man belonged to one group, part to another, and he was bewildered; no longer was there *one* group in which he could sublimate himself. The liberal philosophers, who were quite happy to see an end to feudal belongingness, interpreted this release from the group as freedom. Mayo does not see it this way. To him, the dominant urge of mankind is to belong: "Man's desire to be continuously associated in work with his fellows," he states, "is a strong, if not the strongest, human characteristic."

Whether the urge to co-operate is in fact man's most dominant drive, it does not follow that the co-operation is necessarily good. What is he going to co-operate *about*? What ends is the group working toward? But these questions do not greatly interest Mayo, and he seems to feel that the sheer fact of "spontaneous" co-operation carries its own ethic. "For *all* of us," Mayo states, "the feeling of security and certainty derives *always* from assured membership of a group." (Italics mine.)

Suppose there is a conflict between the individual and the group? Mayo sees conflict primarily as a breakdown in communication. If a man is unhappy or dissatisfied in his work, it is not that there is a conflict to be resolved so much as a misunderstanding to be cleared up. The worker might not see it this way, and most certainly the unions do not, but we have already been told that the individual is a nonlogical animal incapable of rationally solving his own problems or, in fact, of recognizing what the problem is.

At this point the human relations doctrine comes perilously close to demanding that the individual sacrifice his own beliefs that he may belong. The only way to escape this trap would be through the notion that by the process of equilibrium, a clarification of which never seems to detain anyone very long, what's good for the group is good for the individual. In speaking of the primitive group Mayo writes, "The situation is not simply that the society exercises a forceful compulsion on the individual; on the contrary, the social code and the desire of the individual are, for all practical purposes, identical. Every member of the group participates in all social activities because it is his chief desire to do so."

How to get back to this idyllic state? Mayo does not recommend a return to the Middle Ages. Too much water—and damn muddy water too, if you ask Mayo—has flowed under the bridge for that. The goal must be "an *adaptive* society"—a society in which we can once again enjoy the belongingness of primitive times but without the disadvantages of them.

This won't come about naturally. What with the mischief caused by the philosophers of individualism, most contemporary leaders are untrained in the necessary social skill to bring the adaptive society to pass. What is needed is an administrative elite, people trained to recognize that what man really wants most is group solidarity even if he does not realize it himself. They won't push him around; they won't even argue with him—unfettered as they will be of "prejudice and emotion," they won't have any philosophy, other than co-operation, to argue about. They will adjust him. Through the scientific application of human relations, these neutralist technicians will guide him into satisfying solidarity with the group so skillfully and unobtrusively that he will scarcely realize how the benefaction has been accomplished.

When Mayo got down to cases he was entirely consistent with his philosophy. His advocacy of "nondirective counseling" is a good case in point. In the course of their interviewing at Hawthorne, Mayo and his colleagues became impressed with the therapeutic effects the interviews had on the workers and went on to make the interview a management tool. The idea was to have a group of counselors who would be paid by management but who would not report to management what the workers said to them when they spilled their troubles. Since the workers knew this they could feel free to talk out their problems.

Implicit in this technique is the assumption that the worker's problems can indeed be *talked out*. He is to adjust to the group rather than vice versa; and the alternative of actually changing reality is hardly considered. If a worker is sore at his foreman the chances are good that he is not really sore at the foreman because of some rational gripe but is merely venting on the foreman certain repressed feelings. By listening patiently, like a psychiatrist, the counselor helps such persons understand that what they are really sore about flows from inner, subjective conflict. Characteristically, Mayo cites a woman worker who "discovered for herself during an interview that her dislike of a certain supervisor was based upon a fancied resemblance to a detested stepfather."

In similar cases it is possible the worker might not be maladjusted at all. The foreman might have been dividing up the work load problem badly, and maybe he had a few syndromes himself. The nondirective counseling idea, however, pooh-poohs the possibility: if there is a conflict of values that can't be talked out the interview has no provision in it for action to be taken—the setup itself, in short, is a value judgment that adjustment, rather than change, is the desideratum.

For a number of reasons, one being the hostility of the unions to it, the nondirective counseling system as such has never taken hold of the American industry. But the basic idea has. As I hope to demonstrate in later chapters, many of the more popular techniques—such as psychological "personality" testing, conference techniques—are all manifestations of the same principle. The rock is the group and maladjustment is disharmony with it.

Ironically, the primary target of this adjustment has become the managers themselves. While Mayo intended human relations to apply to the workers and managers both, the managers first seized on it as an excellent tool for manipulating the workers into a chronic contentment that would turn them away from the unions. But manipulation is a two-edged weapon; having learned how illogical workers were, managerial pioneers of human relations soon began to ponder the fact that their colleagues weren't so logical either. They needed to belong too—and even more than the worker, for more of their life was involved in the organization. Looking at the neuroses about him, many a progressive young organization man resolved that here, not on the shop floor, was the place that needed human relations most.

The use of psychological tests, if I may get a bit ahead of my story, is symptomatic. Originally, they were introduced by the managers as a tool for weeding out unqualified workers. As time went on, and personality tests were added to aptitude tests, the managers began using them on other managers, present and prospective, and today most personality testing is directed not at the workers, but at the organization man. If he is being hoist, it is by his own philosophy.

Not so long after Mayo and his colleagues documented the importance of the group at Hawthorne, a former student of

Mayo's, anthropologist Lloyd Warner, began coming to remarkably similar conclusions in a study of a New England town. This study, which has had a tremendous impact on social science, was an impressively large-scale undertaking in which some twenty researchers spent three years making a study of Newburyport, Massachusetts. Every conceivable fact about Newburyport was to be dug up, and through scientific evaluation, some objective conclusions were to be arrived at.

Several years before, Warner had studied a tribe of Australian aborigines and had been immensely impressed by the way in which the tribal customs and the unwritten laws kept the individual in harmony with the group. The rituals and sanctions seemed illogical at times, but they shielded man from the kind of individual decisions which a fast-changing industrial society could overwhelm him with.

When Warner began poking around Newburyport, he discovered strong parallels. It was a venerable old New England town rich in tradition and full of people with a strong attachment to the past.[7] There were Memorial Day celebrations instead of the Nurngin totem rites, but in many ways it seemed much the same, and Warner drew the same moral. Of the many conclusions that came out of the study, by all odds the most important finding was the function of social structure in fixing the individual in a satisfying relation to the society. Newburyport did not present altogether as happy a picture of stability as a medieval or primitive society would have. Even though it had been touched by the Industrial Revolution, however, it did provide excellent grist for Warner's argument that the happiness of man depended on the rootedness in a stable group. Like several other old communities, it had lost the economic basis of its early prosperity and thus was frozen somewhat in the mold of previous times.

Warner saw, and charted, seven class divisions in Newburyport, and from these generalized a concept of class and

[7] It was also the home town of J. P. Marquand, a fact which was later to produce *Point of No Return* and some sharp passages about anthropologists studying a venerable old New England town.

status for the country as a whole. The concept has long since been subjected to a thoroughgoing critical analysis by many social scientists; suffice it to say here that Warner's description carried with it a strong note of advocacy. Warner did believe that there should be some mobility between classes and he thought it healthy that a number of people could move up from, say, the upper-middle to the lower-upper. But not *too* many. The class structure would become meaningless in that case, and people would become bewildered for lack of a firm group to relate themselves to.

Conflict, change, fluidity—these are the evils from which man should be insulated. To Warner, the unconscious yearning for belongingness was all-important. During the time he and his associates were at Newburyport, the workers in the shoe factory there went on strike. Ostensibly, the strike was over economic matters; the workers thought they wanted more money. But Warner and his colleagues saw it another way. They saw so many other factors that they produced a book on the subject (called, somewhat flatly, *The Social System of the Modern Factory*). The real cause of the strike, the book implies, was not so much the economic plight of the workers as the social one. Back in the eighteen-hundreds they had enjoyed the status that comes from a firm hierarchy of skills and there had been the steadying hand of the paternal local capitalists. But now increased mechanization, while not rampant in the shoe industry, had downgraded the old high-status jobs; equally unfortunate, the absentee ownership of "Big City capitalism" had supplanted the local oligarchy. Whether they knew it or not, in short, the workers struck because the cohesive society of old had broken down.

Someday someone is going to create a stir by proposing a radical new tool for the study of people. It will be called the face-value technique. It will be based on the premise that people often do what they do for the reasons they think they do. The use of this technique would lead to many pitfalls, for it is undeniably true that people do not always act logically or say what they mean. But I wonder if it would produce findings any more unscientific than the opposite course.

That strike at Newburyport, for example. Warner did devote a couple of sentences to the logical, economic factors, but it's clear in reading the other three hundred pages that he feels that the real cause lay in the fact that there was no longer any "hierarchy of skills" that used to give workers a sense of satisfaction and status. Well, maybe so, but most of the workers who struck didn't happen to have been around to remember the idyllic days of old described by Warner, and it is somewhat debatable if they would have liked them quite as much as Warner seems to believe they would. As far as I can gather from a careful reading of Warner's account of it, the workers acted with eminent logic. They wanted more money; the employers didn't want to give it to them; the workers banded together in strike, and the employers gave in. Is it so very naïve, then, to explain this strike as very much of an economic matter? Any more naïve than to attribute it to a nostalgia for ancient paternalism? Who has the nostalgia?

In fairness to Warner, it should be pointed out that he has subsequently been coming to the view that there is more mobility than Newburyport would suggest. His followers, however, have not been so flexible, and the Warner thesis, for all the defections of its author, remains a very powerful force. Among educators in particular it is one of the principal ideological bases for the belief that only a segment of society should be schooled in the humanities. The majority, goes the idea, should be taught lesser skills; rather than tantalize themselves with aspirations, they should adjust to the fact of a fairly fixed social system.

Neither Warner nor Mayo had much enthusiasm for the union as a social group; in Mayo's case it split loyalties in the factory scheme of things; in Warner's case it split the loyalties of the stable, fixed, small community. It could be argued, however, that if workers needed an embracing group the union had as much right to be it as any other group. Which brings us to the third variation on belongingness—the proposition of Frank Tannenbaum. Unlike Mayo, he is the father of no school; he is an historian rather than a labor leader. But his views are well worth examining all the same; they may not be symptomatic of labor thought but they are symptomatic of the growing quest for belongingness.

In the opening pages of Tannenbaum's *A Philosophy of Labor* (New York: Knopf, 1951) there is the customary salute to the Middle Ages.

> Membership in a guild, manorial estate, or village protected man throughout his life and gave him the peace and serenity from which could flow the medieval art and craft. The life of man was a nearly unified whole. Being a member of an integrated society protected and raised the dignity of the individual and gave each his own special role. Each man, each act, was part of a total life drama, the plot of which was known and in which the part allotted to each was prescribed. No one was isolated or abandoned. His individuality and his ambitions were fulfilled within the customary law that ruled the community to which he belonged.

Then came the Industrial Revolution and paradise lost.

> The Industrial Revolution destroyed the solid moorings of an older way of life and cast the helpless workers adrift in a strange and difficult world. The peasant who had been reared in the intimacy of a small village . . . now found himself isolated and bewildered in a city crowded with strangers and indifferent to a common rule. The symbolic universe that had patterned the ways of men across the ages in village, manor, or guild had disappeared. This is the great moral tragedy of the industrial system.

To make matters worse, Tannenbaum continues, the philosophers of the enlightenment rationalized this breakdown of the old society in terms of individualism. "This doctrine gave the social disintegration then taking place a moral purpose. . . . In its extreme form the theory seemed to advance the idea that the best society was that in which organized human relations and responsibilities were least."

As Tannenbaum rightly points out, this doctrine of self-sufficiency was all very fine for the *bourgeoisie*, but for the workers, self-sufficiency was an illusion. In learning this, however, the workers were taking the first steps to recreating a community. In making them recognize their individual helplessness, the employers made them recognize their common strength. "The trade-union," as Tannenbaum says, "was the visible evidence that man is not a commodity, and that he is not sufficient unto himself."

The kind of sufficiency Tannenbaum is most concerned with is social rather than economic, and thus to him the real promise of the unions lay in their potential as a social unit. But the workers, no less affected by the Protestant Ethic than their employers, had too pressing an agenda to be diverted from bread-and-butter economic matters. Thus, in fighting the unions, the employers were diverting the unions' energies from the ultimate goal. And the employers didn't do it just to save money; they resisted unionization "because a society tends to become an all-embracing way of life."

Now, however, Tannenbaum argues that the unions are at last in a position to become instruments of "governance" rather than instruments of war. "Only when the battle for recognition is finished can the institutional role come into its own. If the trade-union could not fulfill its larger responsibilities, it would have no reason for existence, would not be a true society, would have no moral role, and would disintegrate." The true end, then, is for a society in which the worker, like his ancestors in the Middle Ages, will be firmly rooted in a group with customs, laws, and guides. He will lose his mobility—not for him the upward—and individual—path to the managerial world; the "fluidity," both geographic and social, that we will see in suburbia is precisely the thing Tannenbaum wants to insulate man from. And the trend away from fluidity is not to be denied. "Institutionally the trade-union movement is an unconscious effort to harness the drift of our time and reorganize it around the cohesive identity that men working together always achieve. That is why the trade-union is a repudiation of the individualism of the French Revolution and the liberalism of English utilitarian philosophers."

Tannenbaum seems to be working the other side of the street from Mayo and Warner. But while they are truer to the medieval spirit in wanting the nobility rather than the serfs to be in charge, the outlook is the same. Any dispute is merely jurisdictional; they don't agree on *which* group should do the embracing but they are all of a piece on the idea the embracing should be done—although not by the state, for that would be totalitarian.

I do not mean to deprecate study of the function of groups. One can study something without deifying it, and a recognition that a society can be all embracing doesn't require belief that it should be. The most vigorous criticism of the human-relations doctrine has come from social scientists, and most of them have by no means been uninterested in the power of the group or its value. However one differs with the findings of particular studies, the point at issue should be the findings, not the fact of the studies. An obvious point perhaps, but there does seem too little middle ground between the near-evangelical acceptance of social-science research on the one hand, and the damnation of it as the improper study of mankind because its particulars are found wanting.

Nor do values mar it; the point is to recognize the values that we may judge them. Mayo made his quite explicit, and in fairness to him and the other pioneers of human relations, we must remember the prevailing climate of opinion at the time; as John Dewey was to authoritarian education, so they were to authoritarian industry. Mayo emphasized group cohesiveness and administrative social skill so much because he felt—with considerable justification—that Americans had been slighting these matters. At a time when the people in charge of big organizations clung to the mechanistic views of the efficiency experts, Mayo brought a badly needed shift in perspective; he helped sensitize a steady stream of influential management people to the importance of the whole vast informal network beneath them and the necessity of comprehending it. One does not have to go along with Mayo's philosophy of the adaptive society to recognize the benefits in better management that he helped bring about.

But what was once counter-cyclical is now orthodoxy. Already human relations is a standard part of the curriculum of the business schools and it will not be very long before it is standard in the high schools too. Human relations can mean a lot of things—as one critic defines it, it is any study called human relations to escape the discipline of established theory in the appropriate field. But, generally speaking, most human-relations doctrine is pointed toward the vision of Mayo, and this reinforces what many people are already very well prepared to believe.

Particularly, the organization man. Who is the hero in human relations? In the older ideology, it was the top leader who was venerated. In human relations it is the organization man, and thus the quasi-religious overtones with which he gratefully endows it. The older ideology provided an unsatisfactory view of the system for the large and growing bureaucratic slice of management. The human-relations doctrine, however, not only tells them that they are important, but that they are the key figures. As sociologist Reinhard Bendix has observed, in the new managerial ideology, it is not the leaders of industry that are idealized—if anything, they are scolded—but the lieutenants. The people that the workers are to co-operate with are not the top employers but enlightened bureaucrats.

At times it almost seems that human relations is a revolutionary tool the organization man is to use *against* the bosses. Listen to an unreconstructed boss give a speech castigating unreconstructed bosses for not being more enlightened about human relations, and you get the feeling the speech is a subtle form of revenge on the part of the harried underling who wrote it. For reasons of protocol, organization men publicly extol human relations for the beneficial effects it casts downward, but privately they spend most of their time talking about using it upward. Whenever there is responsible criticism of human relations, there is a hurt response from middle management staff people, and, invariably, the complaint boils down to something like this: Why, why hurt us? Many of the criticisms are true all right—some people have gone haywire on this—but we progressives have a tough enough fight converting the reactionaries on top, and any criticism at this time only gives aid and comfort to them.

It is not an easy complaint to answer—many older executives are indeed reactionary and many are against human relations for strange reasons. What makes the complaint particularly tough to answer, however, is the trusting way organization men assume that only techniques are subject for criticism and that surely the goals must be noncontroversial. If I do not dwell more in this book on the beneficial aspects of human relations, it is because they have been reiterated quite enough already.

In practice, of course, corporations have not changed their ways quite so much as their self-congratulations on human relations suggest, and many a highly publicized program is only a sugar-coating of the mixture as before. Because there remains a divergence between precept and practice, however, does not mean that precept is any the less important. While older men may appropriate the vocabulary of human relations without the underlying philosophy, the younger men believe. They have had an indoctrination their superiors did not, and though experience may disillusion them somewhat they view the day of their ascension with genuine missionary zeal.

The point I am trying to make is not that the corporation, or any other specific kind of organization, is going to be *the* citadel of belongingness. The union of Frank Tannenbaum, the community of Lloyd Warner, the corporation of Elton Mayo—each is in conflict as to which group is going to furnish the vital belongingness, and these three by no means exhaust the roster of groups proposed. Spokesmen in other areas have similarly bewailed the lack of an encompassing, integrated life, and in an excess of good will have asked that their group take over the whole messy job. Many a contemporary prescription for utopia can be summarized if you cross out the name of one group and substitute another in the following charge: Society has broken down; the family, the church, the community, the schools, business—each has failed to give the individual the belongingness he needs and thus it is now the task of ——— group to do the job. It is fortunate there are so many groups; with such competition for the individual psyche it is difficult for any one of them to land the franchise.

But ideologically these pleas do not cancel each other out. For there is always the common thread that a man must belong and that he must be unhappy if he does not belong rather completely. The idea that conflicting allegiances safeguard him as well as abrade him is sloughed over, and for the people who must endure the tensions of independence there is no condolence; only the message that the tensions are sickness—either in themselves or in society. It does not make any difference whether the Good Society is to be represented by a union or by a corporation or by a church; it is to be a society unified and purged of conflict.

To turn about and preach that conflicting allegiances are absolute virtues is not justified either. But at this particular time the function they perform in the maintenance of individual freedom is worthy of more respect. Clark Kerr, Chancellor of the University of California, at Berkeley, has put it well:

> The danger is not that loyalties are divided today but that they may be undivided tomorrow. . . . I would urge each individual to avoid total involvement in any organization; to seek to whatever extent lies within his power to limit each group to the minimum control necessary for performance of essential functions; to struggle against the effort to absorb; to lend his energies to many organizations and give himself completely to none; to teach children, in the

home and in the school, "to be laws to themselves and to depend on themselves," as Walt Whitman urged us many years ago—for that is the well source of the independent spirit.

TOGETHERNESS

It is the organization man, then, more than the worker whom he wishes to serve, who most urgently wants to belong. His quest takes many forms; in this [section] I would like to examine the most concrete one: his growing preoccupation with group work. The group that he is trying to immerse himself in is not merely the larger one—The Organization, or society itself—but the immediate, physical group as well: the people at the conference table, the workshop, the seminar, the skull session, the after-hours discussion group, the project team. It is not enough now that he belong; he wants to belong *together.*

One reason that he is so fascinated with group work, of course, is the simple fact that there is now so much more of it. Organization life being what it is, out of sheer necessity he must spend most of his working hours in one group or another, and out of self-defense, if not instinct, the committee arts must become reflex with him. But more than necessity is involved. Where the immersion of the individual used to be cause for grumbling and a feeling of independence lost, the organization man of today is now welcoming it. He is not attempting to reverse the trend and to cut down the deference paid to the group; he is working to increase it, and with the help of some branches of the social sciences he is erecting what is almost a secular religion.

There are two bases for this movement, one scientific, the other moral. The scientific basis can be stated very simply. It is now coming to be widely believed that *science has proved the group is superior to the individual.* Science has not, but that is another matter. Mistaken or not, the popularized version of the science of the group is a social force in its own right, and it holds that experiments have shown that in human relations the whole is always greater than the sum of its parts and that through "interaction" we can produce ideas beyond our capabilities as individuals. The new dynamism, furthermore, is not to apply merely to the day-to-day work of getting things done; it is, presumably, going to envelop creative work too, and in areas until recently considered sacrosanct to the individual it is already having some effect. The scientific genius, for example. As I will take up in later chapters, there is a growing thought that he is an anachronism—a once valuable, but now unnecessary, prelude to the research team. And not an idle thought; in the name of science, administrators are taking some practical measures to insure that he will in fact be an anachronism.

As is so characteristic of scientism, there is an overriding faith that we are on the brink of superseding discovery. In previous eras people often worked in groups too, and sometimes, though one would not imagine so from current group literature, quite successfully. But they were merely being empirical. If people were successful before, some now exclaim, think what lies ahead! For there now exists, or shortly will, a scientific body of laws by which we can unleash hitherto untapped sources of creativity.

For their theoretical justification, group advocates lean heavily on the work being done in "group dynamics." This is a difficult field to define, all social science having a concern with the group, but generally it describes the work of those whose attention is focused on the face-to-face group. From its beginnings, it has attracted some of the most imaginative men in social science, and through a combination of attitude surveys of organizations and experiments with small groups, they have tackled a whole series of intriguing questions. If a group has high morale, will it produce more? What is the ideal size of the informal group? What is the effect of the group on the deviate?

Over-all, their intellectual ambition has been large. Not

only have they aimed to discover the underlying principles of group activity, they have aimed to do it in a rather short time, and this promise has unduly excited lay followers in the organization world. There have been delays; originally the group-dynamics people had expected the basic program to be over in ten years, but now they feel more time may be needed. Such delays, however, have only made the eventual promise all the more tantalizing to organization people. Another ten years . . .

But the basis of the movement is primarily a moral one. To the organization man the search for better group techniques is something of a crusade—a crusade against authoritarianism, a crusade for more freedom, for more recognition of the man in the middle. The key word is "democratic"; with some justification the organization man argues that the old-style individualist was often far more of a bar to individualism in other people and that in the modern organization the desk-pounding type of leader drastically inhibits the flow of ideas, not to mention making life unpleasant for everybody. As organization men see it, through an extension of the group spirit, through educating people to sublimate their egos, organizations can rid themselves of their tyrants and create a *harmonious* atmosphere in which the group will bring out the best in everyone. This moral urge is not lightly to be dismissed, and though I wish later to suggest other reasons for the group quest, it is only fair to say that most group advocates would be sincerely disturbed at the thought that they are party to anything that would stifle the individual.

But they are. Much of what they say is correct: it is true that the health of organization life depends upon skillful group work; it is true that the group is tremendously effective in bringing out different points of view that would otherwise remain latent, that together members of a group can see more possible lines of action than if they were consulted individually; it is true that genius cannot function in a vacuum and that interaction with others in the field can be vastly stimulating and, indeed, often indispensable.

But other things are true too, and in this chapter I would like to dwell on a few of the aspects of group work that are currently being sloughed over. To anyone who has had to work in an organization, they will not be novel thoughts, but I believe they deserve far more reiteration than they are now getting. It is not so much the fallacies of specific techniques of group work that are critical as the continued imbalance of emphasis, for this emphasis is having a definite molding effect on the organization man.

The organization man is not yet so indoctrinated that he does not chafe at the pressures on his independence, and sometimes he even suspects that the group may be as much a tyrant as the despot it has replaced. It is the burden of the new group doctrine that such misgivings, if they are not maladjustment on the part of the individual, are simply a lack of knowledge, a lack of mastery of managerial techniques. The doctrine may be wrong, but the constant impress of it is helping to undercut the few personal defenses left the individual; more to the point, it is making an organization life increasingly hostile to the nonbeliever who hangs onto his defenses.

The central fallacy, I believe, lies in what can be called false collectivization. When are people in a group? Too often, we insist on treating a person—or ourselves—as a unit of a group when association with the particular group is not vital to the task in question, or may even be repressive. In some cases the group is a key entity—that is, the working together of individuals is necessary to perform the particular function, and in such cases the way each of the people affects the others is inextricably entwined with the total performance. The work of a combat squad is a good example of this. The soldier is conditioned to fight primarily by his group, and just as a contagion of fear drastically alters the individual, so can a unity of courage. In such cases, plainly, the group is primary and it produces something over and above the total of the individuals.

Can we generalize, however, that this is true of all collections of individuals? We are confusing an abstraction with a reality. Just because a collection of individuals can be called a group does not mean it functions as a group or that it should. In many situations the fact of groupness is only incidental. Take, for example, the men who sit together in a college classroom. At times, an *esprit de corps* is helpful in promoting lively discussion, but it is not vital, and the student's important relationship is not with other members of the group but to the content of the course and to the teacher as intermediary.

But this distinction between the functional grouping and the incidental grouping is easily blurred. To follow the example of the class, we find many teachers treating a course less as a worthy discipline in its own right than as a vehicle for stimulating interaction. In many institutions, as a consequence, the yardstick of a teacher's performance is the amount of interaction he develops in the group, and those who keep the students' focus on the discipline are apt to find themselves under censure.

One teacher who had been criticized on this score told me that he was glad in a way, for he had been forced to think through his own position. "If I didn't, I would stand accused as a reactionary. So I had to think out what I had always taken for granted. First, I made the point that in my course—during the first part of it, at any rate—the students were not qualified. I think it would be a mistake to encourage them to think that their opinions are as good as mine at this stage. They aren't, and I want to let them know that before they can question my interpretation, they must master the fundamentals. Sure, I want them to question and to come to their own conclusions, but they have to earn the right; they don't get fundamentals through glorified bull sessions but by hard work. The second point I made was on the value of the interaction that they talk about. What's so very important about it? Of all the groups that we are connected with in our lives, the classroom group is one of the least permanent and least vital ones. Try to remember who sat next to you in your classes at college. You'll have a hard time remembering."

Another example of false collectivization is the way many organizations treat their professional employees. Recently, to cite a typical case, one well-known corporation was worried over a morale problem among its engineers. Now it is convenient to talk of the engineers as a group—just as it is convenient to talk of hundreds of thousands of individuals as a "mass audience." A convenient method of description, however, is not necessarily a reality. The engineers appeared to be a group because physically many of them were housed in the same building, and in the organization charts and pay scales they were classified together for convenience' sake. But their real problem in this instance came from their vertical relationship—that is, their relationship to the particular task and the superiors above them—and their morale problem had very little to do with social harmony among themselves. The company insisted on treating them as a group, however, and in a vain effort to promote morale completely obscured the real nature of the problem. I am sure that many organization men can think of similar confusions.

The most misguided attempt at false collectivization is the current attempt to see the group as a creative vehicle. Can it be? People very rarely *think* in groups; they talk together, they exchange information, they adjudicate, they make compromises. But they do not think; they do not create.

Group advocates would agree that this has been so. But they do not see this as a natural limitation. To them it is a bug of human relations to be cured, and in the expectation that technique is the key, they are engaged in a wholesale effort to tame the arts of discovery—and those by nature suited for it. In part this effort is propelled by the natural distaste of the noncreative man for the creative, but again, there is the moral impulse. Among many there is a real belief that we can teach the individual to create in concert rather than as an individual and that his acceptance of the organization way will produce a combustion of ideas otherwise impossible.

Here would be the ultimate victory of the administrator. The creative individual he does not understand, nor does he understand the conditions of creativity. The messiness of intuition, the aimless thoughts, the unpractical questions—all these things that are so often the companion to discovery are anathema to the world of the administrator. Order, objective goals, agreement—these are his desiderata.

Vital they are to executing ideas, but not to creating them. Agreement? To concentrate on agreement is to intensify that which inhibits creativity. For any group of people to operate effectively some firm basis of agreement is necessary, and a meeting cannot be productive unless certain premises are so shared that they don't need to be discussed and the argument can be confined to areas of disagreement. But while this kind of consensus makes a group more effective in its legitimate functions, it does not make the group a creative vehicle.

Think for a moment of the way you behave in a committee meeting. In your capacity as group member you feel a strong impulse to seek common ground with the others. Not just out of timidity but out of respect for the sense of the meeting you tend to soft-pedal that which would go against the grain. And that, unfortunately, can include unorthodox ideas. A really new idea affronts current agreement—it wouldn't be a new idea if it didn't—and the group, impelled as it is to agreement, is instinctively hostile to that which is divisive. With wise leadership it can offset this bias, but the essential urge will still be to unity, to consensus. After an idea matures—after people learn to live with it—the group may approve it, but that is after the fact and it is an act of acquiescence rather than creation.

I have been citing the decision-making group, and it can

be argued that these defects of order do not apply to information-exchanging groups. It is true that meeting with those of common interests can be tremendously stimulating and suggest to the individuals fresh ways of going about their own work. But stimulus is not discovery; it is not the act of creation. Those who recognize this limitation do not confuse the functions and, not expecting too much, profit from the meeting of minds.

Others, however, are not so wise, and fast becoming a fixture of organization life is the meeting self-consciously dedicated to creating ideas. It is a fraud. Much of such high-pressure creation—cooking with gas, creating out loud, spitballing, and so forth—is all very provocative, but if it is stimulating, it is stimulating much like alcohol. After the glow of such a session has worn off, the residue of ideas usually turns out to be a refreshed common denominator that everybody is relieved to agree upon—and if there is a new idea, you usually find that it came from a capital of ideas already thought out—by *individuals*—and perhaps held in escrow until someone sensed an opportune moment for its introduction.

I have been talking of the extension of the team to a field where it does not belong. Even in fields where the group is vital, however, the current emphasis on the team is having some equally inhibiting effects. Just as it has obscured the role of the individual in creation and discovery in such activities as research and communication, so in the regular work of running an organization it is obscuring the function of leadership.

Such emphasis is particularly unnecessary at this time because the whole tendency of modern organization life is to muffle the importance of individual leadership. In studying an organization, one of the most difficult things is to trace a program or innovation back to its origins, and this is just as true of organization successes as it is of failures. Who started what and when? This kind of question is the kind that makes organization people uncomfortable. To answer it would be an offense against the organization spirit, and even the man himself who first conceived the plan is apt to deny—except perhaps to his wife—that his contribution was really very important. A sense of the fitness of things requires that it be the team, everyone working together, a small part of the inexorable symmetry of the over-all plan. Repeated, time and again, it becomes official, and this is the face of organization—and the moral—that is presented to the apprentices.

But now to this inclination is added the force of ideology. On the surface it seems reasonable enough; the bogy is authoritarianism, and the aim is to free organization people from the pressures imposed on them by opinionated, unilateral people that all may express themselves more freely. But how do you define authoritarianism? In practice, current definitions of the authoritarian leader come perilously close to including anyone who has ideas of his own or who differs with others on basic policy.

Anti-authoritarianism is becoming anti-leadership. In group doctrine the strong personality is viewed with overwhelming suspicion. The co-operative are those who take a stance directly over the keel; the man with ideas—in translation, prejudices—leans to one side or, worse yet, heads for the rudder. Plainly, he is a threat. Skim through current group handbooks, conference leaders' tool kits, and the like, and you find what sounds very much like a call to arms by the mediocre against their enemies.

Let me cite a Bureau of Naval Personnel handbook on "Conference Sense." It is describing, with elephantine cheeriness, the different kinds of types one has to deal with in conferences. Among the bad people we meet is The Aggressor.

The conference leader's remedy: Place Donald Duck at your left (the blind spot). Fail to hear his objections, or if you do, misunderstand them. If possible, recognize a legitimate objection and side with him. Object is to get him to feel that he "belongs." If he still persists in running wild, let group do what they are probably by now quite hot to do, i.e., cut the lug down. They generally do it by asking Little Brother Terrible to clarify his position, then to clarify his clarification, then to clarify his clarification of his clarification, etc., until our lad is so hot and bothered that he has worked himself into role of conference comedian. Then soothe his bruised ego and restore him to human society by asking him questions that he can answer out of special experience.

The good people? One is The Compromiser. He "may offer compromise by admitting his error . . . by obviously disciplining himself to maintain group harmony, or by 'coming halfway' in moving along with the group. . . . This takes courage. Let him know he's appreciated. Give occasional cigar. A fifteen center. He deserves the best."

These defensive gambits against the leader are only a stopgap measure. What some group advocates have in mind is, quite literally, *to eliminate the leader altogether.* For some time the National Training Laboratory in Group Development at Bethel, Maine, has been experimenting with the "leaderless group"—and with such zeal as to make some students of the group a bit uneasy. One of the most astute students of the group, sociologist William Foote Whyte, was moved to write some second thoughts on his experiences at Bethel. He recounts the well-meaning attempt that was made there to turn the group leader into a "resource person." The idea was that as the group jells, the leader would become less necessary and would retire into the background to be consulted, occasionally, for his special *expertise.* When this was tried out, a good bit of chaos resulted, but the group people hoped that the chaos—or "feeling-draining"—would be a valuable catharsis and a prelude to later agreement. But no agreement came. Unfortunately, the group could not agree on a topic to agree upon.

The causes of failure, as Whyte maintained, were not technical. Later he tried similar experiments on his own, and these led him to the conclusion that "if the group is to make progress in its discussions and avoid confusion and frustration, then there must be a well-defined leadership, at least in the sense of co-ordination of activity. . . . In some groups, and this was notably true at Bethel, such a high premium is placed upon fitting into the group and being sensitive to the group's wishes that the individual who shows some initiative on his own becomes suspect and is likely to be discouraged. We must remember that if every member simply wants to do what the group wants to do, then the group is not going to do anything. Somehow, individual initiative must enter into the group. Should we bring it in openly or should we try to bootleg it in an expression of group sentiment?"

The intellectual hypocrisy of the leaderless group has brought forth a new breed; into the very vacuum that they bespeak have moved the professional group expediters. The end they seek is compromise and harmony, but in their controlled way they can be just as militant as any desk-pounder of old, and a lot more self-righteous. Reuel Denney has written a wonderful account in *Commentary* of the puzzlement of an old-style convention-goer when he comes up against them. After attending a preconvention conference with a group of people interested in groups, it slowly dawns on him that "those fellows were deciding a lot of things. Not that they knew it. But they were, for instance, planning a strategy to prevent the bright and talkative men from intimidating the others at the convention; they were going to get participation even if they, in a nice way, had to slug somebody, and the role of slugger —not just a role-playing role, either—was assigned in advance."

The extent of this ferment was forcibly brought home to me several years ago when I encountered my first "buzz session." It was at a management convention. It had started conventionally enough with a panel discussion in which I and two other men spoke. Halfway through the proceedings, the program chairman called an intermission and, with the assistance of several helpers, began rearranging the seating so that the audience would be divided into groups of four, with the chairs turned around so that they faced each other, looking much like a huge bridge tournament with the bridge table removed. When I asked him what was going on, he seemed surprised. Hadn't I ever heard of a "buzz session"? He was an old hand at it, having been one of the first graduates of the National Group Training Laboratory at Bethel. He explained that rather than have a "directed" discussion, we would stimulate ideas through interaction. By breaking the audience into a constellation of face-to-face groups, he said, we would create this interaction. The fact that the seating would be a random mixture of strangers would make no difference; the interaction itself would produce many provocative insights.

At last he banged down the gavel, and some two hundred grown men turned and faced each other for the discussion period. Minutes went by. There was no buzz. Something, obviously, was wrong, and it was only through the heroic efforts of two expediters that any questions from the floor were forthcoming. The chairman was not chastened. After the meeting he told me that the trouble was simply that the groups were too small. Four wasn't up to the ignition level. Next time they would do it with six to eight men.

While it would be wrong to dwell overlong on the more fatuous examples, they are not quite as unrelated to the main trend as many embarrassed organization men would like to believe. The Harwald Group-Thinkometer, for example. Most group-relations people would probably disown it as too stringent a tool, yet it seems a perfectly logical development. The Group-Thinkometer is an electric meter the dial of which is graduated in degrees of interest. Feeding into it are ten remote-control switches which can be distributed around, or under, the table, and by pressing the switch members of the group indicate approval or disapproval. Since the needle on the meter shows only the accumulated group reaction, one can veto a colleague's idea without his being the wiser, and, as the Harwald Company suggests, thus the personality factor is eliminated almost entirely. Extreme? The Harwald Company has only concretized, you might say, the underlying principles of the group philosophy.

Let me now take up the question of morale. Underpinning the current denigration of leadership are some very questionable assumptions about the relationship between morale and productivity. As usually expressed by organization people, these assumptions follow this general sequence. Once we used hard-driving leaders to get things done, but this was because we didn't know any better. As group-dynamics studies have proved, high group morale is the heart of production. This means that the ideal leader should not lead in the old sense—that is, focus his attention and that of the group on goals. He should instead concentrate almost wholly on the personality relationships within the group. If he attends to these and sees to it that the members get along, the goals will take care of themselves.

But the findings of the group-dynamics investigators themselves have been nowhere near as heart-warming as their lay followers would like to believe. Recently, Rensis Likert, Director of the Institute for Social Research at the University of Michigan—heartland of group dynamics—told a management audience of some second thoughts he had had. "On the basis of a study I did in 1937 I believed that morale and production were positively related: that the higher the morale the higher the production. Substantial research findings since then have shown that this relationship is much too simple. In our different studies we have found a wide variety of relationships. Some units have low morale and low production; other units have fairly good morale and low production; still others have fairly good production but low morale; other units have both high morale and high production."

Likert saw many benefits in the increased attention paid morale. Among other things it had led people to expect more opportunities for expression, initiative, and participation. But he had grown suspicious, he said, of the laissez-faire approach in which the supervisor does not lead but tries to keep people happy. In companies in which human-relations training programs have been emphasized, he went on, "some supervisors interpret the training to mean that the company management wants them to keep employees happy, so they work hard to do so. The result is a nice country-club atmosphere in which the leadership function has been abandoned to all intents and purposes. Employees like it and absence and turnover are low, but since little production is felt to be expected, they produce relatively little."

Obviously, the study of group dynamics need not be antithetical to the individual, and here let me again make the distinction between analysis of a phenomenon and deification of it. One can study the group aspect of a man without deprecating his other aspects, and while many students of group dynamics have crossed the line, they don't have to. The more we find out about how a group actually behaves—and the scientific method is of immense help here—the more sophisticated we can become about its limitations, the more armed against its defects. But this won't be done unless there is a far more rigorous questioning of the value premises which underlie most current attacks on the problem. Consider the abstractions that are so taken for granted as good—such as consensus, cooperation, participation, and the like. Held up as a goal without any reference to ends, they are meaningless. Why participate, for example? Like similar abstractions, participation is an empty goal unless it is gauged in relation to the job to be done. It is a means, not an end, and when treated as an end, it can become more repressive than the unadorned authoritarianism it is supposed to replace.

And why should there be consensus? Must consensus per se be the overriding goal? It is the price of progress that there never can be complete consensus. All creative advances are essentially a departure from agreed-upon ways of looking at things, and to over-emphasize the agreed-upon is to further legitimatize the hostility to that creativity upon which we all ultimately depend.

Let me admit that I have been talking principally about the adverse aspects of the group. I would not wish to argue for a destructive recalcitrance, nor do I wish to undervalue the real progress we have made in co-operative effort. But to emphasize, in these times, the virtues of the group is to be supererogatory. Universal organization training, as I will take up in the following chapters, is now available for everybody, and it so effectively emphasizes the group spirit that there is little danger that inductees will be subverted into rebelliousness.

Over and above the overt praise for the pressures of the group, the very ease, the democratic atmosphere in which organization life is now conducted makes it all the harder for the individual to justfy *to himself* a departure from its norm. It would be a mistake to confuse individualism with antagonism, but the burdens of free thought are already steep enough that we should not saddle ourselves with a guilty conscience as well. The hunch that wasn't followed up. The controversial point that didn't get debated. The idea that was suppressed. Were these acts of group co-operation or individual surrender? We are taking away from the individual the ability even to ask the question.

In further institutionalizing the great power of the majority, we are making the individual come to distrust himself. We are giving him a rationalization for the unconscious urging to find an authority that would resolve the burdens of free choice. We are tempting him to reinterpret the group pressures as a release, authority as freedom, and that this quest assumes a moral guise makes it only the more poignant. Of all the forms of wanton self-destruction, the Englishman A. A. Bowman once observed, there is none more pathetic than that in which the human individual demands that in the vital relationships of life he be treated not as an individual but as a member of some organization.

SMALL TOWN IN MASS SOCIETY

Arthur J. Vidich and Joseph Bensman

The community study occupies a special niche in American sociology. Its practitioners, starting with Robert and Helen Merrell Lynd in the 1920's, have creatively adapted anthropological techniques, applying them to segments, enclaves, or "subcultures" within the larger contemporary scene. With their pioneer studies of a Midwestern town, first in the boom time that followed World War I (Middletown) *and again during the Great Depression* (Middletown in Transition), *the Lynds set a high standard of achievement. They demonstrated that a literate society, or sociologically manageable units thereof, could be understood as well as a preliterate society by means of participant observation. The social scientist could settle for a year or two, not just in Tierra del Fuego or the Andaman Islands, but in Muncie, Indiana. Given a certain capacity for relating to people who might not share his general outlook, he could attain rapport and temporary acceptance in an alien environment.*

For social scientists who can maintain dual vision—looking simultaneously inward and outward, remaining detached while getting involved—participant observation is an efficacious method. But Robert Lynd and his wife brought more than

Source: Reprinted from *Small Town in Mass Society* by Arthur J. Vidich and Joseph Bensman by permission of Princeton University Press.

their responsive personalities to community studies. They brought a sophisticated conception of social class, consonant with and directly related to ideas formulated by Thorstein Veblen. A useful method combined with useful theory paid off unforgettably.

The method has been fully assimilated, proving applicable in countless cases. By and by, every region in the United States underwent similar treatment, as did New England, for instance, in Lloyd Warner's Yankee City series. The major chronicler of such work, Maurice R. Stein, in his appropriately entitled survey *The Eclipse of Community*, has sifted and skillfully summarized a number of these studies. Moving chronologically and kaleidoscopically from study to study, Stein makes clear that much is to be gleaned from them all. They are nevertheless most uneven in quality. Indeed, until the latest and best of them, *Small Town in Mass Society* by Arthur J. Vidich and Joseph Bensman, the earliest told us more about our society than did all the others added together.

Part of the trouble with the reports and analyses that issued from the pen of Lloyd Warner, his associates, and his disciples, was that of subject matter. For reasons of economy and methodology, the focus never deviated far from small or, at most, middle-sized communities. We were in a fair way of mastering all that might be known about small towns just when they had practically ceased to matter. Researchers concentrating on small towns seemed to be engaged in antiquarian activity. One could get all around such a town, as one could encompass a small group; doing so was a matter of convenience, to which the researcher deferred by sacrificing relevance. Although an urban industrial revolution had taken place, clearly sociology had not begun to catch up with its meaning.

And yet, as Vidich and Bensman were to show, a small town in upstate New York, in a genuinely rural setting, could help us unlock many a mystery about ourselves. It was mostly a matter of theoretical perspective. Armed with that perspec-

tive, the authors were able to pierce more than one veil covering and coloring provincial reality. They finally wrote not so much of a small town in mass society as of mass society in a small town. For despite appearance and ideology, they found in Springdale hardly any personal or institutional self-determination; and therein lies Springdale's typicality. The mass society reaches into this small town with cultural and corporate tentacles—and extinguishes its autonomy. That process fits into the broader scheme of things as we have recently come to know it. In previously isolated villages and newly created suburbs, we have created, all unintentionally, a state of political, economic, artistic, and recreational dependency. As our society is "rurbanized," the "rural-urban continuum" goes aglimmering. Everywhere we look, life is made up of much the same massified routine. But the citizenry deny it, refusing to believe what their senses tell them. It is therefore remarkable that two sociologists should have freed themselves from the all-encircling public and professional cant of our time long enough to look unblinkingly at things as they are, and as they are made to seem through needful distortion and rationalization.

Artists and scientists are concerned above all with the difference between illusion and reality. To practice art or science (and much of one is always in the other) often proves a thankless job. In the pursuit of that job, escaping the dominant ethos while immersed in it, Vidich and Bensman have admirably acquitted themselves. They learned and unlearned the conventional wisdom. There is apparently no other way to produce a sociological masterpiece.

PERSONALITY AND THE MINIMIZATION OF PERSONAL CONFLICTS

Leadership provides a way in which the major areas of community activity are given a semblance of order and integration, an order and integration that extend into the major institutional areas of community life. While integration thus exists at the institutional level, there is always the possibility that it does not reach down into the personal lives of the community members. In order for community integration to exist it must in some way be achieved in terms of the psychological make-up of individuals. This is not a simple problem, since we have noted that Springdalers live in a world of rich and complicated values that are often determined by both the local and external societies and their major institutions. Regardless of the conflicts between the public values incorporated by the individual and the institutional framework in which he must act, the Springdaler must necessarily somehow resolve the problems of day-to-day living; he must work, marry, have children and find some way of coming to terms with himself and his neighbors. Adhering to publicly stated values while at the same time facing the necessity of acting in immediate situations places a strain on the psychological make-up of the person.

The Social-Psychological Dilemmas of Rural Life

Conflicts between values and institutions can be expressed in four major dilemmas which confront the members of the community. These dilemmas, which are central to small-town life but which are not equally apparent and applicable to all individuals and classes, are as follows:

1. The small-town resident assumes the role of the warm, friendly, sociable, helpful good neighbor and friend. However, the forms of social competition and the struggle for individual success cause each man to examine his neighbors' pocketbook, to estimate his own gains and losses in relation to theirs, to devalue his neighbors' successes, so that by comparison he does not stand in invidious contrast, and to emphasize his own virtues in order the better to absorb his own

defeats. In the light of these contrasting behavior complexes, the individual has the psychological problem of resolving the self-image of the warm community member with the image of himself as a relatively successful member of the community in its various forms of social and economic competition.

2. The goal of success as a major value and meaning in life stands in contrast to the inaccessibility of the means to achieving success. The institutional means to achieving success are limited and are not equally available to all groups. The life career represents a succession of adjustments of success aspirations to immediate realities.

3. The illusion of democratic control over his own affairs given by the formal structure of government stands in sharp contrast to the actual basis of local politics which is controlled by external agencies. Even if the individual is in the favored group within village, town or school politics—that is, an active participant in the decision making process—his personal activity accounts less for his success than the collective activity of his group. The dynamics of political victory result more from the operation of the system than from the activities of the individual. This, of course, holds only for the more favored groups which control the informal government. Other groups have little or no basis for making a link between the illusion of democratic control and the reality of small-town political dependency. The bulk of the local shopkeepers and farmers have a "reality link" to politics only on the issues of low taxes or roads. Most of the professionals, the old aristocrats, workers, traditional farmers and all of the shack people stand entirely outside the decision making process.

4. The belief and illusion of local independence and self-determination prevent a recognition of the central place of national and state institutions in local affairs. The reality of outside institutional dominance to which the town must respond is given only subliminal, pragmatic recognition. The community simply adjusts to mechanisms which are seen

only dimly and rarely understood. Even the successful are successful primarily in accommodating to these factors rather than in initiating independent action.

At certain levels, all of these problems are not abstract and distant from the ordinary person. The farmer is aware of his economic dependence when he buys farm machinery and when he markets his products. Fluctuations in the price system and shortages of consumer goods in war and peace tend to highlight this dependency nexus in concrete fashion for almost everyone. The factory worker is in daily contact with the forces of modern industrial society. Local political and educational leaders are constantly reminded of connections to state and federal agencies through the various systems of financial grants-in-aid to the community. The life experience of everyone includes, as part of his social knowledge, ascents and descents in the class position of individuals, personal failures and aborted ambitions. There is at one level of conversation a resigned acceptance of a democratic malaise—"What good is one vote from one small town?" Hence, these problems in relatively concrete and specific terms represent real problems for specific individuals. But the contradiction between the illusions and the realities of small-town existence are a contradiction at only one level of perception since the things perceived are seen from a point of view which obscures and confuses the issues in conflict.

At another level, the problems involved are problems of simple action, since the "real world" in its totality represents a set of resistances to the personal goals, plans and aspirations of men and their illusions and to the basis around which they organize their experiences and personalities. In a sense, then, these contradictions and dilemmas in different degrees and to different persons represent personal crises at the most intimate and private level. Yet the community appears to function in what appears to be an integrated manner. The psychological techniques of adjustment to these problems take on a variety of forms.

Solutions to the Social-Psychological Dilemmas

IDIOSYNCRATIC MODES OF ADJUSTMENT

Initially it must be noted that a certain number of individuals find their "solution" in pathological behavior disorders. The social life of Springdale claims its toll of alcoholics, sexual perverts, social isolates and other forms of ill-defined disorders. These types, which remain relatively socially hidden and protected from the public view, number only 20 to 30 individuals. Their presence is highlighted and they become publicly visible only in exceptional circumstances connected with acts of violence and "sex scandals." Those who make up the group of social isolates, however, are neither seen nor heard and live their daily existence outside the mainstream of community life. How it is possible for two specific individuals, who may be technically classified as insane, to exist is a mystery to the other residents of the community. The psychological response of the pathologically disabled is based on an incapacity to deal with the problem.

Aside from sheer incapacity to deal with the problem, there are certain socially stylized ways of finding release from the psychological tensions. For some individuals a pattern of avoidance based on a withdrawal from the life of the community can provide a basis for adjustment. Some individuals pursue idiosyncratic hobbies or other forms of highly private activities; others make a fetish of pets; one is totally engaged in the collection and collation of the performance records of twenty years of athletic heroes; another builds innumerable birdhouses which he stores in a shed.

It is characteristic of some members of the old aristocracy to withdraw for years into the private sanctuary of the home, during which time they may be seen by only a handful of other people. As a class, the aristocrats withdraw from the affairs of the community and live in a private world made up of their own vanishing set.

Other groups organize their life around an autonomous ritualization of a given set of activities. Elements in the marginal middle class exhibit this by their fetishistic emulation of middle-class virtues. Life is organized on a perpetually unsuccessful attempt to become a farmer or a businessman, or attempts to achieve respectability are expressed in compulsive expressions of cleanliness, neatness and morality. However, the forms of withdrawal and ritualization present no problem with respect to definitions of individual normality as held by the community at large.

COMMUNITY DEFINITIONS OF NORMALITY

Normality in a community setting has two aspects. The first, the simple concept of insanity or lunacy, requires no explanation. The second, described above as idiosyncratic modes of adjustment, is more complex. In this case, if the "abnormal" is predictable and not immediately threatening to others, it becomes part of the normal setting. The abnormal is a secondary consideration in social situations and the individual dealing with the abnormal calculates for it and takes it into account in the same way that he must necessarily take any significant factor into account as a setting for his action. In this context the abnormality is neither more or less important nor more or less striking than any number of other factors. It is accepted, and in that sense it is normal. When it is necessary to deal with such abnormal personalities as part of one's own normal actions, it is convenient to define the abnormality as quaint, colorful, humorous or as merely another variety of human diversity, in order thereby to permit the normal flow of action. For the abnormal person in such situations this represents social acceptance of his behavior, and his behavior can continue to be regarded as normal by himself so long as it does not threaten the plans and activities of the normal. In still other instances the abnormal can be regarded as normal by the simple technique of not recognizing what for the psychiatrist would appear to be pathological. In this category, for example, would fall the small-town response to symbolic homosexuality, fetishisms, compulsive collecting and extreme forms of self-imposed social isolation. In terms of local perceptions and definitions such behavior is either not seen or, if seen, is socially acceptable.

The idiosyncratics have abandoned or ritualized their place within the social world and by doing so have also abandoned any attempt to compete socially and economically. This does not mean, however, for those whose abnormality is visible, that they are condemned for failing to fulfill the dominant norms of the public ideology since the public statement of the positive segments of the ideology is sufficiently broad to accommodate them. In public evaluations they either fulfill the image of the easy-going, uncompetitive community member and good neighbor or the image of industriousness and constructive work. In either case a basis is provided for social acceptability which, in turn, leads to a publicly acceptable self-image irrespective of the private tensions which may accompany such psychological responses to the dilemmas of small-town life.

CLASS DEVIANCY

The public self-image of the community is not held by all groups. Socially standardized deviance is permitted for one major sub-group, the shack people, even though this deviance is not approved in the dominant public ideology. The shack people openly and defiantly reject the whole fabric of the public life and live a private code of pleasure, relaxation or debauchery. Some of them in extreme reaction to the public ideology openly resist, criticize and attack it; one can assume that the playing out of this role is done with extreme consequences for the individual's psychological balance and may in some cases lead to personality disorganization. With others, on the other hand, the code of the shack is a secure position which can be supported without tension. Since they reject the dominant ideology as irrelevant to their situation and do not feel compelled to attack it, the mainstream of community values lies outside the scope of their perception. Shack life, then, involves the gratification of immediate wants and desires, irregular work habits and the organization of personal affairs around private codes. Shack dwellers do not accept pressures to conformity and scale down their aspirations to a point within the reach of personal attainment. By virtue of their rejection of the public ideology, the shack people, when they are noticed at all, become the focus of a scorn and derision such that as individuals they stand for the concrete embodiment of all that is bad and base in life.

The professional classes, at the other extreme, recognize, though by no means explicitly, the limitations which they face within their own position. They too attempt to resolve their personal conflicts by loosening the economic requirements upon themselves, which amounts to a voluntary reduction of their work load, and when necessary by seeking psychiatric help.

Even though one does not expect the psychiatrist to appear on the rural scene, he exists for and is available to those who want his services; but recourse to such measures remains a fairly closely held secret. However, the professional classes assume that a person does not have to be insane or pathologically disturbed to seek a psychiatrist. Some professionals are aware of their alienation from the dominant values of the public ideology and, partly as a consequence of this alienation, become social "crusaders" who try to reshape the public life of the town by focussing an extreme emphasis on social and cultural reforms and on activities which serve as a substitute for work. They follow this course of action even though this brings down resentment on them by those whom they regard as the less educated and more backward and frequently more successful farmers and businessmen.

THE "STRAIN TO NORMALITY"

Even when those various types of "adjustive" response are taken into account, there remain large segments of the population for whom they are inaccessible or inadequate. The various forms of social release may be inadequate for several reasons. The individual may lack the intellectual background to recognize his problem, or he may not permit himself to engage in deviant behavior because it would involve a loss in prestige. For the person who is pre-eminently concerned with respectability and for whom the normal channels for the expression of deviancy are closed, there exist other breaking points at other thresholds of personality disorganization which, when they occur, take more dramatic forms and are apt to occur suddenly. For still others the act of acting out normalcy becomes a positive value in and of itself. These "normal" types can tolerate the deviancy of others who do not constitute an immediate threat to them so long as they are able to put them in a joking situation and, hence, discount them. However, for these persons, who strive for normalcy, other psychological mechanisms prevent the disorganization of their activity and personality.

Major Modes of Adjustment

THE REPRESSION OF INCONVENIENT FACTS

One of the major modes of adjustment for the individual is to fail to see the problem at an *explicit, conscious* level and to repress from consciousness all those negative elements which intrude into personal activities and images. This does not mean, however, that the individual is unaware of the existence of the problems.

At the level of *action* (as opposed to the level of consciousness) all the factors which make for the recognition of the problems are present in the actions of the individual even though there is never any need or occasion to discuss them. The farmer's actions in relation to the structure of farm prices imply an acute sensitivity to the larger institutional forces of the mass society. He recognizes his dependence upon market conditions by adjusting his daily farm operation to current market trends. The businessman deals with wholesalers and nationally organized distributors in making up the greatest portion of his inventory and sees through these actions the dependence of his business upon the mass producers who advertise his goods and stipulate their prices. Industrial workers engaged in the production of specialized automotive and computing machine parts are forced to recognize some of the basic facts of modern industrial organization —its centralization, its interdependence and the relationship between production and employment schedules and decisions made in remote places. Public officials and the leaders of invisible government imply by their political actions a sharp awareness of the dependency of the town on outside political agencies; when possible they always look for a way to finance local projects with state funds. Indeed because of the experience of war, depression, unemployment and an uncertain dairy products market, almost the entire community is sensitized to the underlying forces which create the chasm between objective realities and socially stylized illusions.

In some circumstances the members of the small community will even discuss these conditions of reality at an explicit level, but usually this occurs only when the relevance of reality is made in impersonalized terms and without reference to any specific individual, unless it be to a personal enemy or at the level of very confidential gossip. Farmers who discuss the practical aspects of farm operations do so in the content of federal supports and subsidies and in relation to current price and credit structures as they are regulated by federal agencies and as they change with changes in administrations. Businessmen talk about outside competition, particularly supermarkets and the newer type of large-scale hard-goods retail outlets, and the consequences for them of federal "easy credit" and "cheap money policies." The reality of the small-town circumstance is clearly verbalized in the business affairs of community organizations. Members of the American Legion realize and publicly admit their powerlessness as a group in the determination of national policy—"the politicians in Washington take care of that." Town and village officials as well as school board members refer to state policy and state fiscal aid in all of their meetings almost as a matter of habit without ever fully realizing the extent of Springdale's administrative and financial dependency on state government.

All these explicit mentions of community dependence are made in the context of highly specific detailed cases. No generalization sums up these detailed statements, so that individuals are not explicitly aware of the total amount of their dependence. Particularizations prevent the realization of the total impression.

The technique of particularization is one of the most pervasive ways of avoiding reality. It operates to make possible not only the failure to recognize dependence but also the avoidance of the realities of social class and inequalities. The Springdaler is able to maintain his equalitarian ideology because he avoids generalizing about class differences. The attributes of class are seen only in terms of the particular behavior of particular persons. Thus a new purchase is talked about only in terms of the individual who makes it, rather than the class style of the purchase. There are, of course, several exceptions. The half dozen aristocratic families are recognized as a class; that is, they are seen as a collection of families who have socially desirable characteristics such as being "old families," having authentically acquired heirlooms and appearing not to be strivers. The members of the book clubs, on the other hand, are almost recognized as a class—they are at least recognized as a clique. Their glaring violation of the norms of equality forces some perception of their existence even though it leads to negative appraisals. In all other cases, however, class phenomena are dissolved into particularizations and "all other cases" involves the major activities of the major groups in the community.

The extent of the community's social, economic and political dependence is frequently made explicit by outside experts who remind the community of its helplessness as a way of exploiting fears for their own ends. The school principal reminds the school board that action which it contemplates taking can be done only at the risk of losing state aid. The milk price administrator reminds farmers that the alternative to rejecting the milk price order is no milk price order at all and a return to marketing chaos. The state road commissioner informs the village board that the new state highways must either pass over main street or bypass the village entirely. At this level, those who are involved accept the reality, but respond by resenting the agents and institutions of mass society. The act of resentment by itself, however, seems to be a psychologically insufficient response. To absorb the shock, other modes of response are available. Springdalers ridicule and joke about the outside experts, behind their backs. The inalterable decision which represents a victory for the outside world may be accepted without any further talk or mention being made of it, as if in denial of its existence. A defeat is turned to victory or is twisted in a way to make it appear to be an advantage for the community either by forgetting the central (and lost) issue or by emphasizing peripheral and pseudo issues; thus the subsidy or the state-supported road is always a victory over urban life.

Only in specialized instances is there an approximation to a conscious and explicit verbalization of the individual's objective relation to reality. Recognition is given to only parts of the reality and in a way which is not personally damaging. On the one hand an individual may highlight his own success by attributing the failure of others to the objective reality of social forces. This occurs particularly among industrial workers. For them in their work it is easy to see those aspects of the dynamics of modern society which favor the person who sees it. Those who are employed in secure industries easily see the objective reality when they contrast themselves with other local workers whose jobs are dependent upon the seasonal fluctuations of the physically remote automotive industry. Similar processes occur among farmers and businessmen who can and do attribute farm and business failures to declining prices, overproduction and inadequate profit margins. The recognition of some societal forces enables the individual to exculpate himself from personal blame by attaching the blame to impersonal forces over which he has no control. While his analysis may be correct in general form, it frequently does not account for the failure of the specific individual in situations where others do not fail.

In situations of extreme personal crisis the individual may verbalize the underlying conditions of his crisis in complete form, especially if his relationship to the informant is that of the stranger. Frustrated hopes, ambitions, and aspirations as well as blockages to opportunity, self-expression and social acceptance are apt to be revealed to the investigator. The loss of a job, a business failure, overcapitalization in a period of declining farm prices, the sudden realization that promotion is not possible, failure to secure tenure, the threat of foreclosure, the realization of hopeless indebtedness, the re-routed highway which bypasses the individual's place of business, the sudden knowledge that one has been the object of adverse gossip by friends, the gnawing awareness that one is excluded from preferred groups, the contact with outsiders who in contrast with oneself appear to be leading exciting lives—anything which places the individual in a situation highlighting his own desperate circumstance tends to raise private fears and anxieties to the public level. Only in such circumstances does the observer realize that these fears and anxieties, which imply at least a subliminal recognition of a negative reality, were present all the time even though the individual in his ordinary daily routine of activities may neither have thought nor talked about them. It is only through such cases that the observer has evidence that these are high degrees of generally unverbalized recognitions of the dilemmas. In ordinary circumstances these inconvenient facts are repressed.

The field worker, like the therapist, frequently comes in contact with more of the intimate and private than other members of the community. In the absence of the therapeutic situation of the interview, individuals do not openly express their anxieties and, in the absence of the field worker who is a stranger, demonstrate an ability to live through these crises without revealing the presence of anxiety in public. As a result the public life is always more "normal" than the private. Since this is the case, any individual who wants to participate in the public life is forced to repress his private anxieties in order to be able to express the public image which is created by similar expressions on the part of others.

With the exception of extreme crisis situations, then, the individual's recognition of the problem is not defined so sharply as to pose unsolvable personal problems which might lead him to the pathological forms of adjustment mentioned earlier. Other psychologically adjustive mechanisms also contribute to the basic pattern of adjustment by avoidance.

THE FALSIFICATION OF MEMORY AND THE SUBSTITUTION OF GOALS

The sharpness of the conflict between illusion and reality is avoided, it appears, by the unconscious altering and falsification of memories. It is a relatively easy matter to reconstruct life histories both by interviewing individuals concerning their own past and by interviewing different individuals in different age groups.

The age of youth is one of aspirations and illusions expressed in their highest and most ambitious form. The ambitions of some of the high-school youth to become scientists, executives, military officers, big league baseball players or farm operators stagger the imagination of even the successful. The limitations imposed on such ambitions by aptitude and intelligence tests at this stage are easily ignored, since parents tend to encourage ambitiousness. Even those least endowed and those with least opportunity, who appear to their elders to lack all ambition, seem rather to merely take for granted in some vague way the inevitability of success. In the stage of a few years beyond high school one still finds would-be actors, businessmen, writers, big name musicians and so forth.

By middle age or even by the age of thirty or thirty-five the youthful illusions are no longer apparent. The would-be scientist is a radio repairman, the executive is a bookkeeper, the artist is a sign painter and the actor takes a part in local drama. The professional man who in his youth imagined fame is now satisfied with a routine, drab practice. The ex-valedictorian, as a way of self-assurance, talks about his brightness in high-school days. For still others whole periods of the past seem to be completely cut off.

The realization of lack of fulfillment of aspirations and ambition might pose an unsolvable personal problem if the falsification of memory did not occur, and if the hopes and ambitions of a past decade or two remained salient in the present perspective. But the individual, as he passes through time, does not live in spans of decades or years. Rather, he lives in terms of seasons, days and hours and the focus of his attention is turned to immediate pressures, pleasures and events. Through a slow and gradual process of altering hopes and aspirations in phase with the reality situation at any given moment, the youthful illusions disappear with time. As they are in process of disappearing, other thoughts of a more concrete and specific nature occupy the individual's attention, and new goals are unconsciously substituted for those that are being abandoned. Hence, simply by thinking of other things, the individual does not come face-to-face with himself as he was and with what he wanted to be ten, twenty or thirty years ago. As a consequence, his present self, instead of entertaining the youthful dream of a 500-acre farm, entertains the plan to buy a freezer by the fall; and perhaps the immediate gratification of the home freezer at a conscious level gives him the satisfaction that the 500-acre farm might have given to the other self of his youth. In times of crisis or in the therapeutic interview the individual frequently recalls past self-images and aspirations. Personal crisis can be accomplished by self-pity and self-depreciation and in these circumstances a person is apt consciously to berate himself for his failure to achieve—a life is verbally reenacted against the standard of the youthful ambition. By collapsing time, the person comes face to face with what he is and what he hoped to be and to have. Such cases illustrate that the abandoned aspirations are never quite forgotten. They are rather repressed and at the unconscious level constitute a constant irritant which must be continuously repressed, but which in critical instances breaks through and threatens the individual's immediate adjustment.

THE SURRENDER OF ILLUSIONS

Sociologists and social psychologists have placed great emphasis upon the conflict between levels of aspiration and levels of achievement, between institutionalized goals and institutionalized means, between the largeness of personal goals and the poverty of institutional means. However, our observations in Springdale would suggest that they fail to recognize the almost infinite capacity of individual social elasticity and adaptability in dealing with immediate situations in such a way as to avoid or suppress what appears to the observer to be an obvious contradiction and a potential basis for intense personal conflict.

To be sure, not all people are equally able to come to terms with their immediate situation and reconstitute their memories. Different individuals and classes have different points and thresholds of surrender in their life cycle.

1. In a manner of speaking, the shack people surrender

their illusions before birth; the process of socialization in Springdale's shack culture does not include an internalization of any high aspirations. This, of course, can apply only to those who are born and raised in the shack. There are also those who descend to the shack and surrender their aspirations within their own lifetime. The fact that this can happen at odd times and in unexpected places serves as a phantom that haunts all other groups. When this type is publicly mentioned at all, he is despised because he is a living reminder of what could happen to oneself. This knowledge, because it is personally dangerous, is repressed and with it goes the repression of the knowledge and recognition of the very existence of the shack people. This becomes a dynamic accounting for the social invisibility of the shack people and the appearance of community integration.

2. Most workers, skilled as well as unskilled, are individuals who in their youth entertained higher aspirations than those achieved. For them their lack of opportunity to go to college or to acquire a technical skill, along with their acceptance of their first job in unskilled labor shortly after graduating from high school—all this at the age of twenty—lead to a surrender of their illusions in the relatively short period of a few years.

3. The old aristrocrats and the traditional farmers, each in their own way, retain their relatively specialized illusions in the face of the present and live exclusively in a falsified past which serves as a basis for giving meaning to their existence in their privately defined present. Their lives are organized around a present conception of the values and virtues of the life of the "good old days." Genealogical fetishisms, tombstone research, and compulsive affirmations of outmoded tastes are the behavioral reflections of private worlds. These forms of behavior are not only accepted but also emulated by other groups; the aristocrats are emulated by the professional group, which lacks local antecedents, and the traditional farmers are envied by the prosperous

farmers who are caught up in the dynamics of mass society. "Upper class," then, stands as a positive symbol for other groups and to this extent is legitimized.

4. The shopkeepers attempted to maintain illusions which are based on a conception of a world which no longer exists. The days of individual opportunity in the expanding frontier and the days prior to the automobile and mass merchandizing on which their present conceptions are based stand as an historical mockery to their failure to surrender. The shopkeepers find a partial escape by their ability to complain openly about their circumstances.

5. The prosperous farmers, up to the age of forty at least, live in the future and not at all in the past. Those who successfully survived the depression experienced a revitalization of their aspirations in the war and postwar years. Those who started in the late depression or early war years have not experienced the process of even temporary disillusionment. For them the opportunity of the frontier still exists. These farmers live in terms of future goals which still seem possible of fulfillment, and live in the present only in terms of immediate plans and daily and seasonal demands. Hence they exhibit a psychology of buoyancy and optimism. They are in a position to be able to claim that they have accomplished something and to give the appearance of self-satisfaction which to others appears as stridency and condescension.

6. The fee professionals, trained and educated outside the town, make their decision to surrender when they make their decision to migrate to and establish their practice in Springdale. What they had hoped for was to achieve a professional monopoly in a place where competition was not too great—"to be a big fish in a little pond." The teacher or other salaried professional publicly signalizes his act of surrender by buying a house in Springdale; he is no longer interested in moving to the preferred city school systems, or up the organizational hierarchy, and he accepts the fate of

slow promotions and small increments in pay characteristic of country school organizations. At this stage the town recognizes his surrender by beginning to treat him as an insider subject to all the forms of local competition.

For some professionals the decision to migrate to the town is based on a romantic image of the rural community; disenchantment comes later with firsthand experience. Some of these disenchanted leave as soon as the experience of rural life has had an impact, a fact attested to by the high rate of turnover among them. Others attempt to face disillusionment brazenly by acting, especially to their urban friends, as if no disenchantment existed; only the virtues of rural life are emphasized. And some, of course, scale down their expectations of small-town life and live affirmatively within it.

The economic reality of mobility ceilings cannot fail to be recognized by the professionals. Social mobility and activity then act as a substitute for economic mobility and activity and provide the area in which personal conflict finds its highest expression.

These processes, as they occur in the various classes, are more than a social-psychological phenomenon. They are a personal and individual phenomenon for every person who confronts illusion with reality within his own life span. When the transition from aspiration to achievement takes place, it coincides with changes in patterns of work, leisure, identification, consumption and, in fact, in almost every aspect of living. When the farmer who rents his farm realizes that there is little hope for farm ownership, he stops devoting all his energies to productive work. He may begin to buy luxury machinery and to beautify his home. He begins to sleep later in the morning and he begins to take fishing trips, or he gives up the idea of a farm completely and seeks employment in industry. In some instances the realization is so crushing that he allows himself to be reduced to the shack culture. There are instances of businessmen who, having reached the uppermost limits of business success in Springdale, have sold out "in the prime of life" and have since lived on savings within a framework of mininum consumption. An industrial worker who for five years willingly accepted factory discipline, remained loyal to the company and was a model worker, after realizing that his attempt to become a foreman would be unsuccessful, now bitterly complains of his bosses and factory work in general. In another parallel case, the individual after years of steady, sober work is now an unreliable worker and well on the path to alcoholism.

In some cases, particularly among farmers, a man who ten years ago was penniless and without illusions is now a highly successful farm operator. For such individuals the once tarnished illusions take on a new reality and reinforce the public image of the public ideology.

However, these processes are also more than personal idiosyncratic events in the life of the town. When a sufficient number of people surrender their hopes and aspirations in a given direction, the psychological and social character of the town is reconstituted and it is at this point that the linkage between social and economic forces and the personal fate of individuals take on a social character. Hence, the social and economic fate of the class of businessmen has been relatively standardized in a given direction over the past thirty years; their individual psychological responses (a scarcity perspective) have followed in the wake of the changing dimensions of the mass society. The class of farmers who have achieved success within the past fifteen years originally stemmed from various segments of the industrial and shack classes. In their transition to the class of prosperous farmer, their psychological character and perspective has changed in the direction of expansiveness. Today they comprise an important segment of the prosperous farmers and in their contemporary actions are easily differentiated from the actions of the groups from which they originated.

MUTUAL REINFORCEMENT OF THE PUBLIC IDEOLOGY

But, due to the social character of systems of illusions, these dynamic processes in character occur relatively slowly. There is silent recognition among members of the community that facts and ideas which are disturbing to the accepted system of illusions are not to be verbalized except, perhaps, as we have noted, in connection with one's enemies. Instead, the social *mores* of a small town at every opportunity demand that only those facts and ideas which support the dreamwork of everyday life are to be verbalized and selected out for emphasis and repetition. People note other people's successes, comment on them with public congratulations and expect similar recognition for themselves. Mutual complimenting is a standard form of public intercourse while failures and defeats, through known to all, are not given public expression. In this process each individual reinforces the illusions of the other. Only at the intimate level of gossip are discussions of failure tolerated.

In terms of unconscious interpersonal technique, this requires that a particular individual have a fairly sensitive knowledge of the illusions held by another person and, in interacting with him, he must act and respond to the illusion as a reality. On the other hand, one does not support a person who has completely lost his illusions. This is a *faux pas* and an insult and contrary to all forms of interpersonal etiquette; in such cases the relationship is carried on on the basis of formal greetings and inconsequential small talk—the weather, hunting or baseball scores. What is thus involved is a series of graded levels of conversation and conversational content between individuals at different levels of adherence to illusions of success. The code of the proper conversational level is as proper as the code of formalities among the Japanese. The social learning necessary to know what conversational tone to take with other individuals is elaborately involved and constitutes the etiquette of public conversation. In his first contacts with the community the outside observer quickly learns the habit of avoiding direct discussions of reality after he meets with negative or blank responses to his own *faux pas* in this area. The observer's adjustment to community life consists in large part of learning these codes of conversational etiquette. In the small town, at least at a subliminal level, people are recognized and evaluated on the basis of their likemindedness with respect to the publicly stated social dream.

AVOIDANCE OF PUBLIC STATEMENTS OF DISENCHANTMENT AND THE EXCLUSION OF THE DISENCHANTED

The public nature of the facts of mutual support are clearly demonstrated by differences in level of discussion depending upon size and composition of group. In personal conversations with intimate friends, expressions of disenchantment are likely to be heard quite frequently. As the group becomes larger and less intimate, the public ideology becomes a more prominent and forceful focus of attention. Individuals who express disenchantment in private conversations are less likely to speak in larger groups, or, if they do, they change their tone. But, even more than this, those individuals and groups who have publicly expressed disenchantment find it difficult both to participate in and to accept the type of rhetoric and exhortation characteristic of public life. As a consequence, the disenchanted withdraw from the public life of the community and, hence, by default leave the field of public and particularly organizational life open to the exponents of the world of illusion. It is for this reason that the public life is dominated by the system of illusion even though many persons do not in an inner way hold to its tenets.

Moreover, public meetings serve as ceremonial occasions

at which all of the illusions enunciated reflect the public ideology. In light of the tenacity with which the exponents of the public ideology cling to it, it becomes understandable why it is possible to hear day after day and week after week what to an outsider appears to be an endless repetition of high-sounding clichés and sentimental rhetoric. The dominant, publicly repeated ideology proclaims Springdale to be "a wholesome friendly place, the best place to bring up children, and made up of ordinary people, just folks, trying to make their community a better place to live. Nobody here has to worry about having friends, all you have to do is be friendly yourself. No problems are too big for Springdale, it's the outsiders that cause all the trouble. People here have a lot of community spirit, you can always get people to take part, but usually the busiest people are the most reliable. One thing about Springdale, nobody is excluded, this is a democratic town. Anybody who tries to run things gets pushed down, but fast. If you join clubs you can learn things and have a lot of fun too. Everybody was invited and fun was had by all." These and other expressions, at a verbal level, conceal the basic dynamics of the town.

THE EXTERNALIZATION OF THE SELF

All of the above forms of avoidance occur only at the verbal and symbolic levels. Adjustment at this level would be inadequate if other forms of action which make possible other forms of involvement and commitment were not available to the exponents of the public ideology. The greatest dangers to a system of illusions which is threatened by an uncompromising reality are introspection and thought. That is, the individual cannot scrutinize himself to the point where he sees facts which would threaten the position he is in and over which he has little control. For, in seeing such facts, in confronting the reality beneath his illusions, in juxtaposing earlier aspirations against the achievement of age, he would find it difficult and painful to follow through on the path which he must take in his present situation to survive in that situation. Hence, he must falsify these facts in order to live in the present. In order to succeed in avoiding the reality of the situation, he must give a major portion of the life span to developing forms and techniques of self-avoidance. However, it is not too difficult to find these techniques and the techniques themselves are not too inconsistent with the public statement of the ideology.

Work as Self-Avoidance / The major technique of self-avoidance is work. The farmer and the businessman drive themselves in their work almost to the point of exhaustion. It would be a mistake to assume that sheer economic advantage even under an economic ideology could produce the fabulous work efforts and activities of these groups. The farmer is always occupied with his plans, his chores or his field work and in this process of activity he always has something external to himself to think about. In the morning, even before eating, he immediately goes to his chores, which he performs in a state of half-sleep. By the time he is awake and aware of himself he already finds himself integrated into a routine of activities which absorb his thoughts. His day represents a continuous succession of activities and tasks. While engaged in the execution of any given task his mind is preoccupied with laying plans for succeeding activities. And so through the hours, the days and the seasons alternatives to self-preoccupation are constantly available. The objects of thought are relatively immediate, practical and mundane things.

Similarly, the businessman applies himself to a great number of diversified activities which provide him with innumerable small jobs which are never finished. He shifts from waiting on a customer, to restocking his shelves, to checking his inventories, to sweeping the floor and so on and on. Such activity partly serves the purpose of enabling a person not to come to terms with himself.

The problem is much more difficult for the industrial worker, whose work on the moving line ties him to a given spot in an activity which is not too personally involving. It is difficult to know what occupies his thoughts during his working hours, but his inability to cope with introspection and self-reflection is indicated by the intensity with which he pursues work outside of the job. His home is a place not just for living, but more important, requires maintenance and constant improvement. Painting, landscaping, gardening, the addition of a new garage, the insulation of the attic—all these and other projects with the passing of seasons make continuous demands for his attention. His automobile is regarded with affection, almost like an intimate companion, and treated with the utmost care. The amount of time given to polishing, maintaining, tinkering with and talking about cars staggers the imagination. One cannot assume even with the capital investment represented in a home and car that these activities can be explained as reflecting economic interests. To an important degree they represent extensions of the personality and have the psychological meaning of making externalization possible by providing meaningful opportunities for a continuous outer involvement.

Sociability and Passivity as Self-Externalization / Productive work is only one of a number of ways of accomplishing the same purpose. Social activities in community organizations and in informal social groups, where emphasis is placed upon the constant exchange of personalities, social forms and "small talk," can be involving for all but the schizoid personalities. Springdale offers a multitude of opportunities for involvement in socially engaging activities. The innumerable committees, organizational meetings, card parties and canvasses are available for those who are not otherwise involved. The continuous emphasis on social and organizational activities by the professional groups can be accounted for not only in terms of their rejection of economic mobility but also as a substitute therapy for the externalization of personality by work. In both instances the form of the therapy is consonant with the ideology.

Religious activities such as suppers, choirs and fund raising involve a great deal of physical and social effort and support the process of continuous externalization. Conversely, the "spiritual" content of a religious doctrine potentially involves the application of purely religious and ethical messages to the life of the individual. The religious can theoretically force introspection and self-awareness by raising the question of how the quality of life is related to God and doctrines. This, however, is a form of introspection and awareness that would threaten the defense of daily living in the community. In order to avoid such confrontation of the self, the purely religious aspects of religion are avoided and de-emphasized while the social and administrative aspects are accentuated; in this way religion contributes to the life of the community and facilitates personal adjustment. This applies to all religious groups in the community except the Baptists. For them religion means a repudiation of the content of community values, but the same psychological techniques used by other groups are used by them with reference to the Baptist community.

The Baptist church is filled with activities whose appearances are less secular, but which have the same objective and external character to which the Baptist can submit. The exaltation of the Baptist's private life in the feeling of salvation enables him to justify his rejection of community values. Moreover, in terms of Baptist fundamentalism, the dilemmas of modern society are not viewed as important; hence, the psychological feeling of salvation is raised to a level which can preclude almost all mundane matters. The importance that the Baptist attaches to theology and the emotion of achieved states of grace can exist only against the background of a feeling of relief from the imminence of the world.

For those who can not or will not participate in the public life of the town there are always the media of mass culture, though these are potentially dangerous because not all forms of private recreation are amenable to the same needs. One can, for example, buy a book by a serious author which, if read, could turn a personality into itself. Reading is an intimate, solitary experience which, if accompanied by thought, can lead an individual into self-reflection and to a consideration of the meaning of his existence in relation to the outer world. But there is little evidence that these processes occur in Springdale. Reading tends to be regarded as a technique of self-improvement, a form of recreation; it can become a part of routine habitual behavior, as, for example, reading the daily newspaper at a given hour in a given chair. Practical books on the techniques of living, do-it-yourself manuals and correspondence course textbooks form the bulk of the literary diet. Fortunately, in addition, since inexpensive books are easily available, the purveyors of the mass media have taken every precaution, it seems, to allow the individual to escape from his immediate situation into worlds of violence, sex, sadism, humor and romanticism.

Sports represent a halfway mark between work and social and passive participation, all of which place a high premium on the otherness and externality of activity. In Springdale training in athletic interests and proficiency begins at an early age. The young adult in the modern age has a legacy of physical skills to fall back on if and when psychological conditions require it. Active sports like baseball play an important part in the years of robust youth. They furthermore constitute an important outlet for the occupationally dissatisfied, the underemployed, and for those for whom other activities are not sufficiently absorbing. Physical skill and effort exhaust the body and prevent meditative self-examination.

Automatization of Personality / In those cases where some form of personality externalization is not present and when at the same time all forms of introspectiveness and self-insight are absent, what is left of the personality is the dulled, autonomic ritualization of behavior where inner control is exercised to such an extent that no disturbing interferences are allowed to enter into thought. The individual adheres to a fixed and repetitive daily, weekly and seasonal routine in which no one day, week or year exhibits any significant deviation from any other. The chief instruments of discipline are the clock, the calendar and the weather which are used as significant signs in guiding the individual from one activity to the next so that thought, even at the level of making elementary choices, can be eliminated. Personal and social life becomes barren, and the personal mechanics and daily routine of living become the end-all of existence. All types of activities whose operation is based upon an objective, external, automatic rhythm to which an individual can bend himself serve the function of enabling him to lose himself in an objective ceremony. Thus an individual avoids dealing with himself except insofar as he does so through the instrument of an external mechanism. The individual can avoid physical isolation and the threat of loneliness which it implies by engaging in the quasi-automatic ritual of social agencies. The rituals of religious practice and their fixed time and place of occurrence, the procedural rituals of formal meetings and the ceremonialisms of parades, spectatorship and the public festivities of holiday occasions—all link the automatic individual to the automatic segments of public life. But more than this, other activities which are not intrinsically rituals are ritualized in order to permit such individuals to function publicly. It is at this point that inoffensive stylized humor, standardized greetings which are given the appearance of intimacy by the cheerfulness with which they are spoken and the sheer volume of talk devoted to the weather and jokes gain meaning as public extensions of private lives organized around external rituals. In these types of adjustment, loss of self becomes the price one pays for attempting to maintain one's equilibrium in an alien world. This aspect of self-externalization is present in the social activities surrounding all classes and institutions; it is almost totally characteristic of the ritualistic segment of the marginal middle class.

Generalized Anxiety / Social and self-understanding is not, however, an easy solution to these problems. There are individuals in Springdale who possess these qualities, but their life in the community involves other types of problems. First, although they may have an understanding of what are the dilemmas in the community, understanding is not a solution to the dilemmas, and so they are left in the position of either trying to determine what to do or of not knowing what to do. As a consequence of the difficulty of finding a solution, they are disturbed about their situation and tend to have free floating anxieties. In addition, they are disturbed because they cannot communicate their insight and perception of the problem to other members of the community because such insight and perception are a threat to the illusions of the externally oriented segments of the population. There are some who, under these circumstances, have sufficient inner strength to be tolerant, kind and understanding. They contain, absorb and live with their own perceptions and insights even though this is at a great cost to themselves. There are a few who are in personal and intimate contact with each other. This is true of one minister and one teacher who both seem to understand the problems facing the community. In their public role neither is permitted an open expression of their understanding since such expression would involve them in conflict and would hurt others. The minister, then, is forced to provide a social religion to the public while he practices a religion for himself which he believes to be consistent with Christianity. The school teacher does occasionally verbalize his understanding. However, his ideas are regarded as so strange and so unrelated to the practical activities of life in the community that he is regarded as a harmless and humorous oddity, and this is a role that he consciously has come to play. He survives in the community by not threatening anyone, but his survival is based on the fact that no one wants to understand him. In finding each other and in gaining a basis for communication, the condition of which is a recognition of reality, such persons create a private world which sustains a detachment, in some sense, from the dominant illusions of the community.

The various patterns of externalization all have one trait in common; *they occur in a continuous sequence in which no single activity or event is likely to resolve the problem for a specific individual for any length of time.* The activities of externalization must continuously be repeated and reinforced with little surcease. This is why illness, retirement and other unusual circumstances which make for prospects of "time on your hands" are dreaded and why social activities are organized to prevent social isolation on such occasions. The organized "visitations" of the ill and the "sunshine" committees of almost all organizations help to keep the bedridden and the incapacitated involved. Retirement from active work, particularly among farmers and businessmen, tends not to occur. Instead, progression into old age is merely marked by a reduction in work load in consonance with the reduction in physical ability. However, old age and retirement among people who are forced to retire at a fixed age creates problems since alternative work patterns are difficult to develop in the advanced ages, and it is for this group that the community does not provide easily available substitute patterns of involvement. It is interesting that the break in continuous activity for this group has in recent years found its resolution in migration to the cities of Florida which hold out the promise of a program of activities for the retired. But, to complete the picture, those who for one reason or another must remain in the town make a successful adjustment by resurrecting and living within an earlier period of their lives. Numerous examples exist among the aged: the man who for all practical purposes of conversation and thought lives in the decade of the Twenties; the woman who talks of living acquaintances, not seen for ten or fifteen years, as she remembers them when last seen; the old-timers who seek each other out to talk of the town as it was forty years ago; and, of course, senility has its normal rate of occurrence. In such cases life is arrested at a point which is consonant with the individual's retreat and withdrawal. This form of resolution is a frequent occurrence which is treated with a sympathetic tolerance by the rest of the community, so that the illusions around which such lives are organized are not challenged.

Social Structure and the Psychology of Adjustment

The emphasis on the continuous nature of work and other socially therapeutic activities indicates that the basic problems confronting the community are unresolved. The dilemmas arising from the contrast between illusion and reality, between idea and experience, are as continuously present as are the means for exorcizing them. This means that all forms of stability in the community are temporary. Minor and violent shifts in the dimensions of community life are always possible, though they may occur after long years of apparent stability during which illusion has been accepted as "reality" and has not been challenged by reality as experienced.

If a sudden, negative and disastrous shift in the outside situation occurs, the defense mechanisms of the affected members of the community may not be able to accommodate to the strains placed upon the personality. A single event such as a collapse of farm prices or an inflationary trend could challenge a whole class of individuals whoes life organization is based on similar illusions. But, since change for those who live through it and perceive it appears to occur slowly, new and unrecognized forms of personal illusion and institutional resolution of personal problems are an ever-recurrent possibility. For this reason bizarre forms of personality disorganization can occur in unexpected ways and at odd times in unexpected quarters. And for this reason, furthermore, the prediction of future events lies outside the scope of simple projection of present trends.

In the meantime the individual in the community must continue to live out his daily life. The various forms of illusion and defense enable him to make the most of his situation in a world over which he has relatively little control. These very same forms of illusion and defense enable him to perform his life in a useful and productive way and, to a certain extent, to live a full and not wholly unenjoyable life. They enable the individual to get along with his friends and neighbors, to be more often than not considerate and helpful. And for those who must bear the burden of uncontrolled events, they constitute the mechanisms by which the person can attempt to gain some of his own goals in a community where the attainment of individual goals is not always consonant with the goals held by others.

The psychological processes are doubly important in terms of the "objective problems" faced by the community. Objectively, the community members live in a world which they do not control. They come to this world, however, with a belief in their ability to shape their own destinies. In fact, in almost every sphere of their lives they find their inherited beliefs and traditions at odds with their institutions and social environment.

But the people of Springdale are unwilling to recognize the defeat of their values, their personal impotence in the face of larger events and any failure in their way of life. By techniques of self-avoidance and self-deception, they strive to avoid facing issues which, if recognized, would threaten the total fabric of their personal and social existence. Instead of facing the issues, they make compromises and modify their behavior in some cases, and reaffirm their traditional patterns in other cases. They do this, however, without any overt conscious recognition of the basic problems.

Because they do not recognize their defeat, they are not defeated. The compromises, the self-deception and the self-avoidance are mechanisms which work; for, in operating on the basis of contradictory, illogical and conflicting assumptions, they are able to cope in their day-to-day lives with their immediate problems in a way that permits some degree of satsfaction, recognition and achievement. There are many ways in which one could note that Springdalers do not achieve the optimum material and psychological rewards for their strivings, but such achievement does not appear to lie within the framework of their social structure. Life, then, consists in making an adjustment that is as satisfactory as possible within a world which is not often tractable to basic wishes and desires.

GROWING UP ABSURD
Paul Goodman

Editors and readers who enjoyed a foretaste of Growing Up Absurd *(parts of which appeared in little magazines like* Dissent *and* Commentary*) knew that they were having no ordinary experience. Here, on display in rational discourse, were half-forgotten qualities of the mind and heart whose bearer was an urban American intellectual. Empathy, luminosity, sensitivity, simplicity, profundity, practicality—all that was apparent in the first few essays to have gained wide attention from the pen of a writer who had already labored long and well but in relative obscurity.*

In 1947 a book called Communitas: Ways of Livelihood and Means of Life *made its appearance. The authors were Percival Goodman, associate professor of architecture at Columbia University, and his younger brother, Paul. Reissued as a paperback in 1960, the book contained a biographical note concerning the junior author, which reads: "Paul Goodman was born in 1911, received a B.A. from the City College of New York and a Ph.D. from the University of Chicago. He is a novelist, poet, critic and playwright. He is the author of many books, including* The Facts of Life, The Structure of Literature, Kafka's Prayer, *and his most recent novel,* The Empire City *(1959)." The sketch necessarily omits more than it tells. We are presumably in the presence of a man with impeccable academic credentials and a literary bent—neither one at that time much noticed by the world. Goodman earned his doctorate in philosophy, and it is therefore not surprising that he should dedicate a technical academic exercise* (The Structure of Literature, *1954*) *to three famous philosophers—Richard McKeon, Rudolph Carnap, and Morris Cohen—capped, to be sure, by the otherwise unknown Dr. J. Klein, "Who taught me what criticism is when he asked our high-school class on* Macbeth, *'Who is the* he *in 'He has no children'?"*

If Goodman is a philosopher, he has rarely chosen to philosophize in the conventional manner. No more has the teacher Goodman, tirelessly addressing students, ever become an academician, or the novelist, poet, playwright, and critic become a workaday man of letters. His early fiction, well received in the little experimental quarterlies, was somewhat surrealist. Years ago, he became an unorthodox clinical psychologist, and as such, co-author of Gestalt Therapy, *with F. S. Perls and Ralph Hefferline. Hardly anyone knew* that *book until recently; now like almost all his work, old and new, it too is in print. Goodman is a geyser; his rich waters spout in every direction; they may even be sinking in here and there, not least of all in the rocky soil of American sociology.*

It is no small achievement to have irrigated such soil. Nevertheless, intelligent laymen and a circle of receptive social scientists have been reached and refreshed by Paul Goodman, whose ideas have induced them to discard many a cherished preconception. Goodman, unencumbered by institutional affiliations, uninterested in foundation grants or federal funds, unattached, freewheeling, crusty, utopian, eccentric, beyond status-striving, contemptuous of timeservers and careerists, remains an unassimilable offbeat pacifist libertarian who has done more for us than any fistful of his "professional" opposites. One wild man like Goodman is worth a dozen hotshots from urban sociology, industrial relations, city planning, and criminology. Yet all these subjects are illuminated even in the first two chapters of Growing Up Absurd *with which we believe we have added luster to this anthology.*

Goodman is enormously suggestive on any topic that falls

within his range, and his range is comprehensive. Since he is politically committed, deeply involved in the unpopular peace movement, a real democratic citizen eager to keep abreast of national and international problems, there is no situation—be it mundane, vulgar, or beautiful—that fails to arouse his interest, no petty injustice that fails to provoke his indignation.

He has a vision of the good life, and of what might be done to attain it. The vision is faulty—less can be done than Goodman sometimes supposes—but sociology has no one else to thank so much for sharpening its perception of what is realizable, and of what may be worthy even though unrealizable. We are all the better, the more civilized, perceptive, and incorruptible for having been influenced by him.

JOBS

1.

It's hard to grow up when there isn't enough man's work. There is "nearly full employment" (with highly significant exceptions), but there get to be fewer jobs that are necessary or unquestionably useful; that require energy and draw on some of one's best capacities; and that can be done keeping one's honor and dignity. In explaining the widespread troubles of adolescents and young men, this simple objective factor is not much mentioned. Let us here insist on it.

By "man's work" I mean a very simple idea, so simple that it is clearer to ingenuous boys than to most adults. To produce necessary food and shelter is man's work. During most of economic history most men have done this drudging work, secure that it was justified and worthy of a man to do it, though often feeling that the social conditions under which they did it were *not* worthy of a man, thinking, "It's better to die than to live so hard"—but they worked on. When the environment is forbidding, as in the Swiss Alps or the Aran Islands, we regard such work with poetic awe. In emergencies it is heroic, as when the bakers of Paris maintained the supply of bread during the French Revolution, or the milkman did not miss a day's delivery when the bombs recently tore up London.

At present there is little such subsistence work. In *Communitas* my brother and I guess that one-tenth of our economy is devoted to it; it is more likely one-twentieth. Production of food is actively discouraged. Farmers are not wanted and the young men go elsewhere. (The farm population is now less than 15 per cent of the total population.) Building, on the contrary, is immensely needed. New York City needs 65,000 new units a year, and is getting, net, 16,000. One would think that ambitious boys would flock to this work. But here we find that building, too, is discouraged. In a great city, for the last twenty years hundreds of thousands have been ill housed, yet we do not see science, industry, and labor enthusiastically enlisted in finding the quick solution to a definite problem. The promoters are interested in long-term investments, the real estate men in speculation, the city planners in votes and graft. The building craftsmen cannily see to it that their own numbers remain few, their methods antiquated, and their rewards high. None of these people is much interested in providing shelter, and nobody is at all interested in providing new manly jobs.

Once we turn away from the absolutely necessary subsistence jobs, however, we find that an enormous proportion of our production is not even unquestionably useful. Everybody knows and also feels this, and there has recently been a flood of books about our surfeit of honey, our insolent chariots, the follies of exurban ranch houses, our hucksters and our synthetic demand. Many acute things are said about this useless production and advertising, but not much about the workmen producing it and their frame of mind; and nothing at all, so far as I have noticed, about the plight of a young fellow looking for a manly occupation. The eloquent critics of the American way of life have themselves been so seduced by it that they think only in terms of selling commodities and point out that the goods are valueless; but they fail to see that people are being wasted and their skills insulted. (To give an analogy, in the many gleeful onslaughts on the Popular Culture that have appeared in recent years, there has been little thought of the plight of the honest artist cut off from his audience and sometimes, in public arts such as theater and architecture, from his medium.)

What is strange about it? American society has tried so hard and so ably to defend the practice and theory of production for profit and not primarily for use that now it has succeeded in making its jobs and products profitable and useless.

2.

Consider a likely useful job. A youth who is alert and willing but not "verbally intelligent"—perhaps he has quit high school at the eleventh grade (the median), as soon as he legally could—chooses for auto mechanic. That's a good job, familiar to him, he often watched them as a kid. It's careful and dirty at the same time. In a small garage it's sociable; one can talk to the customers (girls). You please people in trouble by fixing their cars, and a man is proud to see rolling out on its own the car that limped in behind the tow truck. The pay is as good as the next fellow's, who is respected.

So our young man takes this first-rate job. But what when he then learns that the cars have a built-in obsolescence, that the manufacturers do not want them to be repaired or repairable? They have lobbied a law that requires them to provide spare parts for only five years (it used to be ten). Repairing the new cars is often a matter of cosmetics, not mechanics; and the repairs are pointlessly expensive—a tail fin might cost $50. The insurance rates therefore double and treble on old and new cars both. Gone are the days of keeping the jalopies in good shape, the artist-work of a proud mechanic. But everybody is paying for foolishness, for in fact the new models are only trivially superior; the whole thing is a sell.

It is hard for the young man now to maintain his feelings

of justification, sociability, serviceability. It is not surprising if he quickly becomes cynical and time-serving, interested in a fast buck. And so, on the notorious *Reader's Digest* test the investigators (coming in with a disconnected coil wire) found that 63 per cent of mechanics charged for repairs they didn't make, and lucky if they didn't also take out the new fuel pump and replace it with a used one (65 per cent of radio repair shops, but *only* 49 per cent of watch repairmen "lied, over-charged, or gave false diagnoses").

There is an hypothesis that an important predisposition to juvenile delinquency is the combination of low verbal intelligence with high manual intelligence, delinquency giving a way of self-expression where other avenues are blocked by lack of schooling. A lad so endowed might well apply himself to the useful trade of mechanic.

3.

Most manual jobs do not lend themselves so readily to knowing the facts and fraudulently taking advantage oneself. In factory jobs the workman is likely to be ignorant of what goes on, since he performs a small operation on a big machine that he does not understand. Even so, there is evidence that he has the same disbelief in the enterprise as a whole, with a resulting attitude of profound indifference.

Semi-skilled factory operatives are the largest category of workmen. (I am leafing through the U. S. Department of Labor's *Occupational Outlook Handbook,* 1957.) Big companies have tried the devices of applied anthropology to enhance the loyalty of these men to the firm, but apparently the effort is hopeless, for it is found that a thumping majority of the men don't care about the job or the firm; they couldn't care less and you can't make them care more. But this is *not* because of wages, hours, or working conditions, or management. On the contrary, tests that show the men's indifference to the company show also their (unaware) admiration for the way the company has designed and manages the plant; it is their very model of style, efficiency, and correct behavior. (Robert Dubin, for the U. S. Public Health Service.) Maybe if the men understood more, they would admire less. The union and the grievance committee take care of wages, hours, and conditions; these are the things the workmen themselves fought for and won. (Something was missing in that victory, and we have inherited the failure as well as the success.) The conclusion must be that workmen are indifferent to the job because of its intrinsic nature: it does not enlist worth-while capacities, it is not "interesting"; it is not his, he is not "in" on it; the product is not really useful. And indeed, research directly on the subject, by Frederick Herzberg on Motivation to Work, shows that it is defects in the intrinsic aspects of the job that make workmen "unhappy." A survey of the literature (in Herzberg's *Job Attitudes*) shows that Interest is second in importance only to Security, whereas Wages, Conditions, Socializing, Hours, Ease, and Benefits are far less important. But foremen, significantly enough, think that the most important thing to the workman is his wages. (The investigators do not seem to inquire about the usefulness of the job—as if a primary purpose of *working* at a job were not that it is good *for* something! My guess is that a large factor in "Security" is the resigned reaction to not being able to take into account whether the work on one's hands is useful for anything; for in a normal life situation, if what we do is useful, we feel secure about being needed. The other largest factor in "Security" is, I think, the sense of being needed for one's unique contribution, and this is measured in these tests by the primary importance the workers assign to being "in" on things and to "work done being appreciated." (Table prepared by Labor Relations Institute of New York.)

Limited as they are, what a remarkable insight such studies give us, that men want to do valuable work and work that is somehow theirs! But they are thwarted.

Is not this the "waste of our human resources"?

The case is that by the "sole-prerogative" clause in union

contracts the employer has the sole right to determine what is to be produced, how it is to be produced, what plants are to be built and where, what kinds of machinery are to be installed, when workers are to be hired and laid off, and how production operations are to be rationalized. (Frank Marquart.) There is *none* of this that is inevitable in running a machine economy; but *if* these are the circumstances, it is not surprising that the factory operatives' actual code has absolutely nothing to do with useful service or increasing production, but is notoriously devoted to "interpersonal relations"; (1) don't turn out too much work; (2) don't turn out too little work; (3) don't squeal on a fellow worker; (4) don't act like a big-shot. This is how to belong.

4.

Let us go on to the Occupational Outlook of those who are verbally bright. Among this group, simply because they cannot help asking more general questions—e.g., about utility—the problem of finding man's work is harder, and their disillusion is more poignant.

He explained to her why it was hard to find a satisfactory job of work to do. He had liked working with the power drill, testing the rocky envelope of the shore, but then the employers asked him to take a great oath of loyalty.

"What!" cried Rosalind. "Do you have scruples about telling a convenient fib?"

"No, I don't. But I felt uneasy about the sanity of the director asking me to swear to opinions on such complicated questions when my job was digging with a power drill. I can't work with a man who might suddenly have a wild fit."

. . . "Why don't you get a job driving one of the big trucks along here?"

"I don't like what's in the boxes," said Horatio sadly. "It could just as well drop in the river—and I'd make mistakes and drop it there."

"Is it bad stuff?"

"No, just useless. It takes the heart out of me to work at something useless and I begin to make mistakes. I don't mind putting profits in somebody's pocket—but the job also has to be useful for something."

. . . "Why don't you go to the woods and be a lumberjack?"

"No! they chop down the trees just to print off the *New York Times*!"

(*The Empire City*, III, i, 3.)

The more intelligent worker's "indifference" is likely to appear more nakedly as profound resignation, and his cynicism may sharpen to outright racketeering.

"Teaching," says the *Handbook*, "is the largest of the professions." So suppose our now verbally bright young man chooses for teacher, in the high school system or, by exception, in the elementary schools if he understands that the elementary grades are the vitally important ones and require the most ability to teach well (and of course they have less prestige). Teaching is necessary and useful work; it is real and creative, for it directly confronts an important subject matter, the children themselves; it is obviously self-justifying; and it is ennobled by the arts and sciences. Those who practice teaching do not for the most part succumb to cynicism or indifference—the children are too immediate and real for the teachers to become callous—but, most of the school systems being what they are, can teachers fail to come to suffer first despair and then deep resignation? Resignation occurs psychologically as follows: frustrated in essential action, they nevertheless cannot quit in anger, because the task is necessary; so the anger turns inward and is felt as resignation. (Naturally, the resigned teacher may then put on a happy face and keep very busy.)

For the job is carried on under impossible conditions of overcrowding and saving public money. *Not* that there is not enough social wealth, but first things are not put first. Also, the school system has spurious aims. It soon becomes clear that the underlying aims are to relieve the home and keep the kids quiet; or, suddenly, the aim is to produce physicists. Timid supervisors, bigoted clerics, and ignorant school boards forbid real teaching. The emotional release and sexual expression of the children are taboo. A commercially debauched popular culture makes learning disesteemed. The academic curriculum is mangled by the demands of reactionaries, liberals, and demented warriors. Progressive methods are emasculated. Attention to each case is out of the question, and all the children—the bright, the average, and the dull—are systematically retarded one way or another, while the teacher's hands are tied. Naturally the pay is low—for the work is hard, useful, and of public concern, all three of which qualities tend to bring lower pay. It is alleged that the low pay is why there is a shortage of teachers and why the best do not choose the profession. My guess is that the best avoid it because of the certainty of miseducating. Nor are the best *wanted* by the system, for they are not safe. Bertrand Russell was rejected by New York's City College and would not have been accepted in a New York grade school.

5.

Next, what happens to the verbally bright who have no zeal for a serviceable profession and who have no particular scientific or artistic bent? For the most part they make up the tribes of salesmanship, entertainment, business management, promotion, and advertising. Here of course there is no question of utility or honor to begin with, so an ingenuous boy will not look here for a manly career. Nevertheless, though we can pass by the sufferings of these well-paid callings, much publicized by their own writers, they are important to our theme because of the model they present to the growing boy.

Consider the men and women in TV advertisements, demonstrating the product and singing the jingle. They are clowns and mannequins, in grimace, speech, and action. And again, what I want to call attention to in this advertising is not the economic problem of synthetic demand, and not the cultural problem of Popular Culture, but the human problem that these are human beings working as clowns; that the writers and designers of it are human beings thinking like idiots; and the broadcasters and underwriters know and abet what goes on—

> Juicily glubbily
> *Blubber* is dubbily
> delicious and nutritious
> —eat it, Kitty, it's good.

Alternately, they are liars, confidence men, smooth talkers, obsequious, insolent, etc., etc.

The popular-cultural content of the advertisements is somewhat neutralized by *Mad* magazine, the bible of the twelve-year-olds who can read. But far more influential and hard to counteract is the *fact* that the workmen and the patrons of this enterprise are human beings. (Highly approved, too.) They are not good models for a boy looking for a manly job that is useful and necessary, requiring human energy and capacity, and that can be done with honor and dignity. They are a good sign that not many such jobs will be available.

The popular estimation is rather different. Consider the following: "As one possible aid, I suggested to the Senate subcommittee that they alert celebrities and leaders in the fields of sports, movies, theater and television to the help they can offer by getting close to these [delinquent] kids. By giving them positive 'heroes' they know and can talk to, instead of the misguided image of trouble-making buddies, they could aid greatly in guiding these normal aspirations for fame and status into wholesome progressive channels." (Jackie Robinson, who was formerly on the Connecticut Parole Board.) Or again: when a mass cross-section of Oklahoma high school juniors and seniors was asked which living person they would like to be, the boys named Pat Boone, Ricky Nelson, and President Eisenhower; the girls chose Debbie Reynolds, Elizabeth Taylor, and Natalie Wood.

The rigged Quiz shows, which created a scandal in 1959, were a remarkably pure distillate of our American cookery. We start with the brute facts that (a) in our abundant expanding economy it is necessary to give money away to increase spending, production, and profits; and (b) that this money must not be used for useful public goods in taxes, but must be plowed back as "business expenses," even though there is a shameful shortage of schools, housing, etc. Yet when the TV people at first tried simply to give the money away for nothing (for having heard of George Washington), there was a great Calvinistic outcry that this was demoralizing (we may gamble on the horses only to improve the breed). So they hit on the notion of a real contest with prizes. But then, of course, they could not resist making the show itself profitable, and competitive in the (also rigged) ratings with other shows, so the experts in the entertainment-commodity manufactured phony contests. And to cap the climax of fraudulence, the hero of the phony contests proceeded to persuade himself, so he says, that his behavior was educational!

The behavior of the networks was correspondingly typical. These business organizations claim the loyalty of their employees, but at the first breath of trouble they were ruthless and disloyal to their employees. (Even McCarthy was loyal to his gang.) They want to maximize profits and yet be absolutely safe from any risk. Consider their claim that they knew nothing about the fraud. But if they watched the shows that they were broadcasting, they could not *possibly,* as professionals, not have known the facts, for there were obvious type-casting, acting, plot, etc. If they are not professionals, they are incompetent. But if they don't watch what they broadcast, then they are utterly irresponsible and on what grounds do they have the franchises to the channels? We may offer them the choice: that they are liars or incompetent or irresponsible.

The later direction of the investigation seems to me more important, the inquiry into the bribed disk-jockeying; for this deals directly with our crucial economic problem of synthesized demand, made taste, debauching the public and preventing the emergence and formation of natural taste. In such circumstances there cannot possibly be an American culture; we are doomed to nausea and barbarism. And *then* these baboons have the effrontery to declare that they give the people what the people demand and that they are not responsible for the level of the movies, the music, the plays, the books!

Finally, in leafing through the *Occupational Outlook Handbook*, we notice that the armed forces employ a large number. Here our young man can become involved in a worldwide demented enterprise, with personnel and activities corresponding.

6.

Thus, on the simple criteria of unquestioned utility, employing human capacities, and honor, there are not enough worthy jobs in our economy for average boys and adolescents to grow up toward. There are of course thousands of jobs that are worthy and self-justifying, and thousands that can be made so by stubborn integrity, especially if one can work as an independent. Extraordinary intelligence or special talent, also, can often carve out a place for itself—conversely, their usual corruption and waste are all the more sickening. But by and large our economic society is *not* geared for the cultivation of its young or the attainment of important goals that they can work toward.

This is evident from the usual kind of vocational guidance, which consists of measuring the boy and finding some place in the economy where he can be fitted; chopping him down to make him fit or neglecting him if they can't find his slot. Personnel directors do not much try to scrutinize the economy in order to find some activity that is a real opportunity for the boy, and then to create an opportunity if they can't find one. To do this would be an horrendous task; I am not sure it could be done if we wanted to do it. But the question is whether anything less makes sense if we mean to speak seriously about the troubles of the young men.

Surely by now, however, many readers are objecting that this entire argument is pointless because people in *fact* don't think of their jobs in this way at all. *Nobody* asks if a job is useful or honorable (within the limits of business ethics). A man gets a job that pays well, or well enough, that has prestige, and good conditions, or at least tolerable conditions. I agree with these objections as to the fact. (I hope we are wrong.) But *the question is what it means to grow up into such a fact as: "During my productive years I will spend eight hours a day doing what is no good."*

7.

Yet, economically and vocationally, a very large population of the young people are in a plight more drastic than anything so far mentioned. In our society as it is, there are not enough worthy jobs. But if our society, being as it is, were run more efficiently and soberly, for a majority there would soon not be any jobs at all. There is at present nearly full employment and there may be for some years, yet a vast number of young people are rationally unemployable, useless. This paradox is essential to explain their present temper.

Our society, which is not geared to the cultivation of its young, *is* geared to a profitable expanding production, a so-called high standard of living of mediocre value, and the maintenance of nearly full employment. Politically, the chief of these is full employment. In a crisis, when profitable production is temporarily curtailed, government spending increases and jobs are manufactured. In "normalcy"—a condition of slow boom—the easy credit, installment buying, and artificially induced demand for useless goods create jobs for all and good profits for some.

Now, back in the Thirties, when the New Deal attempted by hook or crook to revive the shattered economy, there was an outcry of moral indignation from the conservatives that many of the jobs were "boondoggling," useless made-work. It was insisted, and rightly, that such work was demoralizing to the workers themselves. It is a question of a word, but a candid critic might certainly say that many of the jobs in our present "normal" production are useless made-work. The tail fins and built-in obsolescence might be called boondoggling. The $64,000 Question and the busy hum of Madison Avenue might certainly be called boondoggling. Certain tax-dodge Foundations are boondoggling. What of business lunches and expense accounts? fringe benefits? the comic categories of occupation in the building trades? the extra stage-hands and musicians of the theater crafts? These jolly devices to put money back to work no doubt have a demoralizing effect on somebody or other (certainly on me, they make me green with envy), but where is the moral indignation from Top Management?

Suppose we would cut out the boondoggling and gear our society to a more sensible abundance, with efficient production of quality goods, distribution in a natural market, counter-inflation and sober credit. At once the work week would be cut to, say, twenty hours instead of forty. (Important People have already mentioned the figure thirty.) Or alternately, half the labor force would be unemployed. Suppose too—and how can we not suppose it?—that the automatic machines are used generally, rather than just to get rid of badly organized unskilled labor. The unemployment will be still more drastic.

(To give the most striking example: in steel, the annual increase in productivity is 4 per cent, the plants work at 50 per cent of capacity, and the companies can break even and stop producing at *less than 30 per cent* of capacity. These are the conditions that forced the steel strike, as desperate self-protection. [Estes Kefauver, quoting Gardiner Means and Fred Gardner.])

Everybody knows this, nobody wants to talk about it much, for we don't know how to cope with it. The effect is that we are living a kind of lie. Long ago, labor leaders used to fight for the shorter work week, but now they don't because they're pretty sure they don't want it. Indeed, when hours are reduced, the tendency is to get a second, part-time job and raise the standard of living *because* the job is meaningless and one must have something; but the standard of living is pretty meaningless, too. Nor is this strange atmosphere a new thing. For at least a generation the maximum sensible use of our productivity could have thrown a vast population out of work, or relieved everybody of a lot of useless work, depending on how you take it. (Consider with how little cutback of useful civilian production the economy produced the war goods and maintained an Army, economically unemployed.) The plain truth is that at present very many of us are useless, not needed, rationally unemployable. It is in this paradoxical atmosphere that young persons grow up. It looks busy and expansive, but it is rationally at a stalemate.

8.

These considerations apply to all ages and classes; but it is of course among poor youth (and the aged) that they show up first and worst. They are the most unemployable. For a long time our society has not been geared to the cultivation of the young. In our country 42 per cent have graduated from high school (predicted census, 1960); less than 8 per cent have graduated from college. The high school trend for at least the near future is not much different: there will be a high proportion of drop-outs before the twelfth grade; but *markedly more* of the rest will go on to college; that is, the stratification will harden. Now the schooling in neither the high schools nor the colleges is much good—if it were better more kids would stick to it; yet at present, if we made a list we should find that a large proportion of the dwindling number of unquestionably useful or self-justifying jobs, in the humane professions and the arts and science, require education; and in the future, there is no doubt that the more educated will have the jobs, in running an efficient, highly technical economy and an administrative society placing a premium on verbal skills.

(Between 1947 and 1957, professional and technical workers increased 61 per cent, clerical workers 23 per cent, but factory operatives only 4½ per cent and laborers 4 per cent.—Census.)

For the uneducated there will be no jobs at all. This is humanly most unfortunate, for presumably those who have learned something in schools, and have the knack of surviving the boredom of those schools, could also make something of idleness; whereas the uneducated are useless at leisure too. It takes application, a fine sense of value, and a powerful community-spirit for a people to have serious leisure, and this has not been the genius of the Americans.

From this point of view we can sympathetically understand the pathos of our American school policy, which otherwise seems so inexplicable; at great expense compelling kids to go to school who do not want to and who will not profit by it. There are of course unpedagogic motives, like relieving the home, controlling delinquency, and keeping kids from competing for jobs. But there is also this desperately earnest pedagogic motive, of preparing the kids to take *some* part in a democratic society that does not need them. Otherwise, what will become of them, if they don't know anything?

Compulsory public education spread universally during the nineteenth century to provide the reading, writing, and arithmetic necessary to build a modern industrial economy. With the overmaturity of the economy, the teachers are struggling to preserve the elementary system when the economy no longer requires it and is stingy about paying for it. The demand is for scientists and technicians, the 15 per cent of the "academically talented." "For a vast majority [in the high school]," says Dr. Conant in *The Child, the Parent, and the State,* "the vocational courses are the vital core of the program. They represent something related directly to the ambitions of the boys and girls." But somehow, far more than half of these quit. How is that?

9.

Let us sum up again. The majority of young people are faced with the following alternative: Either society is a benevolently frivolous racket in which they'll manage to boondoggle, though less profitably than the more privileged; or society is serious (and they hope still benevolent enough to support them), but they are useless and hopelessly out. Such thoughts do not encourage productive life. Naturally young people are more sanguine and look for man's work, but few find it. Some settle for a "good job"; most settle for a lousy job; a few, but an increasing number, don't settle.

I often ask, "What do you want to work at? If you have the chance. When you get out of school, college, the service, etc."

Some answer right off and tell their definite plans and projects, highly approved by Papa. I'm pleased for them, but it's a bit boring, because they are such squares.

Quite a few will, with prompting, come out with astounding stereotyped, conceited fantasies, such as becoming a movie actor when they are "discovered"—"like Marlon Brando, but in my own way."

Very rarely somebody will, maybe defiantly and defensively, maybe diffidently but proudly, make you know that he knows very well what he is going to do; it is something great; and he is indeed already doing it, which is the real test.

The usual answer, perhaps the normal answer, is "I don't know," meaning, "I'm looking; I haven't found the right thing; it's discouraging but not hopeless."

But the terrible answer is, "Nothing." The young man doesn't want to do anything.

—I remember talking to half a dozen young fellows at Van Wagner's Beach outside of Hamilton, Ontario; and all of them had this one thing to say: "Nothing." They didn't believe that what to work at was the kind of thing one *wanted.* They rather expected that two or three of them would work for the electric company in town, but they couldn't care less. I turned away from the conversation abruptly because of the uncontrollable burning tears in my eyes and constriction in my chest. Not feeling sorry for them, but tears of frank dismay for the waste of our humanity (they were nice kids). And it is out of that incident that many years later I am writing this book.

BEING TAKEN SERIOUSLY

1.

The simple job plight of these adolescents could not be remedied without a social revolution. Therefore it is not astonishing if the most well-intentioned public spokesmen do not mention it at all. In this book we shall come on other objective factors that are not mentioned. But it is hard to grow up in a society in which one's important problems are treated as nonexistent. It is impossible to belong to it, it is hard to fight to change it. The effect must be rather to feel disaffected, and all the more restive if one is smothered by well-meaning social workers and PAL's who don't seem to understand the real irk. The boys cannot articulate the real irk themselves.

For instance, what public spokesman could discuss the jobs? The ideal of having a real job that you risk your soul in and make good or be damned, belongs to the heroic age of capitalist enterprise, imbued with self-righteous beliefs about hard work, thrift, and public morals. Such an ideal might still have been mentioned in public fifty years ago; in our era of risk-insured semimonopolies and advertised vices it would be met with a ghastly stillness. Or alternately, to want a job that exercises a man's capacities in an enterprise useful to society, is utopian anarcho-syndicalism; it is labor invading the domain of management. No labor leader has entertained such a thought in our generation. Management has the "sole prerogative" to determine the products and the machines. Again, to speak of the likelihood or the desirability of unemployment, like Norbert Wiener or J. K. Galbraith, is to be politically nonprofessional. Yet every kid somehow knows that if he quits school he won't get ahead—and the majority quit.

During, let us say, 1890–1936, on Marxist grounds, the fight for working conditions, for security, wages, hours, the union, the dignity of labor, *was* mentioned, and it gave the worker or the youth something worth while. But because of their historical theory of the "alienation of labor" (that the worker *must* become less and less in control of the work of his hands) the Marxist parties never fought for the man-worthy job itself. It is not surprising now if workmen accept their alienation, and are indifferent also to Marxist politics.

2.

When the objective factors cannot be mentioned, however, other rhetoric is used instead, and in this chapter let us examine its style, as applied, for instance, to juvenile delinquency, on which there is a good deal of oratory.

In our times the usual principle of such speech is that the others, the delinquent boys, are not taken seriously as existing, as having, like oneself, real aims in a real world. They are not condemned, they are not accepted. Instead they are a "youth problem" and the emphasis is on their "background conditions," which one can manipulate; they are said to be subject to "tensions" that one can alleviate. The aim is not to give human beings real goals that warrant belief, and tasks to share in, but to re-establish "belonging," although this kind of speech and thought is precisely calculated to avoid contact and so makes belonging impossible. When such efforts don't work, one finally takes some of the boys seriously as existing and uses force to make them not exist.

Let me give a childish but important illustration of how

this works out. A boy of ten or eleven has a few great sexual adventures—*he* thinks they're great—but then he has the bad luck to get caught and get in trouble. They try to persuade him by punishment and other explanations that some different behavior is much better, but he knows by the evidence of his senses that nothing could be better. If he gives in, he lives on in a profound disbelief, a disbelief in their candor and a disbelief even of his own body feelings. But if he persists and proves incorrigible, then the evidence of his senses is attached to what is socially punished, explained away; he may even be put away. The basic trouble here is that they do not really believe he has had the sexual experience. That objective factor is inconvenient for them; therefore it cannot exist. Instead, this is *merely* a case of insecure affection at home, slum housing, comic books, and naughty companions: tensions and conditions. My hunch, as I shall discuss later, is that this kind of early sexual adventure and misadventure is fairly common in delinquency. It is called precocious, abnormal, artificially stimulated, and so forth—an index of future delinquency. In my opinion that's rubbish, but be that as it may; what is important in a particular case is that there is a stubborn new fact. Attempting to nullify it makes further growth impossible (and *creates* the future delinquency). The sensible course would be to accept it as a valuable part of further growth. But if this were done, they fear that the approved little hero would be a rotten apple to his peers, who now would suddenly *all* become precocious, abnormal, artificially stimulated, and prone to delinquency.

The sexual plight of these children is officially not mentioned. The revolutionary attack on hypocrisy by Ibsen, Freud, Ellis, Dreiser, did not succeed this far. Is it an eccentric opinion that an important part of the kids' restiveness in school from the onset of puberty has to do with puberty? The teachers talk about it among themselves, all right. (In his school, Bertrand Russell thought it was better if they had the sex, so they could give their undivided attention to mathematics, which was the main thing.) But since this objective factor does not *exist* in our schools, the school itself begins to be irrelevant. The question here is not whether the sexuality should be discouraged or encouraged. That is an important issue, but far more important is that it is hard to grow up when existing facts are treated as though they do not exist. For then there is no dialogue, it is impossible to be taken seriously, to be understood, to make a bridge between oneself and society.

In American society we have perfected a remarkable form of censorship: to allow every one his political right to say what he believes, but to swamp his little boat with literally thousands of millions of newspapers, mass-circulation magazines, best-selling books, broadcasts, and public pronouncements that disregard what he says and give the official way of looking at things. Usually there is no conspiracy to do this; it is simply that what he says is not what people are talking about, it is not newsworthy.

(There is no conspiracy, but it is *not* undeliberate. "If you mean to tell me," said an editor to me, "that *Esquire* tries to have articles on important issues and treats them in such a way that nothing can come of it—who can deny it?" Try, also, to get a letter printed in the *New York Times* if your view on the issue calls attention to an essential factor that is not being generally mentioned.)

Naturally, the more simply true a statement is in any issue about which everybody is quite confused, the less newsworthy it will be, the less it will be what everybody is talking about. When the child in the story said, "But the Emperor has no clothes!" the newspapers and broadcasts surely devoted many columns to describing the beautiful new clothes and also mentioned the interesting psychological incident of the child. Instead of being proud of him, his parents were ashamed; but on the other hand they received $10,000 in sympathetic contributions toward his rehabilitation, for he was a newsworthy case. But he had a block in reading.

Where there is official censorship it is a sign that speech

is serious. Where there is none, it is pretty certain that the official spokesmen have all the loud-speakers.

3.

But let us return to our theme of vocation and develop it a step further. Perhaps the young fellows *really* want to do something, that is, something worthwhile, for only a worthwhile achievement finishes a doing. A person rests when he has finished a real job. (The striking illustration of this is that, statistically, the best mental health used to be found among locomotive engineers, and is now found among air-line pilots! The task is useful, exacting, it sets in motion a big machine, and when it is over, it is done with.) If the object is important, it gives structure to many a day's action and dreaming—one might even continue in school. Unfortunately our great society balks us, for it simply does not take seriously the fact, or the possibility, that people want this; nor the philosophic truth that except in worthwhile activity there is no way to be happy. For instance, in a standard questionnaire for delinquents, by Milton Barron, in a hundred headings there do not appear the questions, "What do you want to be? What do you want to work at? What do you want to achieve?" (But Donald Taft's *Criminology,* which Barron is adapting, has the sentence: "Absence of vocational interest at the age when it is normal . . . is tell-tale of a starved life.")

In despair, the fifteen-year-olds hang around and do nothing at all, neither work nor play. Without a worthwhile prospect, without a sense of justification, the made-play of the Police Athletic League is not interesting, it is not their own. They do not do their school work, for they are waiting to quit; and it is hard, as we shall see, for them to get part-time jobs. Indeed, the young fellows (not only delinquents) spend a vast amount of time doing nothing. They hang around together, but don't talk about anything, nor even—if you watch their faces—do they passively take in the scene. Conversely, at the movies, where the real scene is by-passed, they watch with absorbed fantasy, and afterward sometimes mimic what they saw.

If there is nothing worth while, it is hard to do anything at all. When one does nothing, one is threatened by the question, *is* one nothing? To this insulting doubt, however, there is a lively response: a system of values centering around threatened grownupness and defensive conceit. This is the so-called "threatened masculinity," not in the sense of being called a girl, but of being called, precisely, "boy," the Negro term of insult. With this, there is an endless compulsion to prove potency and demand esteem. The boys don't talk about much of interest, but there is a vast amount of hot rhetoric to assert that oneself is "as good as anybody else," no more useless, stupid, or cowardly. For instance, if they play a game, the interest in the game is weak: they are looking elsewhere when the ball is served, there are lapses in attention, they smoke cigarettes even while playing handball. The interest in victory is surprisingly weak: there is not much glow of self-esteem. But the need for proof is overwhelming: "I won you, didn' I? I won you last week too, didn' I?"

During childhood, they played games with fierce intensity, giving themselves as a sacrifice to the game, for play was the chief business of growth, finding and making themselves in the world. Now when they are too old merely to play, to what shall they give themselves with fierce intensity? They cannot play for recreation, since they have not been used up.

The proving behavior is endless. Since each activity is not interesting to begin with, its value does not deepen and it does not bear much repetition. Its value as proof quickly diminishes. In these circumstances, the inevitable tendency is to raise the ante of the compulsive useless activity that proves one is potent and not useless. (This analysis applies equally to these juveniles and to status-seeking junior executives in business firms and on Madison Avenue.)

It is not surprising then, that, as Frederic Thrasher says in *The Gang*, "Other things being equal, the imaginative boy has an excellent chance to become the leader of the gang. He has the power to make things interesting for them. He 'thinks up things for us to do.' "

4.

Last summer, after a disastrous week when there were several juvenile murders, the Governor of New York made the following statement (*New York Times*, September 2, 1959):

We have to constantly devise new ways to bring about a challenge to these young folks and to provide an outlet for their energies and give them a sense of belonging.

The statement is on the highest level of current statesmanship—that is why I have chosen it. It has been coached by sociologists and psychologists. It has the proper therapeutic and not moralistic attitude, and it does not mention the cops. (The direct appeal to force came a couple of weeks later, when there were other incidents.)

The gist of it is that the Governor of New York is to play the role that Thrasher assigns to the teen-age gang leader. He is to think up new "challenges." (The word could not have been more unfortunate.) But it is the word "constantly" that is the clue. A challenge can hardly be worth while, meaningful, or therapeutic if another must constantly and obsessively be devised to siphon off a new threat of "energy." Is not this raising the ante? Solidly meeting a real need does not have this character.

("The leader," says Thrasher, "sometimes controls the gang by means of summation, i.e., by progressively urging the members from one deed to another, until finally an extreme of some sort is reached.")

My guess is that in playing games the Governor will not have so lively an imagination as the lad he wants to displace as leader; unlike the grownups, the gang will never select him. One of the objective factors that make it hard to grow up is that Governors are likely to be men of mediocre humane gifts.

The psychology of the Governor's statement is puzzling.

There are no such undifferentiated energies as he speaks of. There are energies of specific functions with specific real objects. In the case here they might be partly as follows: In adolescents a strong energy would be sexual reaching. For these boys, as for other adolescents, it is thwarted or imperfectly gratified, but these have probably not learned so well as others to cushion the suffering and be patient; so that another strong energy of the delinquents would be diffuse rage of frustration, perhaps directed at a scapegoat. If they have been kept from constructive activity making them feel worth while, a part of their energy might be envious and malicious destructiveness of property. As they are powerless, it is spite; and as they are humiliated, it is vengeance. As they feel rejected and misunderstood, as by governors, their energy is woe; but they react to this with cold pride, and all the more fierce gang-loyalty to their peers. For which of these specific energies does the Governor of New York seriously plan to devise an outlet? Their own imaginative gang leader presumably does devise challenges that let off steam for a few hours.

What is the sociology of "belonging" here? In the great society they are certainly uprooted. But in the gang their conformity is sickeningly absolute; they have uniform jackets and uniform morals. They speak a jargon and no one has a different idea that might brand him as queer. Since they have shared forbidden behavior, they are all in the same mutually blackmailing plight and correspondingly guilty and suspicious toward the outsider. It is a poor kind of community they have; friendship, affection, personal helpfulness are remarkably lacking in it; they are "cool," afraid to display feeling; yet does the Governor seriously think that he can offer a good community that warrants equal loyalty?

5.

More aware of what challenging means, the New York Youth Board has had a policy more calculated to succeed. Its principle is provisionally to accept as *given* the code of the gang and the kids' potency-proving values and prejudices; and then, as an immediate aim, to try to distract their overt behavior into less annoying and dangerous channels. This immediate aim is already valuable, for it diminishes suffering. For instance, there is less suffering if a youth' addiction is changed from heroin to alcohol, so long as heroin is illegal and alcohol is legal; the youth is less in danger and the store that he would rob to pay for the criminally overpriced narcotic is out of danger.

Then there is the further hope that, accepted by the wise and permissive adult, the adolescents will gradually come to accept themselves and the spiral of proving will be arrested. Further, that the friendship of the trusted adult will evoke a love (transference) that can then be turned elsewhere. I take it that this is the Youth Worker philosophy. In many cases it should succeed.

I am skeptical that it can widely succeed. For here again the young people are not taken seriously as existing, as having real aims in the same world as oneself. To the Youth Board, in their own real world (such as it is), the code is *not* acceptable, and the teen-age vaunts and prejudices cannot lead to growth in any world. To pretend otherwise is playing games and continuing to exclude them from one's own meant world. How then can the boys be trusting and feel they are understood? Not being morons, they know they *cannot* be understood in their own terms, which are empty to themselves. They know there is another world beyond, as square and sheepish as they might please to rationalize it, but which is formidable and enviable. (Actually, apart from the code itself and the sphere of their delinquencies, the kids are models of conventionality in their tastes, opinions, and ignorance.) And though they have a childish need for sympathetic attention and are proud of having compelled it—"We're so bad they give us a youth worker"—they are too old not to demand being taken seriously.

There is a valuable nondirective approach which makes

no judgments or interpretations and gives no advice, but which simply draws the patient out and holds up a mirror; and this is no doubt also part of the philosophy of the Youth Board. But then, it must be a therapy, it must hold up the mirror and risk the explosion of shame and grief, or the impulsive defenses against them, violent retaliation or flight. In youth work this is very impractical. It is a different thing to go *along* with the patient, or worse to seem to go along with him, and provide only the reasurance of attention.

The philosophy of the Youth Board can succeed only if the worker can hold out some real objective opportunity, something more than "interpersonal relations," and make the boy finally see it. (E.g., at P.S. 43 in New York there has been an experiment of simply urging the kids to go to college—a far-off goal—showing that it is economically possible for them, and promising that the school will follow up. This alone has resulted in rapid academic advance, increases in I.Q., and less truancy.)

My hunch is that the occasional spectacular success occurs not because of the "accepting" method, but because the youth worker does not really belong to the world of the Youth Board either, and his acceptance is bona fide. For whatever motive, he confronts the young people as real. He may be a covert accomplice with the same inner dilemma as his gang, and can pass on a more practical worldly wisdom. He may be emotionally involved with some of them, so they are in fact important. He may be so deeply compassionate or so inspired a teacher that he creates new interests and values altogether, *not* the meant world of the Youth Board which is, after all, just what had proved unsatisfactory to begin with.

6.

Our society has evolved a social plan, a city plan, an economy and a physical plan, of which this delinquent youth is an organic part. The problem is *not* to get them to belong to society, for they belong a priori by being the next generation. The burden of proof and performance is quite the other way: for the system of society to accommodate itself to all its constituent members. But can it be denied that by and large the official practice is to write these boys off as useless and unwanted and to try to cajole or baffle them into harmlessness?

Suppose we look at it the other way. Like any other constitutional group, they exert an annoying pressure, but they are inarticulate. In some dumb way they are surely right, but what the devil do they want? Has much effort been made to ask them and help them find words? We can guess that they want two broad classes of things: changes in the insulting and depriving circumstances that have made them ornery, spiteful, vengeful, conceited, ignorant, and callous—unable to grow; and objective opportunities in which to grow.

Let us go back to the Governor. On the same occasion mentioned above, he issued to the press the following formal statement:

> The problem of juvenile delinquency has no easy remedy. There is no quick or overnight solution. It is compounded of neglect by parents, broken homes, poor living conditions, unhealthy background, economic deprivation, mental disturbance, and lack of religious training.

This is not a bad list of background conditions; it satisfies every popular and scientific theory of etiology. The question is, does the Governor seriously not understand how organic these conditions are in our society? They cannot be remedied by gimmicks or the busy kind of social work that offers no new vision or opportunity. He speaks of broken homes; has he some plan to improve the institution of modern marriage, especially among folk for whom it is hardly an institution? The present-day urban poor are largely Negro and Spanish, they are excluded from many unions, they often earn less than the minimum wage, they are unschooled; naturally there is economic deprivation, poor living conditions. How is their religion relevant if it is irrelevant to the basic community functions of vocation and war, and wrong on sex? There is no community and not even a community plan; naturally there is unhealthy background.

What great concerted effort is being led by the Governor to remedy these conditions, not overnight, but in the next five, ten, or twenty years?

Indeed, *official* policy has often worked to increase delinquency rather than remedy it. For instance, in a characteristically earnest analysis, our best authority on housing, Charles Abrams, has shown how the public-housing policy has had this effect. Slums have been torn down wholesale, disrupting established community life. By not building on vacant land and by neglecting master planning, our officials have created insoluble problems of relocation and have vastly increased the number of one-room flats, making decent family life impossible. (Suppose you were fifteen years old and returned home at 11 P.M., as the Mayor urges, to a room with Mama and Papa in one bed and two little brothers in your bed and a baby yowling; you might well stay out till four in the morning.) Also, families are ousted from public housing when their incomes increase, thus eliminating and penalizing the better models; and on the other hand, other families are expelled on irrelevant moral criteria, without thought of what becomes of them. And the original income segregation in large blocks was itself bound to increase tension, like any segregation. All of this has been *official* policy. The picture gets even grimmer if we turn to the quasi-official graft in Title I that for two- and three-year stretches has stalled either demolition or construction, while families pay rent in limbo.

The trouble with Abrams' analysis is that he, Mumford and others have been saying it aloud for twenty years, while the New York City Planning Commission has gone on manufacturing juvenile delinquency.

7.

Now finally (January 1960), the Governor's practical antidelinquency youth program is offered for legislation. Let me summarize its chief points: (1) Reduce the age of felonies to fifteen. (2) Space for 390 more in the forest camps (added to the 110 now there). (3) Admit a few older to these camps. (4) Establish "Youth Opportunity Centers"—residences for youths "on the verge of delinquency." (5) Provide "halfway houses" for those in transition from institutions to freedom. (6) Certified boarding houses to which the court can direct youngsters. (7) Ease compulsory continuation school. (8) Permit after-school work from fourteen to sixteen. (9) Encourage work-and-study programs "to keep potential drop-outs in school long enough to prepare for employment." (10) Centralize probation services. (11) Increase probation staff.

Of these eleven points, eight seem to be aimed primarily at punishment or control: the boys are really unwanted, the problem is to render them harmless. Only two (8 and 9) envisage, very unimpressively, any substantive change whatever. What on earth has happened to the program of "constantly devising new ways to challenge these young folks"? But let me call attention to the forest work-camps (2 and 3). There is good evidence that these are excellent and have provided a rewarding experience. But then certainly they should be made available not for convicted delinquents as such, but for all kids who want to work there a year. Naturally, however, there is no money—not even for more than five hundred delinquent boys altogether. The question is whether or not such a program of camps for many thousand boys is less important than one of the Park Commissioner's new highways to Westchester. Until they will face that question, our public officials are not serious.

8.

Positively, the delinquent behavior seems to speak clearly enough. It asks for what we can't give, but it is in *this* direction we must go. It asks for manly opportunities to work, make a little money, and have self-esteem; to have some space to bank around in, that is not always somebody's property; to have better schools to open for them horizons of interest; to have more and better sex without fear or shame; to share somehow in the symbolic goods (like the cars) that are made so much of; to have a community and a country to be loyal to; to claim attention and have a voice. These are not outlandish demands. Certainly they cannot be satisfied directly in our present system; they are baffling. That is why the problem is baffling, and the final recourse is to a curfew, to ordinances against carrying knives, to threatening the parents, to reformatories with newfangled names, and to 1,100 more police on the street.

CRISIS IN BLACK AND WHITE

Charles E. Silberman

On the dust jacket of Crisis in Black and White *is a wide assortment of testimonials. The eminently respectable Eugene Carson Blake, former president of the National Council of Churches, and Whitney Young, executive director of the National Urban League, are cheek by jowl with Malcolm X, the fearsome Black Muslim leader, and the Reverend Ralph D. Abernathy, aide to Dr. Martin Luther King and proponent of passive resistance. The applause for Charles E. Silberman's achievement comes from various sources, and for various reasons. It even emanates from Harvard University: the distinguished psychologist, Professor Jerome Bruner, doubtless speaks for every reader when he asserts: "*Crisis in Black and White *is a powerful and unsparing analysis of 'the Negro problem' in America. It is one of the finest books on American society that has appeared in several years. 'The Negro problem' is not something that can be separated from the 'main pattern' of our style of life. If one began Mr. Silberman's book with such an easy assumption one finally puts it down convinced that to change 'the status of the Negro' is to face the necessity of much deeper changes in the American way. Such changes, Mr. Silberman urges, are possible, but they require first that we face our problems honestly. His book is a model of just such honesty."*

The praise is well deserved and all the more impressive for a book that must contend vigorously for attention. Almost overnight, with the rise of Negro militancy and public anxiety, books, articles, monographs, studies, and plays based on "the Negro problem" are in superabundant supply. To rise above the flood of race-relations literature that comes cascading off American presses at this moment is in itself an achievement. Conscientious citizens doubtless wish to learn as much as they can about a bewildering social problem that threatens to get out of hand. But they are rapidly approaching satiety; there is a limit to the number of mediocre analyses that will appeal to them. When that limit has been reached and thoughtful people have put the dross aside, one may confidently predict that they will continue to read Silberman.

Another work devoted to "the Negro problem and modern democracy" has already passed the rigorous test of time. We refer, of course, to the monumental report submitted in 1944 by a young Swedish economist, Gunnar Myrdal. Seven years earlier, the Carnegie Corporation had decided to commission the best man it could find for a difficult and delicate inquiry into a deep-rooted problem that no American could approach with detachment. For this purpose, Myrdal was nearly heaven-sent. He brought a higher degree of objectivity and a greater measure of passion to his task than most scholars could be expected to muster. Being outside, Myrdal looked inside with incomparable acuity, and produced *An American Dilemma*. His encyclopedic survey will stand as a permanent landmark of the dilemma and the agony we seem unable to dispel. Updated for a reprinting in 1962, *An American Dilemma*—to our everlasting shame—needed little revision. Things had not changed all that much in the ensuing decades. And those things that had changed had not necessarily changed for the better.

Twenty years after World War II, and amidst unparalleled prosperity, there was deep poverty for millions of Americans. Many were whites, but by far the largest proportion were *dark-skinned. More and more, Negroes found their oppression intolerable. How was one to bear not just relative deprivation, but* increasing *residential and therefore educational segregation —even now, when legal steps at last were being taken to alleviate a hideous condition that nevertheless continued to fester. Whether that condition led to apathy or anger, violence or nonviolence, law or a principled violation of law, the tragedy remained.*

Before and after Myrdal's towering achievement, American sociologists spawned many valuable little studies of Negro-white relations. They learned to shake off the racism that afflicted many of their forebears in a discipline which at the turn of this century harbored no more enlightenment than did most other sectors of American society. After the Supreme Court decision of 1954, directing that desegregation of the public schools which has yet to keep pace with the new and greater residential segregation, they undertook scarcely any research in the field of race relations. Today, for the most part, such research is smuggled in under more fashionable headings like Poverty and Delinquency. Nonsociologists—novelists, poets, journalists, and civil-rights workers—have typically and providentially ventured into territory where most sociologists (with honorable exceptions) dared tread but gingerly, if at all.

Among those who hold the big picture up before us in horrifying detail, few are more important than Charles Silberman, an occasional teacher of economics and a full-time editor of Fortune *magazine. No respecter of foolish academic boundaries, he ranges far and wide with admirable mastery of the facts and unusual courage in interpreting them while he remains fully aware of their sad significance.*

THE NEW MAJORITY

And if a stranger sojourn with thee in thy land, ye shall not do him wrong. The stranger that sojourneth with thee shall be unto thee as one from among thee, and thou shalt love him as thyself; for ye were strangers in the land of Egypt: I am the Lord thy God.

Leviticus XIX, 33–34

It was only eight years after the founding of the Republic when a member of the House of Representatives took the floor to complain about the riff-raff flooding the big cities. Unrestricted immigration might have been satisfactory when the country was new and unsettled, he declared; but now that the United States had reached maturity and was fully populated, the nation's well-being required an end to immigration.

The congressman was not the first to voice these sentiments. Concern over the flood of foreign riff-raff had been growing throughout the eighteenth century; it was to remain a recurrent theme down to our own day. As early as 1718, "proper" Bostonians worried that "these confounded Irishmen will eat us all up"; and in 1729, a mob prevented the docking of several ships bringing immigrants from Belfast and Londonderry. Pennsylvanians were equally outraged by the flood of German immigrants into their territory: in the middle of the century, the great Benjamin Franklin delivered a number of attacks on "the Palatine Boors," *i.e.*, the Germans, migrating to Pennsylvania. Jefferson, too, opposed mass immigration fearing that it would expose the new nation to the corrupting influence of a decadent Europe. And the first Congress heard a plea to bar admission of "the common class of vagrants, paupers, and other outcasts of Europe."

Thirty years later, things seemed to be going from bad to worse. "This inlet of pauperism threatens us with the most overwhelming consequences," the Managers of the Society for the Prevention of Pauperism in the City of New York reported in 1819. The immigrants, they added, "are frequently found destitute in our streets; they seek employment at our doors; they are found in our almshouses, and in our hospitals; they are found at the bar of our criminal tribunals, in our bridewell, our penitentiary, and our state prison. And we lament to say that they are too often led by want, by vice, and by habit to form a phalanx of plunder and depredation, rendering our city more liable to the increase of crimes, and our houses of correction more crowded with convicts and felons."

And the "inlet of pauperism" had barely begun! In the next decade, 152,000 immigrants entered the United States—half again as many as in the three preceding decades. Ten years later, the number of immigrants jumped to 599,000. And then the deluge began. Betwen 1850 and 1860, over 2.5 million immigrants entered the United States. By the 1880's the number exceeded five million; and in the first decade of this century, nearly nine million men, women, and children came to these shores. All told, some forty-two million immigrants have settled in the United States since 1820, the first year in which accurate records were kept.

The immigrants came for many reasons. Some came to seek political asylum, some because they had been forced off the land by famine or technological change, some because of religious persecution, some because the trip to America was a means of escaping jail or the debtors' prison. In the early years of the nation, some immigrants came because they were literally snatched off the streets of London and other towns to find themselves "slaveys"—indentured servants in the new land. But in every period, the immigrants came because the new nation, and especially its growing cities, needed their labor to build its streets and offices, lay its railroad tracks, service its homes and restaurants, and do all the dirty, menial jobs that the older residents disdained.

But the city did more than use its newcomers; it equipped them to take their places as fully participating members of United States society. Doing this—bringing people from society's backwaters into the main stream of American life—has always been the principal business, and the principal glory, of the American city. Cities have always had to create their own stable, cultivated citizenry from whatever raw material lay at hand. For the American city during the past hundred fifty years, the raw material was the stream of immigrants pouring in from Britain, Ireland, Germany, Norway, Italy, Russia, Poland, and a dozen other lands. Thus, most of the huge middle class that dominates American life today was manufactured in the big-city slums of yesteryear. Indeed, a great epoch of American history is now drawing to a close: the epoch of the ethnic groups. Increasingly the sons and grandsons and great-grandsons of immigrants find their identity through membership in one of the three main religions, as well as through ethnic affiliation. Election of a Catholic as President completed the transformation of the United States from a Protestant society with an Anglo-Saxon tradition to a pluralistic society with a Protestant tradition.

A new epoch is beginning, dominated instead by race. The immigrants still pour in—not from County Cork, or Bavaria, or Sicily, or Galicia, but from Jackson, Mississippi, and Memphis, Tennessee, and a host of towns and hamlets with names like Sunflower, Rolling Fork, and Dyersburg. No single European ethnic group ever increased as rapidly, or accounted for as large a proportion of the big cities' population as the current wave of newcomers. The new immigrants however, are distinguished from the older residents neither by religion nor by national origin; they are Protestant, for the most part, and can boast of an American ancestry much older than that of the established city dweller. Their sole distinguishing feature is color: the newcomers are black.

The new immigration is changing the character of the big cities as much as did the older immigration from Europe. It is also profoundly altering the nature of race relations in the United States. Only twenty years ago, Professor Myrdal reported "a sense of hopelessness in the Negro cause," stemming from the fact that Negroes "can never expect to grow into a democratic majority in politics or in any other sphere of American life." No longer; Negroes are beginning to see themselves as riding the wave of the future. They can begin to see the day when they will be in the majority in most large cities; already, they hold the political balance of power, although they have not yet learned how to take full advantage of the fact. Thus, the Negro vote catapulted an unknown, Jerome Cavanagh, into the mayoralty of Detroit in 1961, defeating a candidate backed by both businessmen and the United Automobile Workers. Negroes supplied 118,000 of the 139,000-vote plurality by which Chicago's Mayor Richard Daley won re-election in 1963.

The Negro migration to the city actually began about seventy-five years ago, when the Jim Crow system first began to take shape in the South and white men moved actively and brutally to force the Negro back into his pre-Reconstruction place. Contrary to the popular view that Southern folkways are immutable, the quarter-century following the Civil War had seen a considerable relaxation of the barriers between the races as the South accommodated itself to a new order. Negroes were accepted at the polls, in the courts and legislatures, in the police and militia, and on the trains and trolleys. Col. Thomas Wentworth Higginson of Boston, a noted abolitionist who had been one of John Brown's "Secret Six" before Harper's Ferry, went south in 1878, and reported in *The Atlantic Monthly* his pleasant surprise at how well Negroes were being treated, as compared with his native New England. "How can we ask more of the states formerly in rebellion," he wrote, "than that they should be abreast of New England in granting rights and privileges to the colored race?" In 1885, T. McCants Stewart, a Negro newspaperman from Boston, returned to the South for a visit and found traveling "more pleasant than in some parts of New England . . . I think the whites of the South," he reported, "are really less afraid to [have] contact with colored people than the whites of the North." Negroes were treated particularly well in Virginia. Thus in 1886 the Richmond *Dispatch* took what today would be considered a pro-Negro position:

Our State Constitution requires all State officers in their oath of office to declare that they "recognize and accept the civil and political equality of all men." We repeat that nobody here objects to sitting in political conventions with negroes. Nobody here objects to serving on juries with negroes. No lawyer objects to practicing law in courts where negro lawyers practice . . . Colored men are allowed to introduce bills into the Virginia Legislature; and in both branches of this body negroes are allowed to sit, as they have a right to sit.

Racism was still widespread, of course, in all its ugliness. But it was held in check by a number of forces: Northern liberal opinion; the prestige and influence of Southern conservatives, with their tradition of *noblesse oblige* and their distaste for the venomous race hatred of the poor whites;[1] and the idealism of Southern radicals, who for a time dreamt of an alliance of all the propertyless against the propertied class. As a result of these competing pressures, Negroes were able to retain the suffrage they had won during Reconstruction. While Negroes were increasingly defrauded and coerced, they did continue to vote in large numbers, and Southern conservatives and radicals competed for their support. "The Southern whites accept them precisely as Northern men in cities accept the ignorant Irish vote," Colonel Higginson wrote, "not cheerfully, but with acquiescence to the inevitable; and when the strict color line is once broken, they are just as ready to conciliate the Negro as the Northern politician to flatter the Irishman. Any powerful body of voters may be cajoled today and intimidated tomorrow and hated always," the abolitionist added, "but it can never be left out of sight."

Beginning around 1890, however, the forces that had kept Southern racism and fanaticism in check rapidly weakened and became discredited. In the North, the desire for sectional

[1] "It is a great deal pleasanter to travel with respectable and well-behaved colored people than with unmannerly and ruffianly white men," a Charleston, South Carolina, paper observed, suggesting that "the common sense and proper arrangement . . . is to provide first-class cars for first-class passengers, white and colored."

reconciliation persuaded liberals to drop their interest in the Negro, who was the symbol of sectional strife; increasingly, liberals and former abolitionists began espousing the shibboleths of the Negro's innate inferiority in the pages of *The Atlantic Monthly, Harper's, The Nation,* and *The North American Review;* and this, in turn, encouraged the more virulent Southern racists. "Just as the Negro gained his emancipation and new rights through a falling out between white men," wrote historian C. Vann Woodward, "he now stood to lose his rights throught the reconciliation of white men."[2] Not only did the Negro serve as a scapegoat to aid the reconciliation of Northern and Southern white men; he served the same purpose in aiding the reconciliation of estranged white classes in the South itself. The battles between the Southern conservatives and radicals had opened wounds that could be healed only by the nostrum of white supremacy.

The first and most fundamental step was the total disfranchisement of the Negro; disfranchisement served both as a symbol of "reform" and as a guarantee that no white faction would ever again seek power by rallying Negro votes against another group of whites. Because of the Federal Constitution, the Southern states had to rob Negroes of their vote through indirection: through the use of the poll tax, the white primary, the "grandfather clause," the "good character clause," the "understanding clause," and other techniques, some of which are still in use in states like Mississippi and Alabama. But while the methods were roundabout, the purpose was not. When the Mississippi Constitution was revised in 1890, for example, the purpose of revision was stated quite baldly: "The policy of crushing out the manhood of the Negro citizens is to be carried on to success." Addressing the Virginia Constitutional Convention eleven years later, the young Carter Glass, then a member of the Virginia State Senate, was no less blunt:

[2] Professor Woodward's *The Strange Career of Jim Crow* (New York: Oxford University Press Galaxy Book, 1957) is a brilliant analysis of the origins of the Jim Crow system.

"Discrimination? Why that is precisely what we propose; that, exactly, is what this convention was elected for—to discriminate to the very extremity of permissible action under the limitations of the Federal Constitution, with a view to the elimination of every Negro voter who can be gotten rid of, legally, without materially impairing the numerical strength of the white electorate." By the winter of 1902, the Convention had achieved its purpose. By 1910, the Negro was disfranchised in virtually every Southern state. In Louisiana, for example, the number of registered Negro voters dropped abruptly from 130,334 in 1896 to only 1,342 in 1904.

Disfranchisement was preceded and accomplished by an intensive campaign of race hatred, designed in good measure to allay the suspicions of the poor whites that they, too, were in danger of losing the vote. Although the regime of the carpetbaggers had been over for twenty years or more, all the old horror stories were revived and embroidered; the new generation of Southerners (and each succeeding one) was made to feel that it, too, had lived through the trauma of Reconstruction. Newspapers played up stories of Negro crime and "impertinence." The result was a savage outbreak of anti-Negro violence. In Atlanta, white mobs took over the city for four days, looting and lynching at will; in New Orleans, mobs rampaged for three days. And rigid segregation rapidly became the rule. Until 1900, Jim Crow laws had applied only to railroad travel in most Southern states; indeed, South Carolina did not require Jim Crow railroad cars before 1898, North Carolina before 1899, and Virginia before 1900. Until 1899, only three states required separate waiting rooms at railroad terminals. In the next six or eight years, however, Jim Crow laws mushroomed throughout the South, affecting trolleys, theaters, boarding houses, public toilets and water fountains, housing; in Atlanta Jim Crow extended even to the ultimate absurdity of providing separate Jim Crow Bibles for Negro witnesses to swear on in court, and, for a time, to requiring Jim Crow elevators in buildings.

In short, the South, whose leaders today deny the possibility as well as the desirability of rapid change, transformed the pattern of race relations almost overnight. Men's hearts changed as swiftly as their actions. As late as 1898, for example, the Charleston, South Carolina, *News and Courier,* the oldest newspaper in the South, ridiculed the whole idea of segregation of the races. "As we have got on fairly well for a third of a century, including a long period of reconstruction," the editor wrote, "we can probably get on as well hereafter without it, and certainly so extreme a measure [as Jim Crow railroad cars] should not be adopted and enforced without added and urgent cause." The editor went on to discuss the absurd consequences that would follow, once the principle of Jim Crow were accepted. "If there must be Jim Crow cars on the railroads, there should be Jim Crow cars on the street railroads. Also on all passenger boats." Warming to his task, he continued: "If there are to be Jim Crow cars, moreover, there should be Jim Crow waiting saloons at all stations, and Jim Crow eating houses . . . There should be Jim Crow sections of the jury box, and a separate Jim Crow dock and witness stand in every court —and a Jim Crow Bible for colored witnesses to kiss," and separate Jim Crow sections in government offices so that Negroes and whites would not have to mingle while paying their taxes. "In resorting to the tactics of *reductio ad absurdum,*" Professor Woodward has commented, "the editor doubtless believed that he had dealt the Jim Crow principle a telling blow with his heavy irony." But the real irony was unintended: what the *News and Courier* editor regarded as an absurdity in 1898 very rapidly became a reality, down to and including the Jim Crow Bible. So rapidly did the change occur, in fact, that in 1906—only eight years later—the paper had swung completely around. Segregation was no longer ridiculous; it was merely inadequate. Only mass deportation could solve as grave a problem as the presence of Negroes in South Carolina. "There is no room for them here," the paper declared.

There *was* room in the North—and thus began the great migration. There had been a steady trickle of Negroes from the eleven states of the Old Confederacy since the end of the Civil War; emancipation had cut many Negroes loose from the land and started them wandering from place to place. In the last decade of the century, however, the number of Negroes leaving the Old Confederacy jumped to more than two hundred thousand from fewer than sixty thousand in the 1880–1890 period, and the number of migrants increased somewhat in the first decade of the twentieth century. The migrants included a great many of the preachers and politicians who had sat in Southern legislatures during Reconstruction and its aftermath, as well as less distinguished Negroes who had occupied minor political posts. But the majority were half-educated or illiterate country folk too restless or too proud to accept life on Southern terms.

It was World War One that broke the social and economic fetters that had bound Negroes to the rural South almost as effectively as slavery itself, for the war created an enormous demand for previously untapped sources of labor. Business was booming as the United States supplied the Allies with weapons and matériel; but combat had cut off the flow of immigrants from Europe. With labor the scarce factor of production even before American entry into the war, Northern industries began sending labor agents into the rural South, recruiting Negroes just as they had recruited white workers in Ireland and Italy during the nineteenth century. The labor agents promised jobs and frequently offered free railroad tickets. Negroes began to move North in such numbers—emigration from the eleven states of the Old Confederacy jumped from 207,000 in 1900–1910 to 478,600 in 1910–1920—that white Southerners began to fear a shortage of labor in their own region and took measures to stop the Northern labor recruiters. In Macon, Georgia, an ordinance was passed requiring labor recruiters to pay a license fee of $25,000 and barring their admission unless recommended by ten local ministers, ten manufacturers, and twenty-five businessmen. In Montgomery, Alabama, fines and jail sentences were imposed on anyone found guilty of "enticing, persuading, or influencing labor" to leave the city, and throughout Mississippi, agents were arrested, ticket agents were intimidated to keep them from selling tickets to Negroes, and trains were actually stopped.

The Negroes kept leaving nevertheless. Besides the agents for Northern firms, Northern Negro newspapers also encouraged the migration editorially, as well as through advertisements offering employment. *The Chicago Defender*, in particular, exhorted Negroes to leave the oppression of the South for the freedom of the North. Copies of the *Defender* were passed from hand to hand, and from all over the South, Negroes wrote to its editor, Robert S. Abbott, asking for help and advice. "I would like Chicago or Philadelphia. But I don't Care where so long as I Go where a man is a man," wrote a would-be migrant from Houston, Texas. From the Black Belt of Mississippi came this letter, showing the hopes that moved the migrants:

Granville, Miss., May 16, 1917

Dear Sir:
This letter is a letter of information of which you will find stamp envelop for reply. I want to come north some time soon but I do not want to leve here looking for a job where I would be in dorse all winter. Now the work I am doing here is running a guage edger in a saw mill. I know all about the grading of lumber. I have been working in lumber about 25 or 27 years. My wedges here is $3.00 a day, 11 hours a day. I want to come north where I can educate my 3 little children, also my wife. Now if you cannot fit me up at what I am doing down here I can learn anything any one els can. also there is a great deal of good women cooks here would leave any time all they want is to know where to go and some way to go. please write me at once just how I can get my people where they can get something for their work. There are women here cookeing for $1.50

and $2.00 a week. I would like to live in Chicago or Ohio or Philadelphia. Tell Mr. Abbott that our pepel are tole that they can not get anything to do up there and they are being snatched off the trains here in Greenville and a rested but in spite of all this, they are leaving every day and every night 100 or more is expecting to leave this week. Let me here from you at once.

American's entry into World War One stimulated migration still more. As men were drafted, the labor shortage was intensified. And the draft brought thousands of Negro soldiers to Army bases in the North, opening a vision of a world beyond that of the small town in which, until then, their lives had been bound. The heavy traffic of Negroes moving North in turn persuaded others living along the main routes to join the trek. A migrant from Decatur, Alabama, reported that perhaps a third of the city's Negro population decided to leave after seeing all the migrants riding through. "And when the moving fever hit them," he said, "there was no changing their minds."

While Negroes were being pulled to the North by job opportunities, they were also being pushed off the land in the South. The full impact of the agrarian revolution was reaching the Southern cotton farmer, and the Negro was hit hardest of all. Farmers in the hot, dry climate of New Mexico and Arizona were producing a longer staple, better quality cotton than the farmers in the old Black Belt could produce, and so cotton production of Negro-operated farms east of the Mississippi began to decline. Mechanization of agriculture also hurt the Negro farmers, most of whom were sharecroppers and tenants. Finally, the ravages of the boll weevil, which plagued the Black Belt after 1910, intensified the Negro cotton farmer's already desperate plight. "The merchant got half the cotton, the boll weevil got the rest," went a Negro ballad. And as if the boll weevil weren't enough, a series of floods during the summer of 1915 added to the Negroes' woes.

The Negro was pushed off the land—but he could find no

place in the cities of the South, for poor whites who were also being forced off the land pre-empted the jobs opening up in Southern industry. Indeed not only were Negroes barred from jobs in the new textile mills and other industries springing up in the South, but they found their traditional occupations as well—as barbers and waiters, as carpenters, masons, and painters, as saw-mill operators—taken over by the desperate whites. And so the North, for all its faults, looked more and more like the promised land.

Once the forces of ignorance and inertia were overcome and a new pattern of behavior opened up, the movement northward rapidly gained momentum. The pull of demand continued after the end of the First World War, when the Immigration Exclusion Acts of the early twenties ended once and for all the immigration from Southern and Eastern Europe. And the agrarian revolution continued to push Negroes off the land, while discrimination barred them from jobs in Southern industry. Nearly 800,000 Negroes left the eleven states of the Old Confederacy during the 1920s, and almost 400,000 moved away during the Depression of the 1930s. Thus, the 1940 Census revealed that the Negro population outside the Old Confederacy had more than doubled in the preceding thirty years, increasing from 1.9 to 4 million. Within the Old Confederacy, by contrast, the Negro population had increased only 12 per cent. Yet these eleven states still contained over two-thirds of all Negro Americans.

World War Two really opened the floodgates. With ten million men in uniform and industry operating in full blast, labor again was a scarce and precious commodity. Negroes flocked to the assembly lines in Detroit, now turning out tanks and jeeps instead of autos; to the shipyards in Oakland, New York, and Camden; to the steel mills in Pittsburgh, Gary, and Chicago; to the aircraft plants in Los Angeles. After the war had ended, industry continued to boom; in the late forties and early fifties the auto companies sent labor agents fanning through the South to recruit Negroes for the busy assembly lines. In New York, Philadelphia, Chicago, and most other big cities, employment agencies still do a brisk business directing a steady flow of Negro women and girls to work as domestic servants in a newly affluent society.

Within the South itself, moreover, mechanization of agriculture has been forcing millions of people, black and white, off the land, even when there are no jobs in the cities. Thus, the number of farms in the United States declined by one-third during the fifties. As always, the Negro farmers were hardest-hit: the number of Negro farm operators dropped 41 per cent in the five years from 1954 to 1959, the latest year for which figures are available. Sharecropping—once the predominant method of Negro farming—has almost disappeared: the number of sharecroppers, black and white, dropped from 541,000 in 1940 (and 776,000 in 1930) to a mere 122,000 in 1959.

The result has been an enormous shift of population from rural to urban areas: no fewer than 78 per cent of the counties of the United States suffered a net out-migration of population during the decade of the fifties. In the South itself, nearly four and a half million whites and two million Negroes moved from rural to urban places in the 1950s. The rural whites, for the most part, moved to Southern cities and towns, (through some 1.4 million left the South). Negroes on the other hand, left the South altogether: only 150,000 Negroes moved to Southern cities during the 1950s, since competition from white migrants, when added to traditional Southern discrimination, made it impossible for Negroes to find jobs in the Southern cities. In all, some 2.75 million Negroes left the South between 1940 and 1960.[3] Thus, the Negro population outside the Deep South has increased five-fold since 1910; it has nearly tripled just since 1940. Part of this expansion, of course, has come from natural increase

[3] The statistics, of course, refer to *net* changes in population. A good many rural Southern Negroes moved to Southern cities, taking the place of Negroes who had moved to the North.

rather than migration; but it is the migration of Negroes of child-bearing age that enabled the natural increase to occur outside the South. Within the South itself, migration has caused a substantial decline in the Negro population in rural areas; as a result, the population living in cities has jumped from 21 per cent in 1940 (and only 7 per cent in 1910) to 41 per cent in 1960.

Most of the Negroes moving to the North have crowded into the slums of the twelve largest cities, which in 1960 held 60 per cent of the Negroes living outside the Deep South. Between 1940 and 1960 the Negro population of New York increased nearly two and a half times to 1.1 million, or 14 per cent of the city's population. The Negro population of Chicago increased more than two and a half times to 890,-000, or 24 per cent. In Philadelphia, between 1940 and 1960, the number of Negroes doubled to 529,000, or 26 per cent. The Negro population of Detroit has more than tripled to nearly a half-million, or 29 per cent of the city's population; and the Negro population of Los Angeles County has increased a phenomenal 600 per cent between 1940 and 1960, from 75,000 to 464,000. In recent years, moreover, Negro migration has fanned out to a host of smaller cities—Buffalo and Rochester, Toledo and Akron, Newark, New Haven, Fort Wayne, Milwaukee, Kansas City, Wichita.

The migration continues; Newark, which was 34.4 per cent Negro at the time of the 1960 Census, is now over 50 per cent Negro. But even if Negro migration were to stop completely (and it's bound to slow down), the Negro population of the large cities would continue to grow at a rapid rate, and Negroes would account for a steadily increasing proportion of the cities' population. For the Negro population is considerably younger than the white population of these cities; in addition, the Negro birth rate is considerably higher than the white. (In New Haven and Buffalo, for example, Negroes represent one person in eight out of the total population, but account for one birth in four.) Thus, Professor

C. Horace Hamilton of the University of North Carolina, has predicted that Negro population outside the South will have doubled again by 1980, and that by the year 2,000, nearly three Negroes in four will be living in the North and West.

Were it not for the increase in their Negro population, the large cities would be losing residents at a rapid clip. For the stream of Negroes moving into the big cities has been paralleled by a stream of whites moving out to the suburbs. In the twenty-four metropolitan areas with a half-million or more residents, for example, the "central cities" lost 2,399,000 white residents between 1950 and 1960, a drop of 7.3 per cent.[4] They gained 2,641,000 new Negro residents in the same period, a rise of over 50 per cent; Negroes now account for over 20 per cent of the population of these cities. In the suburbs, by contrast, the white population grew by nearly 16 million, or 65 per cent; Negro population increased by 800,000, or better than 60 per cent, but remained a small proportion—under 5 per cent—of the total suburban population.

The dimensions of the suburban population explosion, incidentally, make it clear that the white exodus from the city has *not* been due primarily to the Negro influx, as sensitive Negroes (and a good many white liberals) frequently assert. On the contrary, the flight to the suburbs has been one of the dominant facts of city life for a century or more. Almost as soon as city dwellers become members of the middle class, they seen to long for a house and patch of land, no matter how small. Hence the middle class has always been on the move, abandoning its homes near the center of town for sites farther out. The opening of an Illinois Central railway station at Fifty-fourth Street and Lake Park Avenue in 1856,

[4] The twenty-four are New York, Los Angeles, Chicago, Philadelphia, Detroit, San Francisco-Oakland, Boston, Pittsburgh, St. Louis, Washington, D.C., Cleveland, Baltimore, Newark, Minneapolis-St. Paul, Buffalo, Houston, Milwaukee, Paterson-Clifton-Passaic, Seattle, Dallas, Cincinnati, Kansas City, San Diego, and Atlanta.

and another at Forty-seventh Street, in 1859, led to the creation of the first suburbs south of Chicago's Loop; Hyde Park Village was incorporated in 1861, and by 1890, shortly before its annexation by the city of Chicago, boasted that its population of 85,000 made it the largest village in the world. In New York, as early as the 1870s, citizens were lamenting the exodus of men of "moderate income to the suburban towns," and complaining that the city was becoming the habitat only of the very rich and the very poor. (Manhattan reached its peak population in 1910 and has been losing residents ever since). To be sure, until the 1930s or 1940s, cities were able to recapture a large portion of their self-exiled residents by annexing the new suburbs to which the former urbanites had moved. But they depended for their growth on the steady stream of immigrants.

Like all previous immigrant groups, the Negroes have settled in the traditional "port of entry"—the oldest, least desirable section of the city, generally in or around the central business district. That is where the cheapest housing usually is to be found; more important, that is the only place the newcomers can find a place to live, since prejudice as well as income keeps them out of the "better" neighborhoods. (Immigrants, Negroes included, have always paid more for their housing, comparatively, than the established city dwellers. No urban industry is quite as profitable as slum manufacturing.) In Detroit, for example, the number of Negroes within an eight-mile radius of the central business district has increased eightfold since 1930, while the number of white residents has been halved.

As did each European immigrant group, moreover, the new Negro residents also figure disproportionately on the police blotters, the relief rolls, the truant officer's case load, the registers of rundown housing, the commitments for drug addiction, etc. In St. Louis, for example, Negroes represented 29 per cent of the population in 1959, but accounted for over 50 per cent of the crime. In Detroit, where Negroes make up about 30 per cent of the population, they comprise some 80 per cent of the people on relief. (One Negro in four in Chicago is receiving public assistance of some sort.)

To be sure, it is not Negroes alone who find the move painful. In New York, the Puerto Rican population has swelled from perhaps 100,000 in 1940 to over 700,000 in 1960; with this increase has come a host of social problems. And Cincinnati, Baltimore, St. Louis, Columbus, Detroit, and Chicago, among other cities, receive a steady stream of impoverished white hillbillies from the Southern Appalachian Mountains. These Appalachian whites—the oldest and purest Anglo-Saxon stock in the United States—have at least as much initial difficulty adjusting to the city as do the Negroes and Puerto Ricans. Consider this report, from *Harper's*,[5] on the hillbillies in Chicago:

> Settling in deteriorated neighborhoods where they can stick with their own kind, they live as much as they can the way they lived back home. Often removing window screens, they sit half-dressed where it is cooler, and dispose of garbage the quickest way. Their own dress is casual and their children's worse. Their housekeeping is easy to the point of disorder, and they congregate in the evening on front porches and steps . . .
>
> Their children play freely anywhere, without supervision. Fences and hedges break down; lawns go back to dirt. On the crowded city streets, children are unsafe, and their parents seem oblivious. Even more, when it comes to sex training, their habits—with respect to such matters as incest and statutory rape—are clearly at variance with urban legal requirements, and parents fail to appreciate the interest authorities take in their sex life . . .
>
> "Skid row dives, opium parlors, and assorted other dens of iniquity collectively are as safe as Sunday school picnics compared with the joints taken over by clans of fightin', feudin' Southern hillbillies and their shootin' cousins," said one ferocious exposé in the Chicago *Sunday Tribune*. "The Southern hillbilly migrants," the story continued, ". . . have the lowest standard of living and moral code (if any), the biggest capacity for liquor, and the most savage tactics when drunk, which is most of the time."

[5] Albert N. Votaw, "The Hillbillies Invade Chicago," *Harper's*, February, 1958, pp. 65–66.

It is the explosive growth of their Negro populations, however, that constitute the large cities' principal problem and concern. The Puerto Rican and Appalachian whites affect only a limited number of cities, usually only in a limited way; but every city has a large and growing Negro population. In every city, white residents and civic leaders are concerned about the physical deterioration of neighborhoods inhabited by Negroes; about the rising adult crime and juvenile delinquency rates in Negro neighborhoods that spill over into the rest of the city, making the parks and sometimes even the streets unsafe; about the tensions unleashed by suits to force school desegregation and the fiscal strain of building classrooms fast enough to hold the mushrooming enrollments in Negro areas, and the difficulty of hiring teachers to teach in these schools; about the burden of welfare payments and the horror they feel as they watch second- and third-generation relief recepients grow up without ever knowing, or even seeing, what it means to be self-supporting. And in every city, Negro residents are bitter about the high rents they have to pay for rundown and shamefully neglected tenements in segregated sections of the city; about the discrimination by business and trade unions alike that bars them from skilled crafts and white-collar jobs; about the overcrowding and lack of standards in the schools their children attend; about the snubs and hurts and humiliations—big and small, real and imagined—that are their daily lot; about the general indifference to their plight. There is no large city, in short, which does not have a large and potentially explosive Negro problem.

THE BEER CAN IN THE COTTON PATCH

To be a Negro in this country and to be relatively conscious is to be in a rage almost all the time.

JAMES BALDWIN

Migration to the large city has always been painful, both to the migrants and to the people among whom they settled. A good many sociologists, city planners, and others concerned with urban problems have concluded, therefore, that the difficulties Negroes are having with the city, and the city with its Negro residents, represent simply one more chapter in the long saga of urban migration—a chapter which will end as happily as the preceding ones. The foremost proponent of this point of view is Professor Philip M. Hauser, Chairman of the Sociology Department of the University of Chicago, and Director of its Population Research and Training Center. According to Professor Hauser, "The problems which confront the Negro today, although perhaps differing in degree, are essentially the same kinds of problems which confronted our migrant groups in the past," and they will be solved in essentially the same way. Professor Hauser concedes that Negro migrants do not need "Americanization," as did their European predecessors, but he argues that they *do* need "acculturation" (some professors prefer the term "urbanization" or "accommodation"). This need for acculturation, in his view, forms the heart of the Negro problem of the large city. For Negroes have "been drawn from a primitive folk culture into a metropolitan way of life" in little more than a single generation—"as severe a problem of acculturation," Hauser argues, "as any group in history has ever faced." To solve "the Negro problem," he concludes, "the older residents must teach the newcomers what is expected of them in the city," thereby equipping them "to enter into the opportunities of the dominant culture." Unless the new Negro residents receive the proper instruction from their cultural superiors—so the theory runs—they are bound to make undesirable neighbors; for their "primitive folk culture" permits or even encourages behavior that clashes with the needs and standards of city life. "A Negro in the Mississippi Delta," Hauser suggests by way of illustration, "tosses his empty whisky bottle or beer can in a cotton patch, and what difference does it make? But on the asphalt pavements of a city it can make a difference, esthetically and with respect to safety. If physical violence is accepted in the south as a means of resolving conflict," Hauser continues, "nobody cares much; but in the urban community, such acts become felonies, with much more serious consequences." In one variant or another this theory that Negroes need "acculturation" underlies most of the public and private programs now being developed in Northern cities to ameliorate the Negro-urban problem. The Ford Foundation, for example, has committed a portion of its huge resources and influence to an attempt "to do in one generation for the urban newcomer what until now has taken three." The Foundation makes no distinction between the problems faced by Negroes and those faced by other contemporary migrants. The metropolis, Dr. Paul N. Ylvisaker, Director of the Foundation's Public Affairs Program, has told city planners and civic leaders, should be viewed "as a continuous system of attracting the newcomer (once the Scotch, the Irish, the Jew, the Italians, now the Negroes, the Puerto Ricans, the mountain whites, the Mexicans, and the American Indians) and of assimilating this newcomer to all that is up-to-date and sought after in the urban culture."

The "acculturation theory" can provide a useful perspective. Measured against the backdrop of history, the gangs and crime and squalor of today seem almost benign. Americans who have been shocked to read that women employees of the Supreme Court have been officially advised to secure a police escort before leaving the Court building at night should at the very least know that muggings and robberies in the capital antedate the recent Negro influx. In 1858, for example, when the Negro residents of the nation's capital still wore the fetters of slavery, a Senate committee investigated the city's rising crime rate. "Riot and bloodshed are of daily occurrence," the committee reported, "innocent and unoffending persons are shot, stabbed, and otherwise shamefully maltreated, and not infrequently the offender is not even arrested." And during the week-long Draft Riots in New York in 1863, when the Irish immigrants of Hell's Kitchen revolted against authority, federal troops had to be recalled from the front to restore order. Ninety-seven years later, the grandson of Irish immigrants was elected President of the United States. If the most backward, downtrodden, and discriminated-against European immigrant groups have now all moved up into the great American middle class—so the reasoning seems to go—then why not the Negroes, too?

Reasoning by analogy can be dangerously misleading, however; history does not usually repeat itself. Too many historians and sociologists—and far too many civic leaders—are using the "acculturation theory" as a license to look away from the uncomfortable fact of race and so to avoid the hard and painful decisions. Government officials can hardly be blamed for taking the easy way when academic authorities offer the bland reassurance that time and history will solve everything. To be sure, Hauser admits that the Negro's problem of adjustment may be more difficult than that of the European immigrants. But "forces are in motion," he assured the United States Civil Rights Commission, "that will enable the Negro to win his place as a full-fledged member of the American society." The motion Hauser is talking about is a lot slower than Negroes may be willing to accept, however. The process of acculturation, he told a Washington, D.C., audience in 1961, "requires time—time measured in human generations rather than years. I am displeased to report this," he dutifully added, "but it is the only honest thing to do."

Harvard's Professor Oscar Handlin offers much rosier lenses. "The experience of the past," he wrote at the end of *The Newcomers*,[6] a study of Negro and Puerto Rican migration to New York City, "offers a solid foundation for the belief that the newest immigrants to a great metropolis will play as useful a role as any of their predecessors. They themselves

[6] Oscar Handlin, *The Newcomers*, Cambridge, Mass.: Harvard University Press, 1959.

need only show the will and energy, and their neighbors the tolerance, to make it possible."[7]

It will take a lot more than that. To suggest that good will alone will solve the urban Negro problem is fatuousness of the worst sort. Good will can never be relied upon to solve any hard problem, and the question of the Negro's place in America is the hardest problem this country has ever faced. It is equally fatuous to pretend that color is irrelevant, as so many adherents of the "acculturation theory" seem to do, The plain fact is that the Negro faces a problem different in kind, and far more complex, than that faced by any of his European predecessors.

There are many differences. For one thing, the United States has far less need for unskilled labor today than it had when European immigrants were flooding our shores. It took no great transfer of skill for an Irish or Italian peasant to become a laborer on a construction gang. It takes an enormous transfer of skill, however, to enable a sharecropper from Mississippi to find a job as a computer programmer. And the gap is widening between Negro education and training, on the one hand, and the requirements of the labor market, on the other. Automation, new management techniques, and changes in consumer spending patterns are all reducing the demand for unskilled and semiskilled labor and increasing employment in professional, managerial, clerical, and sales jobs, many of which require considerable education and training. These white-collar occupations account for no less than 97 per cent of the total increase in employment that occurred between 1947 and 1963. The professionalization of the labor force accelerated during the mid-fifties, and will pick up momentum in the middle and late sixties. But Negroes are badly prepared for this change. Seven Negro men in ten now work in unskilled or semiskilled blue-collar jobs, compared

[7] Professor Handlin's optimism reflects pedantry as well as naïveté. "It is often necessary in social science," he wrote in the opening sentence of *The Newcomers*, "to obscure reality in the interest of clarity of analysis." In real life, reality must be faced squarely, not obscured.

to three out of ten white men; and more than half the Negro men over the age of twenty-five (*vs.* 21 per cent of white men) have had less than a grammar school education. Small wonder that in Northern industrial centers one out of every three Negro workers has suffered unemployment in the last several years, or that in some Negro neighborhoods, the unemployment rate may run as high as 40 per cent. To anyone walking through the Negro neighborhoods of any large city—and to the children who grow up in them—few sights are more familiar than the groups of idle Negro men congregating at street corners, or the lonely Negroes sitting on their front stoops all day long, sipping wine from bottles discreetly hidden in brown paper bags.

Negroes' lack of education and training and their concentration in unskilled occupations—conditions produced by past discrimination—do not entirely account for Negro poverty, however. Neither does the inadequate growth of the economy, which has caused high unemployment among unskilled whites as well as among Negroes. On the contrary, the Negro unemployment rate is higher than the white rate in *every* major occupational group. Among craftsmen and foremen, for example, Negro unemployment ran to 9.7 per cent in 1962, compared to 4.8 per cent for whites; among clerical workers, 7.1 per cent *vs.* 3.8 per cent; among unskilled laborers, 15.8 per cent *vs.* 11 per cent. While a great many Negroes cannot find jobs because they lack the necessary skills, all too many Negroes who do have the education and training are unable to put their skills to work.

It is a lot harder for Negroes today to bear their poverty and lack of status than it was for the European immigrants. If you have to be poor, John Kenneth Galbraith has quipped, at least have the good sense to be born during a time when *everybody* is poor. The European immigrants showed this good judgment; they arrived at a time when the great majority of the population was poor. The Negro migration, by contrast, is occurring in an affluent society. Hence the Negroes are an economic as well as a racial minority—the first minority poor the world has ever known. Two out of three Negro households earn less than $4,000 a year, and one Negro male in nine is out of work. This poverty and insecurity are particularly galling to the Negro, who sees the white society that surrounds him grow increasingly affluent while he remains mired in squalor. Contrary to popular impression, the Negroes' economic position has actually deteriorated over the last ten years, relative to that of whites. Negroes did make enormous advances during World War Two and the boom years that followed, for the shortage of labor drew them into factory and white-collar jobs that had always been barred to them. As a result, Negro income increased 80 per cent faster than white income, and the median income of Negro families jumped from only 37 per cent of white income in 1939 to 57 per cent in 1952. But this escalation halted with the general slowdown of the economy after the Korean war. As a result, the median income of Negro families dropped from its high of 57 per cent of white income in 1952 to 53 per cent in 1962.

The slum in which the Negro lives, moreover, has been bequeathed to him by the Italians and Poles, the Slovaks and Jews of yesteryear who have left for greener pastures. In contrasting his lot with theirs, the Negro is positive that "the man"—the white man—has stacked the cards against him.

Among the great mass of working-class Negroes, therefore, and among many of the middle class as well, apathy exists side by side with a growing, festering resentment of their lot. These Negroes are more and more convinced that they should have a better life; they are less and less convinced that they themselves can do anything about it.

2.

Most important of all, however, the Hauser-Handlin-Ylvisaker approach, which sees the Negro problem as similar in kind to the problem faced by European immigrants in the past, or white migrants today, diverts attention from what is surely the central fact. The Negro is unlike any other immigrant group in one crucial regard: he is colored. And that makes all the difference. The Irish immigrants, to be sure, faced job discrimination as severe as the Negro faces today. A century ago, in fact, Negroes apparently were preferred over Irishmen. A want ad in the New York *Daily Sun* of May 11, 1853, for example, seeking a woman for general housework, specified "English, Scotch, Welsh, German or any country or color except Irish." But once the Irishman was "Americanized," his problem could be fairly easily resolved. He could lose his brogue and, if he so desired, change his name; and when his income permitted, he could move away from the slum and lose himself in the crowd. So, today, can the Appalachian whites and even most Puerto Ricans. But no Negro has ever made that much money in the United States; no matter how wealthy—or how educated, how "acculturated"—he may become, he cannot lose himself in the crowd. He remains a Negro. Sociologists and political scientists, for example, commonly refer to "Irish-Americans" or "Italian-Americans" or "Polish-Americans"—but to "American Negroes." The accent is always on "Negro."

The European ethnic groups, in short, could move into the main stream of American life without forcing beforehand any drastic rearrangements of attitudes or institutions. For the Negro to do so, however, will require the most radical changes in the whole structure of American society. The mere presence of a Negro in a white residential neighborhood unleashes fears and hatreds of the most elemental sort, and leads almost without exception to an exodus of the white residents. Residential segregation of Negroes has actually increased over the past several decades, despite the improvement in their economic position. This is in sharp contrast with the experience of European immigrant groups—or with the current experience of Puerto Rican immigrants. Traditionally, migrants have settled initially in ethnic ghettos in the slums of the central city and worked at the worst-paid and most menial occupations; but as they and their descendants move up the occupational ladder, they also move away from the ghetto to less and less segregated neighborhoods. Not so with the Negroes; the contrast between Negro experience and that of other immigrant groups is all the more striking in view of the fact that ethnic organizations generally have tried to *maintain* their ethnic colonies intact, whereas most major Negro organizations have been fighting for residential dispersal. And there seems to be little doubt that residential segregation in turn helps bar the Negro's assimilation into the economy and society at large.

The problem is double-barreled. On the one hand, "acculturation" is not enough; for all his culture or wealth, the educated Negro remains an alien in his own land.[8] But on the other hand, the process of acculturation doesn't seem to "take." Thus, Negroes have not been moving up the socioeconomic ladder as rapidly as might have been expected; second- and third-generation Negro city dwellers achieve less in school than the second- and third-generation offspring of immigrants; the crime rate in settled Negro areas is high and rising; and so on. Consider the following report:

> It cannot be denied that the main results of the development of the Philadelphia Negro since the war have on the whole disappointed his well-wishers. They do not pretend that he has not made great advance in certain lines, or even that in general he is not better off today than formerly . . . Yet there is a widespread feeling that more might reasonably have been expected in the line of social and moral development than apparently has been accomplished. Not only do they feel that there is a lack of positive result, but the relative advance compared with the period just before the war is slow, if not an actual retrogression; an abnormal and growing amount of crime and poverty can justly be charged to the Negro; he is not a large taxpayer, holds no conspicuous place in the business world or the world of letters, and even as a workingman seems to be losing ground.

[8] Statistically speaking, Negroes are now more urbanized than whites; that is, a slightly larger proportion of Negroes than of whites now live in urban areas.

The war in question was the Civil War, not World War Two; the writer was the great Negro sociologist, W. E. B. Du Bois, in his classic study of *The Philadelphia Negro*, published in 1899.

Du Bois' observations remain uncomfortably pertinent. An increasing proportion of Negroes, moreover, are city-born and raised, but too many occupy the same relative position in society as did their parents and grandparents. In 1960, for example, 44 per cent of the Negro residents of Chicago were born in Illinois, and perhaps two-thirds of the older Negroes (those over forty-five) had lived in metropolitan areas for twenty years or more. Yet fully one-quarter of the Negro families in Chicago are receiving public welfare assistance; Negroes account for 25 per cent of the city's population, but over 80 per cent of the relief recipients. Negroes also account for a disproportionate amount of crime.

Much the same is true of Harlem, once the largest Negro community in the United States and still in a sense the intellectual and cultural center of American Negroes. Harlem receives a steady flow of migrants from the South (some seventy-five hundred came between 1955 and 1960), but it is predominantly a community of established city dwellers, with over two hundred fifty churches and some fifty-four social agencies in its service.[9] Only 4 per cent are recent migrants from the South—yet Harlem's juvenile delinquency rate is nearly two and one half times the city average, its venereal disease rate is nearly seven times as high. Considerably more than one-third of all Harlem births are illegitimate, a ratio nearly five times that of the city as a whole. Harlem's infant mortality rate—generally considered the best single measure of the state of a community's health—is nearly twice as high as that for New York City as a whole.

By any measure of social disorganization, in short, Harlem

[9] Harlem has approximately 200,000 residents, of whom about 125,000 are church-affiliated; an estimated 70,000 to 80,000 receive help from one or more of the social agencies.

is a slum sunk in apathy and steeped in crime, narcotics addiction, poverty and disease. "Don't let this Harlem git you," a motherly Harlem matron advises the young hero of Ellison's *Invisible Man,* just recently arrived from the South. "I'm in New York, but New York ain't in me, understand what I mean? Don't get corrupted." But many do. And the worst corruption of all is not the crime but the apathy; not even the Black Muslims can attract any sizable membership in Harlem. The hopelessness seems to increase with the passage of time. "Yes, we've progressed," James Baldwin has quipped. "When I was a boy in Harlem, Negroes got drunk and cursed each other out. Now they become junkies and don't say anything."

They do not read anything, either—in part because they never learn to read fluently. In the New York City public schools, New York-born Negro youngsters read as poorly as immigrant youngsters; by the sixth grade, both groups, on average, score at about the fourth-grade level, nearly two years below the national norm.[10] The fact that the city-born youngsters read no better than recent arrivals from the South is all the more striking in view of the fact that the former have somewhat higher IQs—in the sixth grade, an average of 90, compared to 85.8 for the in-migrants. Thus, the native-born children perform at a lower level relative to capacity than the newcomers. Residence in the Northern city seems to dull rather than to stimulate achievement.

If Negroes remain outside the main stream of city life, therefore—if they appear amoral, if their behavior clashes with city standards—the blame can be placed less and less on what Professor Hauser calls the "primitive folk culture" of the Negro South. A growing body of research—most notably, the studies of the Negro family in Washington, D.C., by Hylan Lewis and associates—suggests that urban Negroes in fact do share in middle-class values and aspirations. They, too, value

[10] White middle-class children in the New York metropolitan area tend to score about two years *above* the national average, so the Harlem youngster, be he native-born or in-migrant, is further below the city norm than the nationwide tests indicate.

financial success; they, too, want their children to be educated; they, too, are ashamed of illegitimacy, to cite a few examples. To be sure, lower-class Negroes do not always act accordingly; they do drop out of schools and they do have more illegitimate children than members of the middle class. But the reason, in many cases, is that their poverty—intellectual and cultural as well as financial—gets in the way. Some Negroes know what they want (according to middle-class standards) but do not know how to achieve these wants. Others know both, but their daily struggle for existence drains them of the energy they need to achieve their aspirations. These people, in Hylan Lewis' phrase, are "frustrated victims of middle-class values." Precisely because they have been acculturated into middle-class values, their inability to climb out of the lower-class slum persuades them that the cards are stacked against them, or reinforces their sense of worthlessness. In either case, the evidence of their lives suggests that there is no use in trying.

But the slum-dwelling Negro's behavior stems from something deeper-rooted, and harder to overcome, than poverty: his hatred of "the man," the white man, who seems determined to keep him in his place. Take Professor Hauser's tale of the Negro from Mississippi, who once threw his empty whisky bottle or beer can in the cotton patch and who, as Hauser puts it, now must be taught not to hurl it out his Chicago tenement window. There may well be some Negroes in Chicago who throw beer cans out of windows because they do not know any better; the great majority who do so, however, know perfectly well that their act is anti-social; that is precisely why they do it! They throw the beer can not through ignorance but through hate—because throwing it out the window is an act of defiance, a readily available means of social protest. There are other means of protest, of course: misbehaving in school, or dropping out of school altogether; not showing up for work on time, or not showing up at all (and lying about the reason); breaking school windows or ripping telephone receivers out of outdoor phone booths; or the oldest form of protest of all, apathy—a flat refusal to co-operate with the oppressor or to accept his moral code. "You can force a man to live in a prison," says Saul Alinsky of the Industrial Areas Foundation, "but you can't make him contribute to its upkeep."

Against what are the beer-can throwers or the drop-outs protesting? In a word, everything: the world about them, which dooms them to defeat and humiliation (or which they believe dooms them, which amounts to the same thing); and the weakness in themselves, which accepts humiliation, and so makes defeat inevitable. Something happens to the Negro in Harlem (or the South Side of Chicago, or North Philadelphia, or their equivalents in a dozen cities)—something which stifles the ambition and kills the spirit, and suffuses the whole personality with despair and emptiness. Like the immigrants of old, the Negro migrants, many of them, come in search of the promised land. But their aspirations are quickly trampled on. In one of the short stories in his *Eight Men,*[11] the late Richard Wright described what moving to Chicago did to him.

> While working as a porter in Memphis I had often stood aghast as a friend of mine had offered himself to be kicked by the white men; but now, while working in Chicago, I was learning that perhaps even a kick was better than uncertainty . . . I had elected, in my fevered search for honorable adjustment to the American scene, not to submit and in doing so I had embraced the daily horror of anxiety, of tension, of eternal disquiet.
>
> To solve this tangle of balked emotion, I loaded the empty part of the ship of my personality with fantasies of ambition to keep it from toppling over into the sea of senselessness. Like any other American, I dreamed of going into business and making money; I dreamed of working for a firm that would allow me to advance until I reached an important position . . . Yet I knew—with that part of my mind that the whites had given me—that none of my dreams were possible. Then I would hate myself for allowing my mind to dwell upon the unattainable. Thus the circle would complete itself.
>
> Slowly I began to forge in the depths of my mind a mechanism than repressed all the dreams and desires that the Chicago streets, the newspapers, the movies were evoking in me. I was going through

[11] Richard Wright, *Eight Men,* New York: World, 1960.

a second childhood; a new sense of the limit of the possible was being born in me. What could I dream of that had the barest possibility of coming true? I could think of nothing. And, slowly, it was upon exactly that nothingness that my mind began to dwell, that constant sense of wanting without having, of being hated without reason. A dim notion of what life meant to a Negro in America was coming to consciousness in me, not in terms of external events, lynchings, Jim Crowism and the endless brutalities, but in terms of crossed-up feeling, of emotional tension.

Despair and apathy, of course, are basic ingredients of any lower-class community, and a good many problems attributed to Negroes because of their race in fact are due to their class. But there is a special quality to the despair of the Negro slum that distinguishes it from any other. For the youngster growing up in Harlem or any other Negro slum, the gates of life clang shut at a terrifyingly early age. For one thing, the children become aware almost from infancy of the opprobrium Americans attach to color. They feel it in their parents' voices as they are warned to behave when they stray beyond the ghetto's wall. They become aware of it as they begin to watch television, or go to the movies, or read the mass-circulation magazines; beauty, success, and status all wear a white skin. They learn to feel ashamed of their color as they learn to talk, and thereby to absorb the invidiousness our very language attaches to color. White represents purity and goodness, black represents evil. The white lie is the permissible misstatement, the black lie the inexcusable falsehood; the black sheep is the one who goes astray (and when he goes astray, he receives a black mark on his record); defeat is black (the stock market crashed on "Black Thursday"), victory white. Even James Weldon Johnson's "Negro National Anthem" speaks of Negroes "treading our path through the blood of the slaughtered/ . . . Till now we stand at last/ *Where the white gleam of our bright star is cast.*" [Emphasis added]

Language aside, Negro children learn soon enough—from their father's menial job, or lack of it, from his mixture of fear and deference and hate of "the man"—that the world is white and they are black. And the odds are small indeed that a Negro child can grow up without being abused or patronized, without being convinced by a hundred big and small humiliations, that he has no worth and no chance. "One did not have to be very bright," Baldwin has written of his childhood in Harlem, "to realize how little one could do to change one's situation; one did not have to be abnormally sensitive to be worn down to a cutting edge by the incessant and gratuitous humiliation and danger one encountered every working day, all day long." He continues:

> The humiliation did not apply merely to working days, or workers; I was thirteen and was crossing Fifth Avenue on my way to the Forty-second Street library, and the cop in the middle of the street muttered as I passed him, "Why don't you niggers stay uptown where you belong?" When I was ten, and didn't look, certainly, any older, two policemen amused themselves by frisking me, making comic (and terrifying) speculations concerning my ancestry and probable sexual prowess, and for good measure, leaving me flat on my back in one of Harlem's empty lots.[12]

And if the child should grow up somehow without confronting prejudice and discrimination directly, he meets it soon enough as an adult. He meets it whether he stays in the slum or moves to the top, for white men in authority do not always distinguish between Negroes who are "acculturated" and those who are not. The police are an ever-present threat; there is hardly a Negro community in the United States which does not regard the local police with suspicion, if not with hate. Consider the following report from the New York City *Amsterdam News* of December 8, 1962:

> Two young white cops were suspended from the New York City Police force last Wednesday after they were indicted and arrested on charges of brutal assault on a 30-year-old prominent Negro engineer in a West Side police station when he went in to complain about being unlawfully searched and assaulted by them earlier in the street . . .

[12] James Baldwin, *The Fire Next Time*, New York: Dial Press, 1963.

Victim of the police brutality was Marshal Whitehead, 30, of 116 W. 87 St., a prominent designing engineer with a Hempstead, L.I., firm.

The brutality incident occurred last August 8 when Whitehead after returning home from a neighborhood softball game decided to run around the block and loosen up.

As he was trotting in the area of 87th St. and Amsterdam Ave., the tactical police force car with four officers stopped, and several got out and slugged him and searched him, and then told him to get off the street.

Whitehead, whose photo is to be on the cover of the forthcoming Emancipation issue of a popular magazine, wrote the police car number down and went home.

Whitehead later went to the stationhouse to complain and was sent to a Detective Keogh, who after interviewing him, denied any knowledge of the police car number and tore up the slip containing the license number.

As Whitehead was about to leave, he saw the four cops who had slugged him earlier, entering the stationhouse and identified [them].

The cops reportedly said: "If you want something to complain about, then we'll give you something to complain about" and allegedly took him to the basement of the stationhouse, where Whitehead was brutally assaulted about the head and body, and later arrested for disorderly conduct and resisting arrest. [The charges were later dismissed.]

The occasional acts of police brutality, however, hurt less than the constant flow of petty indignities—indignities that seem to demonstrate, a dozen times a year, that no matter what a Negro does, no matter what he achieves, no matter what he is, the white world will never accept him. He can be Ralph Bunche, and still be refused a room in an Atlanta hotel while his secretary's reservation is immediately accepted. He can be a distinguished sociologist, yet in a restaurant two blocks from the White House be ushered to a table alongside the kitchen door while the front tables are all unoccupied. Experiencing hostility wherever they go, many Negroes begin to *expect* hostility wherever they go. They lose their ability to distinguish a real from a fancied injury; as James Baldwin has put it, "every American Negro risks having the gates of paranoia close on him," and he takes affront from anything and everything. Appearing in court to answer charges of assaulting a white musician, for example, the band-leader Charlie Mingus angrily turned on his own lawyer, who had described Mingus as "a great jazz musician." "Don't call me a *jazz* musician," he told the startled lawyer. "To me the word *jazz* means nigger, discrimination, second-class citizenship, the whole back-of-the-bus bit . . . I'm just a musician, man."

The worst indignity of all is being patronized by whites who "know how to handle Negroes." The housekeeper inspecting my wife's hospital room was obviously pleased with the way the Negro porter had cleaned the room. "You're a good boy, Jimmy," she told him by way of compliment; and Jimmy said, "Thank you, Ma'am." Jimmy was forty-eight years old. Perhaps he had become so used to being treated like a boy that he took the insult as a compliment. Or perhaps he had merely learned, for his own well-being, to hide his anger behind a mask of servility. In any case, he knew that no supervisor would say, "You're a good boy, Jack," if the white orderly did a good job of mopping up after a patient. "There is a form of oppression which is more painful and more scathing than physical injury or economic privation," Rabbi Abraham Heschel told the first National Conference on Religion and Race. "It is public humiliation." Ancient Jewish law understood and underscored this fact. According to the Talmud, one should prefer to throw oneself alive into a burning furnace than to embarrass another person publicly. Indeed, the same Hebrew word denotes both murder and insult.

Negroes are given humiliation, insult, and embarrassment as a daily diet, and without regard to individual merit. They are convinced, as a result, that most whites never see them as individuals, that all Negroes look alike to whites; the theme of "facelessness" and "invisibility" runs through Negro literature. "No more fiendish punishment could be devised, were such a thing physically possible," the philosopher William James once wrote, "than that one should be turned loose in society and remain unnoticed by all the members thereof." The Negro is noticed, of course, for in rejecting him, white society must thereby notice him. But the Negro, too often, is noticed only to be rejected. "The dehumanized image of the Negro which white Americans carry in their minds, the anti-Negro epithets continuously on their lips," Richard Wright has written, "exclude the contemporary Negro as truly as though he were kept in a steel prison."

This sense of rejection by American society, a sense which dominates the lower-class Negro's life, tends to destroy his feeling of responsibility to law and authority; law and authority are always white and middle class and always seem designed to keep the lower-class Negro in his place. It also creates a good deal of class conflict and antagonism within the Negro community. Lower-class Negroes tend to resent Negroes who have achieved economic success, especially if the success is in the white world, for they are convinced that whites have so stacked the cards against Negroes that none can rise through ability or merit. Hence, if another Negro has "made it" in the white world it must be because of favoritism, because he pandered to white prejudice or white vanities, and thereby betrayed his own race. (Since ability counts for naught in the white world, why else has he advanced while I'm held back?) This kind of intra-group hostility is fairly typical of disadvantaged groups—witness the "shanty Irish" resentment of the "lace-curtain Irish" a generation or two ago. And lower-class Negroes' resentment of "dickety" Negroes frequently exists side-by-side with a vicarious delight that "one of our boys has made it."

Most important of all, however, the Negro reacts to exclusion with anger and hate. Nor is it just the sullen, apathetic tenement dweller who hates "the man." On the contrary, it is hard to imagine how any Negro American, no matter how well born or placed, can escape a deep sense of anger and a burning hatred of things white. Some are better able to repress it than others, but few escape its demonic force. "To be a

Negro in this country and to be relatively conscious," James Baldwin has written, "is to be in a rage almost all the time." With those Negroes who deny their hatred, the essayist-novelist J. Saunders Redding has written, "I have no quarrel . . . it is simply that I do not believe them." Some Negroes, he concedes, may be able to order their lives so as to avoid the experience of prejudice and discrimination—but to do so, in his view, requires an effort so great as to bring them to a psychopathic brink. "One's heart is sickened," he writes, "at the realization of the primal energy that goes into the sheer business of living as a Negro in the United States—in any one of the United States." It is impossible, in Redding's view, for a Negro to avoid a dual personality; inevitably, one part of him reacts to people and events as an individual, the other part reacts as a Negro.

The inevitability and the horror of this fact—the unending consciousness of color—were driven home to Redding by a traumatic experience he describes in his moving essay, "On Being Negro In America." The incident occurred during the thirties, when Redding was teaching at a Negro college in Louisville. His office window overlooked a white slum beginning at the edge of the campus. Standing at the office window one quiet winter Saturday, he saw a young woman lurching and staggering in his back yard, until she fell face down in the snow. He couldn't tell whether she was sick or drunk. "Pity rose in me," he relates, "but at the same time something else also—a gloating satisfaction that she was white. Sharply and concurrently felt, the two emotions were of equal strength, in perfect balance, and the corporeal I, fixed in a trance at the window, oscillated between them." The gloating won out. Redding decided not to go to her aid, but salved his conscience by calling the police to report "a drunken woman lying in the back yard of a house on Eighth Street." An hour later, the police came—and the next morning, Redding read on a back page of a newspaper that the woman had died of exposure following an epileptic seizure. "One can wash his hands," Redding concludes, "but the smudges and scars on the psyche are different."

Redding was troubled by the conflict between his instincts as a Negro and his instincts as a human being, and scarred by his decision to follow the former. A good many Negroes would have felt no such qualms of conscience afterward, nor would they have felt beforehand the tug of war Redding describes, between his desire to help the woman and his glee that a white person was in trouble. On Sunday, June 3, 1962, when news was flashed around the United States that a chartered airplane bound from Paris to Atlanta had crashed, killing 130 of the 132 aboard, Malcolm X, then the number two man in the Black Muslim movement, now leader of his own black nationalist group, was delivering a sermon to fifteen hundred Muslims in Los Angeles. He immediately shared the good news with his audience:

> I would like to announce a very beautiful thing that has happened . . . Somebody came and told me that [God] had answered our prayers in France. He dropped an airplane out of the sky with over 120 white people in it because the Muslims believe in an eye for an eye and a tooth for a tooth. But thanks to God, or Jehovah or Allah, we will continue to pray and we hope that every day another plane falls out of the sky . . . We call on our God—He gets rid of 120 of them at one whop.

Whites have generally been shocked by the animal-like hatred Muslim leaders have expressed on this and other occasions. They should be upset; but they shouldn't be surprised. There's no reason to assume that black men are more immune to the cancer of hate than white men, and we have seen more than enough examples of white hatred and brutality in recent years: in mobs rioting in Oxford, Mississippi, to block James Meredith's admission to the University, and in the obscene insults flung at him by his fellow students—the flower of Mississippi gentry—throughout his stay there; in the famous pictures of three Birmingham policemen forcing a single Negro woman to the ground, and pinning her there with their knees;

in crowds in Chicago hurling rocks to try to stop a Negro from moving into a previously all-white neighborhood. And Malcolm X's pleasure at the plane crash was no more vengeful than the glee expressed by Eugene "Bull" Connor, then-Commissioner of Public Safety of Birmingham, Alabama, when he learned that Rev. Fred T. Shuttlesworth, Alabama Negro leader, had been injured by a spray of water from police hoses. Connor was sorry that he hadn't been present to see the event —he'd been waiting all week to see Shuttlesworth hurt, he said—and he expressed regret that Shuttlesworth was carried away in an ambulance, instead of a hearse. The Black Muslims' hatred, in short, is the mirror image of white hatred.

To be sure, the Muslims have been able to enroll no more than 100,000, and perhaps as few as 50,000, Negroes as active members. But they have captured the sympathy of an enormous segment of Northern urban Negroes, who are unwilling to embrace the Muslim's strict discipline and religious tenets but who are delighted to hear the anger they feel being expressed so clearly. "I don't know how many followers he's got," a Harlem cabdriver told *Life* photographer Gordon Parks, who had just left Malcolm X, "but he has sure got a hell of a lot of well wishers." The cabbie was one of the latter. "Those Muslims or Moslems, 'ever what you call 'em, make more sense to me than the NAACP and Urban League and all the rest of them put together," he told Parks. "They're down on the good earth with the brother. They're for their own people and that Malcolm ain't afraid to tell Mr. Charlie, the FBI or the cops or nobody where to get off. You don't see him pussy-footin' 'round the whites like he's scared of them." Asked whether the Muslims hated all white men, the cabbie replied succinctly that "if they don't, they should, 'cause [the whites] sure don't waste no love on us. I used to live in Mobile and I lived in Memphis and I've lived in New York for fifteen years," the driver finished, "and I've come to one conclusion. No matter where the white man is, he's the same—the only thing he respects is force. And the only things gonna change him is some lead in the belly."

Nor are the relatively uneducated the only ones to respond to the Muslim's siren song of hate. On the contrary, the Muslims have struck a responsive chord in the most sophisticated Negro circles—among men and women in the forefront of the drive for integration, as well as in those who have held themselves aloof from any contact with "the problem." "Malcolm says things you or I would not say," a former president of the New York NAACP chapter confesses in admiration. "When he says those things, when he talks about the white man, even those of us who are repelled by his philosophy secretly cheer a little outside ourselves, because Malcolm X really does tell 'em, and we know he frightens the white man. We clap."

3.

To be a Negro in the United States, therefore, is to be angry —if not all the time, then most of the time. More than that, to be a Negro is to suspect, and even to hate, white men. ("Maybe freedom lies in hating," Ralph Ellison speculates in *Invisible Man.*) The anger and the hatred are facts—uncomfortable facts, but facts nonetheless. They must be taken into account in any effort to improve Negro-white relations; they must be taken into account in any program to help disadvantaged Negro youngsters or adults climb out of the slum; they must be taken into account in any program to help Negro adults. For the anger and hate are there; unless they find some constructive outlet, they inevitably poison and corrode the spirit. Unless they are recognized and dealt with, they doom to failure the best-intentioned attempts at speeding "acculturation," for Negroes regard doing the things that "acculturation" implies as "going along with Mr. Charlie's program."

Well-intentioned whites are surprised by the depth of Negro anger and frequently talk as if it were something new;

they read James Baldwin with a shock of discovery, not knowing that Richard Wright was saying the same things twenty-five and thirty years ago. Negro anger is not new; it has always been there. What *is* new is simply the Negro's willingness to express it, and his ability to command white attention when he does. For three and a half centuries, Negroes were taught to hide their true feelings. Under slavery, an expression of anger carried the risk of severe beating, of being sold away from family and friends, even of death. Knowing and fearing the consequences, the slave commonly suppressed any expression of rage or aggression; the surest way of avoiding the consequence was to replace anger with submission and humility. Nor did Emancipation change matters significantly in this regard. As recently as two decades ago, the Negro still took great pains not to provoke the white. Writing after America's entry into World War Two, Gunnar Myrdal reported that "it is the custom in the South to permit whites to resort to violence and threats of violence against the life, personal security, property, and freedom of movement of Negroes." (There are a good many areas in Mississippi and Alabama where the custom still holds.) Any white man, Myrdal went on to say, can strike or beat a Negro, steal or destroy his property, cheat him, and in some communities even take his life without fear of reprisal; how a white man handles "his niggers" is his business, and anyway, the Negro must have deserved whatever punishment was meted out. Even Negro leaders, Myrdal reported, were forced to be accommodating in their approach. "It is a political axiom," Myrdal wrote, "that Negroes can never, in any period, hope to attain more in the short-term power bargain than the most benevolent white groups are prepared to give them."

For their own protection, therefore, Negroes, no matter how rich or how poor, had to avoid any form of provocation. But the anger and hate were there (increased by Negroes' hatred of their own submissiveness) and had to find some outlet. They found expression by being directed against other

Negroes—thus, in a sense, against themselves. Until very recently, a very large proportion of Negro crime involved violence against other Negroes. This outlet was encouraged by the Southern tradition of ignoring Negro criminality as long as white lives or property were not involved; crime and violence *within* the Negro community were tolerated with a "Nigras will be Nigras" attitude.

Increasingly, however, Negroes are losing their fear of "the man"; increasingly, they are directing their anger against its real object. The turning point was World War Two. A war fought in the name of the Four Freedoms, but managed so as to preserve segregation, was bound to increase the American Negro's already ample store of hate. When the war began, Secretary of the Navy Knox stated that Negroes were acceptable aboard ship only as messmen, *i.e.*, as officers' servants; Admiral Nimitz defended the Navy's discrimination as "in the interests of harmony and efficiency." An Army spokesman informed a group of Negro newspapermen in 1941 that "The Army did not create the [race] problem . . . The Army is not a sociological laboratory; to be effective it must be organized and trained according to principles which will assure success." (Apparently treating Negroes as men would not have assured success.) As the war progressed, the most blatant discrimination was abolished; Negroes were accepted as combat soldiers and sailors, but almost always in segregated units. And the majority of Negro servicemen were assigned to menial or construction labor rather than to combat. Negroes were usually barred from the USO on the nights white soldiers were there—unless separate recreation facilities were provided for white and colored servicemen; a Negro who entered a USO or service club on his post might be arrested and court-martialed. The Red Cross, universal symbol of help and healing, "helped" by operating segregated entertainment centers and "healed" by segregating blood from white and colored donors. Negro soldiers even suffered the ultimate humiliation of seeing Nazi prisoners of war treated with more respect than they received.

The prisoners were allowed to eat with white soldiers and civilians in railroad dining cars or in station restaurants while the Negro soldiers—assigned to guard the Nazis en route to Southern POW camps—were barred. Witter Bynner dramatized one such incident in his poem "Defeat":

> On a train in Texas German prisoners eat
> With white American soldiers, seat by seat,
> While black American soldiers sit apart,
> The white men eating meat, the black men heart.
> Now, with that other war a century done,
> Not the live North but the dead South has won,
> Not yet a riven nation comes awake.
> Whom are we fighting this time, for God's sake?
> Mark well the token of the separate seat.
> It is again ourselves whom we defeat.[13]

World War Two also destroyed whatever illusion American Negroes may have had remaining about white sincerity, about white Americans' willingness to grant them equality. "White folks talking about the Four Freedoms," Negroes cynically observed, "and we ain't got none." Being drafted only increased the Negro's cynicism and discontent. "You ain't even a second-class citizen any more," a character in John Oliver Killens' bitter novel about World War Two, *And Then We Heard the Thunder,*[14] observes; "You're a second-class soldier."

Killens' book is a weak novel but a powerful sociological tract. Killens' hero, Solly Saunders, an ambitious and handsome young idealist, had been graduated from New York's City College. The model of the completely acculturated Negro, he had entered the Army as an anti-fascist, believing in the "Double V"—victory over the enemy abroad and the enemy at home. In the beginning, the enemy at home is the idea of

[13] Witter Bynner, "Defeat," in *Take Away the Darkness,* New York: Alfred A. Knopf, Inc., 1947.

[14] John Oliver Killens, *And Then We Heard the Thunder,* New York: Alfred A. Knopf, Inc., 1963.

racism; at the end, the enemy is the white man—*any* white man—as Saunders discovers that to whites his acculturation is irrelevant; he is still just a Negro. He reacts with hate. "You hate me because I'm white, and I don't blame you," Saunders' white mistress complains after he rudely rejects her protestation of love, "but it isn't fair—it just isn't fair." "Fairness is a thing no white man has a right to ask of colored," Saunders tells her. "I mean, look—who's been unfair to whom? Who's been unfair to my mother and her mother and my father and his father and who'll be unfair to my son and his children? 'Fairness' is a word that should choke in the white man's throat. I'm not asking any white man to be fair with Solly Saunders, baby. I live with no such false illusions."

World War Two not only shattered Negroes' illusions about white sincerity, it destroyed their fear of white authority as well. In the beginning, Killens' soldiers are angry but docile. "Charlie's got a plantation and you all his slaves, and ain't a damn thing you can do about it," one man cautions the rest. "You sure can't rise up against him and make a revolution." But in the end the soldiers do make a revolution, and quite a revolution it is! Stationed in Australia after a long tour of combat in the South Pacific, the Negro soldiers are angered when they find themselves received as men by the Australians, but still treated as *niggers* by their white superiors. When one of the company is arrested by military police for visiting a local pub at which they are welcomed, but which the Army had declared off limits, the company goes to his rescue. A bloody battle ensues when a company of southern whites is turned loose to subdue the black rebels. Killens' hero, Solly Saunders, gets word of the revolt at the apartment of his Australian mistress. "All my life, everything that ever happened to me, has brought me to this very moment," he tells her as he gets dressed to join the fray. But the full meaning of the battle is not revealed to Saunders until he reaches the scene and finds his buddies all dead. Then comes the moment of truth, the realization that his color takes precedence over everything else, that in trying to play the game according to the white man's rules—in trying to please white officers to gain a commission for himself, in trying to act out his role as an "acculturated" Negro—he had been betraying his soul.

> And now he knew what he hoped he never would forget again. All his escape hatches from being Negro were more illusion than reality and did not give him dignity. All of his individual solutions and personal assets, Looks, Personality, Education, Success, Acceptance, Security, the whole damn shooting match, was one great grand illusion, without dignity . . . If he signed a separate treaty with Cap'n Charlie, would it guarantee him safe conduct through the great white civilized jungle where the war was raging, always raging? Would his son also get safe passage? Anywhere any time any place? He had searched in all the wrong places.

Killens' account is fictional only in the specific details; it is based on a racial explosion that occurred in Brisbane, Australia, in 1943. Nor was this the only Negro revolt during World War Two, by any means. Thousands of spontaneous and individual rebellions went unrecorded and unnoticed, except perhaps by War Department statisticians surprised at the unusually heavy casualties suffered by white officers who led Negro soldiers into battle. (Pentagon statisticians, analyzing the casualties after the fact, had no way of determining by whose bullets the officers had died.) Other revolts were too formal to be ignored, though news of them was suppressed rather systematically, and the details frequently kept out of Army records. Deaths resulting from race riots were ascribed to "motor vehicle accident" or some such category when they occurred within the United States, to combat when they occurred abroad. War Department files dealing with Negro discontent and with racial conflict were classified to prevent their use or dissemination. Within the United States, race riots occurred at the Mobile Naval Yard and at Fort Bragg, Fort Dix, Camp Davis, Camp Lee, and Camp Robinson; abroad, there were riots at Wiltshire, England, in October of 1943, and at the Guam Naval Base on December 24 and 25, 1945.[15] At Mabry Field, Florida, and Port Chicago, California, Negro servicemen refused to perform work they felt had been assigned them solely because of their color. At Freeman Field, Indiana, a hundred Negro officers of the 47th Bomber Group were arrested and placed in the stockade when they entered a "For White Only" officers club; they were cleared after being held for some time, but were transferred to a Southern post as punishment.

Acts of defiance aside, the war drastically altered the relations between Negroes and whites. By 1945, a million Negroes were in uniform. Men who had been decorated for "outstanding courage and resourcefulness" at Bastogne, who had built the Lido Road in Southeast Asia or manned the "Red Ball Express" in France or landed in the first invasion wave at Okinawa were not likely to be quite as afraid of white authority as their fathers. What Negroes discovered during the war (and what they have been rediscovering ever since) was their power to intimidate—not by violence, but by their very presence. Writing about the First World War, W. E. B. Du Bois spoke of "the deep resentment mixed with the pale ghost of fear which Negro soldiers call up in the white South." What was true of World War One was even truer of World War Two. And as Negroes began to sense this, their own attitude changed: one need not fear—and certainly not respect—the man who fears you.

Thus, Negroes in civilian life, as well as those in uniform, lost their fear of speaking up and acting out. When the country began its defense preparation after war broke out in Europe, Negroes were systemically denied employment; in contrast

[15] More recently—on the night of September 6, 1963—a Southern white Air Force man was killed during a riot between white Air Force men and Negroes belonging to an Army Quartermaster company stationed at the United States Air Force base at Evreux, sixty miles outside Paris. The riot was touched off by an argument over Alabama Governor George Wallace's defiance of the late President Kennedy over desegregation of the Alabama public schools.

to the situation at the beginning of World War One, there was still a large pool of unemployed whites from which to draw. Early in 1941, therefore, A. Philip Randolph, President of the Brotherhood of Sleeping Car Porters, advanced the idea of assembling fifty to a hundred thousand Negroes to march on Washington to demand employment of Negroes in defense industries. Governmental alarm matched Negro enthusiasm; the officials understood only too well the embarrassment that would be caused the United States if the march were to come off. Randolph could not be dissuaded until President Roosevelt issued his famous Executive Order 8802, prohibiting discrimination in defense industries and establishing a Fair Employment Practices Committee. The Executive Order was relatively unimportant in itself, since it lacked any real enforcement provisions. But its issuance was enormously significant: it represented the first time since Reconstruction that the Federal Government had intervened on behalf of Negro rights; and it demonstrated that Negro militancy could pay off. The seeds of the protest movements of the 1950s and 1960s were sown by the March on Washington. As the war progressed, Negroes were drawn into better-paying and higher status jobs in the cities of the North and West. Thus, the Negro population of Los Angeles County doubled during the course of the war.

And now, as might be expected, the closer Negroes come to full equality, the angrier they become over the disparities that remain. Their anger is expressed in a variety of ways. Testifying before a congressional committee studying the integration of Washington, D.C., public schools, a pitifully naïve white principal told how a "Negro girl will stand in the aisle and dare a white girl to pass her . . . Or walking down the halls and stepping on their heels. Little things that show an antagonism for which I can see no reason." Sometimes the hostility takes a more direct and dangerous form, exploding in a paroxysm of violence, as in the 1962 Thanksgiving Day race riot in Washington, following the defeat of an all-Negro public-high-school football team by a predominately white parochial-school team. Here is one reporter's description:

> Inside the stadium, the shouting mob had fought its way into the St. John's seats and forced retreating white spectators to jam up the exit ramps. Racing up an aisle to reach the petrified whites, a colored woman, approximately 45 years old, slapped a white teen-age girl, added her hateful reason: "You're white."
>
> Pushing, shoving and purse snatching characterized the stampede to clear the stadium, which suffered little damage. Trampled under foot were combs, lipsticks and rosary beads that had fallen out of ripped open purses. Spectators were called "you white bastard," or "you white sonofabitch," or "white mother f——r."
>
> On the broad, uncluttered streets, parking lots, and plazas outside the stadium, the riot broke out in full fury . . . "It was nothing short of pure terror," said one frightened father as he observed some of the harm inflicted. A sample of the terror:
>
> Because he wanted to sit with some of his friends for the second half of the game, 15-year-old Lawrence Linson, a St. John's freshman, made arrangements to meet his family at the car after the game. As he was waiting by the car, young Linson was pummelled by ten Negroes. He suffered a compound fractured jaw and lost three teeth from the simultaneous blows.
>
> Michael Belmore, 15-year-old student at Montgomery Northwood High School, was in a party of six teenagers who stopped their car at a traffic light at 17th Street. A gang of fourteen Negroes approached the car and the leader said to Belmore, "Gimme a cigarette." Answering that he did not smoke, Belmore was promptly hit in the mouth. He required six stitches in his upper lip.
>
> A fourteen-year-old white boy was chased for a quarter of a mile by a band of twenty-five Negroes. Hemmed in by the approaching mob, the youth's only recourse was to run, fully clothed into the Anacostia River. The hoodlums stood on the bank, jeered at him, then left.
>
> Three religious brothers who are substitute teachers at St. John's were beaten by six Negroes. Trying to protect the girl cheerleaders . . . the brothers were punched and shoved to the ground.

The riots in Birmingham in the spring of 1963, moreover, showed how quickly anger can erupt into violence—and how much Negroes have lost their fear of whites. The rioters were the unemployed and the poor and the uneducated—those who had always suppressed their hatred to protect their own skulls. They had had no part in the non-violent demonstrations led by Martin Luther King and his followers, and the ministers wanted no part of them. But for two weeks they had watched the police dogs and the police hoses at work, and their hatred built up; they had watched the disciplined young ministers of King's organization defy the police, and they had seen shiny-faced school children marching off to jail, and their courage built up. The spark was ignited when the Gaston Motel and the home of Dr. King's brother were bombed. And when the Birmingham cops ran for cover under a barrage of rocks and bottles, instead of opening fire in return, the Negro revolt entered an entirely new stage. The echoes were wide and far. In Chicago, a few days later, two Negroes assaulted the Mayor's eighteen-year-old nephew, shouting "This is for Birmingham." It was for Birmingham, all right—but it was for three hundred fifty years of history before Birmingham as well.